RADICAL PHILOSOPHY

RADICAL PHILOSOPHY

AN INTRODUCTION

CHAD KAUTZER

Routledge
Taylor & Francis Group

LONDON AND NEW YORK

6/6/17
ww
$30.95

First published 2015 by Paradigm Publishers

Published 2016 by Routledge
2 Park Square, Milton Park, Abingdon, Oxon OX14 4RN
711 Third Avenue, New York, NY 10017, USA

Routledge is an imprint of the Taylor & Francis Group, an informa business

Library of Congress Cataloging-in-Publication Data

Kautzer, Chad, author.
   Radical philosophy : an introduction / Chad Kautzer.
      pages cm
   Includes bibliographical references and index.
   ISBN 978-1-61205-742-2 (hardcover : alk. paper) —
   ISBN 978-1-61205-915-0 (lib. ebook)
   1. Radicalism. 2. Communism. 3. Feminism. 4. Queer theory.
I. Title.
   HN49.R3K38 2015
   303.48'4—dc23

                                                                2014042164

ISBN 13: 978-1-61205-742-2 (hbk)
ISBN 13: 978-1-61205-743-9 (pbk)

Dedicated to Jenny Weyel

CONTENTS

Acknowledgments   ix

Introduction   1
   From Philosophical to Scientific Knowledge   6
   Scientific Revolution and Subject Formation   9
   Radical Philosophy, Praxis, and Conflict   16

1 Critical Methodology   20
   Hermeneutics and Standpoint   24
   Phenomenology   30
   Dialectics   33
   Materialism   40

2 Marxism and Class Critique   46
   Alienation and the Phenomenology of Labor   50
   Fetishism and the Hermeneutics of Value   55
   Surplus Value and Class Conflict   62
   Post-Capitalism, Communism, and Autonomism   70

3 Feminism and Queer Theory   75
   Bodies, Performance, and Normalization   79
   Objectification, Praxis, and Masculinity   86
   Law, Patriarchy, and Labor   97

4 Antiracism and the Whiteness Problem 105
    Colonialism, Mastery, and the Hermeneutics of Race 110
    Whiteness as Property, Sovereignty, and Fetish 122

Notes 135

Bibliography 182

Index 205

ACKNOWLEDGMENTS

I would like to thank Paradigm Publishers for supporting this project, and my colleagues at the University of Colorado Denver for creating an exceptionally nurturing and supportive philosophy department. In particular, I want to acknowledge Candice Shelby, Sarah Tyson, Robert Metcalf, Maria Talero, Sam Walker, Brian Lisle, Mark Tanzer, Gabriel Zamosc-Regueros, and especially David Hildebrand. For reading and commenting on parts of this text, I thank Daniel Loick, Julie Carr, Sarah Tyson, Robert Metcalf, Markus Redlich, and above all Jenny Weyel. Jenny's labor and incisive critiques are gratefully reflected in most of these pages, and her bountiful support throughout the writing process is reflected in my seeing it through. The cover design is by Denver-based artist Deidre Adams, with whom I became friends through the Colorado Foreclosure Resistance Coalition; the cover art is taken from her "Composition VIII." For her editorial assistance, I want to thank Rachel Shanahan. For their inspirational work on the streets of Denver, I want to thank Janet, Terese, Fred, Steve, Darren, Mikel, Billie, Roshan, Saadia, Jonathan, Katrina, Michael, Candace, Antony, Marcus, Benjamin, Stephen, and Tim. For their love and friendship, I am deeply grateful to Jenny, Pam, David, Ian, Shawn, Steve, Christina, Hunter, Kaitlyn, Jane, Elke, Matthias, Lena, Markus, Jurek, Jolanda, Manuel, Farnaz, Dascha, Daniel, Reggie, Ivana, Katrin, and Nina.

INTRODUCTION

When we turn from anger we turn from insight . . .
                        —*Audre Lorde,* Sister Outsider[1]

The starting point of theoretical reflection is opposition, negativity, struggle. It is from rage that thought is born, not from the pose of reason. . . . We start from negation, from dissonance.
        —*John Holloway,* Change the World without Taking Power[2]

Plato and Aristotle argued long ago that wonderment inspires philosophical reflection, but with radical philosophy it is something akin to anger, disobedience, and resistance that cultivates a desire for knowledge that can help us in a fight.[3] "Anger expressed and translated into action in the service of our vision and our future," writes Audre Lorde, "is a liberating and strengthening act of clarification."[4] It is in this spirit that I write this introduction to a group of radical philosophies engaged in acts of self-clarification within practical struggles.

Radical philosophical projects often disorient those unaccustomed to them, because they challenge disciplinary boundaries and the merely contemplative notion of philosophy itself. The explanations and organization of this text are intended to be helpful to readers coming to it for different reasons and with various interests, and my discussions are mostly limited to the United States and its colonial history.[5] My own interest in writing this book arises from the conviction that there are underappreciated commonalities among various critical social theories and social movements that when recognized are both insightful

1

and empowering. This book does not, however, develop a test to determine whether or not *individuals* are radical. Thankfully, we are complicated creatures with varied interests and projects, and thus defy such generalizations. Rather, this book is an effort to draw some important distinctions; make explicit relevant values, interests, and traditions; and thereby help readers navigate a vast array of existing and often confusing theories and methods. This is the kind of book I wish I had when I was new to philosophy and political engagement and was animated by anger at injustice.

As bell hooks writes of her own past, "Then and now I understand my rage to be a necessary aspect of resistance struggle. Rage can act as a catalyst inspiring courageous action."[6] While hooks was first enraged by white supremacy, for me it was, in the beginning, class exploitation in the devastating wake of deindustrialization in the Midwest. When unfocused, rage can be self-defeating, and when purely destructive, it eliminates the possibility for its own resolution. It is thus important to identify how anger and rage can be harnessed to support emancipatory projects directed toward the underlying injustices engendering them. This is not an easy task when we are unaccustomed to radical philosophy; a new vocabulary must be learned and new critiques and social relations developed. With that in mind, a warning for readers who don't yet have a tolerance for the technical language of philosophy: Chapter 1 will be especially difficult. It is intended to deepen the understanding and broaden the historical context of the radical philosophical projects discussed in subsequent chapters, but if you begin to find it demoralizing, I suggest reading the chapter's introductory pages and skipping the rest for now. With that said, let me sketch here what I mean by *radical philosophical project,* sometimes simply referred to as *radical philosophy,* and how it differs from more traditional notions of philosophy.

The way I use the term *radical* here is intended to capture the Latin origin of the word, *radix,* which means "root." To be radical means to be about the root, origin, or foundation of something. We could say that a radical critique targets the root of a problem, rather than just a symptom. For example, a radical critique of the "beauty" industry would not be that it perpetuates sexual objectification and cultivates physical standards impossible to satisfy, thus creating widespread shame, alienation from one's own body, or self-hatred. It surely does these things, but these are symptoms and the root of the problem lies deeper. A radical critique views the beauty industry's destabilization and immiseration of social existence, particularly of women's lives, as a way to stabilize and empower a hierarchical social order that primarily benefits men, the able-bodied, whites, straight people, and the beauty industry itself. The latter, for example, intentionally and relentlessly promotes the very physical insecurities its products are supposed to help us overcome. The radical *change* related to this radical critique involves overcoming not only the lived experiences of alienation, objectification, and self-hatred, but also the more fundamental systems of oppression responsible for those experiences as well.

The term *project* is used here to include both of these moments; the theoretical and practical, the critique and the transformation, and the word *philosophy* is derived from the Greek φιλοσοφία, which roughly translates as the "love (*philo*) of wisdom (*sophia*)." Such wisdom is, however, often characterized as distinct from lived experience, or even impractical, contributing to the image of the philosopher as either a hermit or a fool. Take the famous story about Thales of Miletus, considered the first Western philosopher by some, who is said to have fallen in a well while gazing at the sky.[7] Commenting on this story, Socrates states, "It really is true that the philosopher fails to see his next-door neighbor; he not only doesn't notice what he is doing; he scarcely knows whether he is a man or some other kind of creature. The question he asks is, What is Man? What actions and passions properly belong to human nature and distinguish it from all other beings? This is what he wants to know and concerns himself to investigate."[8] For a much more contemporary example, we have the "Philosophers' Football Match" skit by the Monty Python comedy group that is hilarious precisely because it almost entirely lacks any action.

On the other side of the coin there is the famous cave allegory in Plato's *Republic,* which describes the unphilosophical individual as one who is "since childhood, fixed in the same place, with their necks and legs fettered, able to see only in front of them, because their bonds prevent them from turning their heads around."[9] These prisoners see only the shadows of objects cast by the sunlight coming from the entrance to the cave and so "in every way believe that the truth is nothing other than the shadows of those artifacts."[10] To be philosophically educated is, then, to be "released from their bonds and cured of their ignorance" so they can now distinguish mere appearance from truth.[11] Emancipation in Plato's famous allegory is education as critical reflection; unlike radical philosophy, there is neither a social theory of the structures and material conditions of one's lived experiences, which can identify possibilities for their transformation, nor collective emancipatory struggles to enact such transformation. These additional concerns typically fall beyond the boundary of traditional and academic philosophy.

This orientation toward critical social theory and collective action is one of a set of commitments that together set radical philosophy apart. These include—and here I'll be formulaic—the combination of a critical methodology; focus on particular social structures, practices, and material conditions; emancipatory intentions; and the relation to a practical context of collective action in which these intentions can be realized. These four components—methodology, specific social context, emancipatory intent, and practical means—are interrelated and mutually informing. Indeed, radical philosophy emerges dialectically from active resistance, which is an educative experience in itself, and therefore the order of the above list is not indicative of the directionality of projects themselves. Neither theory nor practice is sovereign here, and both are continually subject to revision as social actions have unpredictable outcomes and reveal new possibilities.[12] Of course, there are times when social antagonisms have not yet become manifest in outright conflict and subject positions have not yet formed around their fault lines. It is also possible for particular social forces to become so repressive that critical resistance is severely limited or that the work of survival consumes the entirety of one's time and energy. Under such conditions, however, radical critique can still sustain reflective practice and cultivate a radical social imagery.

Of the above four commitments, the concern with practical emancipation is the most significant deviation from the *contemplative* notion of philosophy or the task of explaining existence and justifying claims about it.[13] To speak of emancipation is to speak of emancipation *from* something—namely, from oppression and injustice.[14] Therefore, radical philosophies have a decidedly negative or interventionist relation to existing social conditions. Their emancipatory interests often include forms of collective self-determination, mutual aid, a social (or nonsovereign) form of freedom, and horizontalist social relations as well as the material conditions necessary to enact them. As essentially oppositional and counter-hegemonic, radical philosophy seeks to undermine or dismantle that which it opposes through successful, theoretically informed political struggle or what I will call *critical resistance*. This is why Étienne Balibar has, for example, described the radical philosophy of Karl Marx as *anti*-philosophy.[15] It is not that Marxism is unphilosophical, but rather the critical intent of Marxist philosophy is to become actualized in praxis and thus overcome the oppressive conditions calling for theorization in the first place. In his famous "Eleventh Thesis on Feuerbach," Marx wrote that the point of philosophy is to not only interpret the world, but also to change it.[16] The flipside is that if you change the world, you change philosophy. As Jean-Paul Sartre writes, "A philosophy remains efficacious so long as the praxis which has engendered it, which supports it, and which is clarified by it, is still alive. But it is transformed, it loses its uniqueness, it is stripped of its original, dated content to the extent that it gradually impregnates the masses so as to become in and through them a collective instrument of emancipation."[17] Radical philosophy's intention, then, is to eventually render itself superfluous—or at least to work toward that end in practical acts of self-negation—making its own concrete success in emancipation and the elimination of oppression its own undoing as a project.

The inclusion of this practical, emancipatory moment into its very constitution means that radical philosophy has a *pluralistic* and *interdisciplinary* component. To develop a social theory of contemporary forms of oppression that can articulate alternatives and identify the mode and directionality of critical resistance requires knowledge derived from other disciplines, experiences, and perspectives.[18] Radical philosophy thus utilizes the work of disciplines such as history, sociology, anthropology, and economics, even as it takes a critical stance toward the methods they employ and the material interests that they serve. Radical philosophical projects must also achieve something much more challenging: continual revision and growth in dialogue with the voices, experiences, and informal knowledge of others. Since our own social positions limit our understanding of the struggles and oppositional knowledge of others, regardless of who we may be, radical philosophy derives its strength and relevance from bringing together this knowledge and working together with the people who possess it. There are traditions of practical and oppositional knowledge that have been marginalized or concealed, historically and within our own communities today—what Michel Foucault calls "subjugated knowledge."[19] It comes in different forms and relates to different kinds of struggle and forms of survival. Bringing them into conversation raises the challenge of facing and embracing difference.[20] Difference "must not be merely tolerated," writes Audre Lorde, "but seen as a fund of necessary polarities between which our creativity can spark like a dialectic. Only then does the necessity for interdependency become unthreatening. Only within the interdependency of different strengths, acknowledged and equal, can the power to seek new ways of being in the world generate, as well as the courage and sustenance to act where there are no charters."[21] This interdependency is *prefigurative* in the sense that the relations of trust, respect, safety, and solidarity we desire to see in the world beyond the movements are fought for within the movements themselves. In short, the ends toward which we strive must be reflected in the movements we cultivate to achieve them.

Much of what I have said thus far about radical philosophy has been in contrast to traditional conceptions of philosophy and the so-called scientific method, so allow me to say a few more things about these traditions against which radical philosophy defines itself. This is useful for identifying the historical origins and contested nature of various disciplinary methods, self-understandings, and justifications, and it is part and parcel of the historical and reflexive nature of radical philosophy itself. In particular, we see how radical philosophy involves a revival of the praxis-oriented theory found in the classical tradition of practical philosophy, albeit with an expanded horizon that integrates the material conditions and social structures in and against which critical resistance operates. This classical tradition was largely eclipsed by the growth of empirical scientific discourses, not only in the natural and social sciences, but also within various philosophical schools of thought. The modern academic disciplines and their positivist methods laid claim to objective and disinterested knowledge production: their methods and claims to truth were supposedly universal, and their work was said to be for the betterment all of humankind. In contrast, radical philosophy does not understand itself to be disinterested, and neither does it uncritically accept assertions of disinterest in other philosophies or in the natural and social sciences. "A critical social theory," writes Nancy Fraser, "frames its research programme and its conceptual framework with an eye to the aims and activities of those oppositional social movements with which it has a partisan though not uncritical identification. The questions it asks and the models it designs are informed by that identification and interest."[22] Knowledge production is enabled and constrained by institutional logics, social relations of power, and discourses about truth and objectivity, regardless of the subjective intentions of the theorists and scientists themselves. As Foucault argues, "There is no power relation without the correlative constitution of a field of knowledge, nor any knowledge that does not presuppose and constitute at the same time power relations."[23] Radical philosophy makes explicit these dimensions of power and knowledge production in its critiques, and makes clear its own practical interests in its projects. After a brief historical excursion in the following, we can better appreciate both the distinctiveness and historical origins of this approach.

From Philosophical to Scientific Knowledge

In the influential philosophy of Aristotle (384–322 BCE), *theōria*, or theory, does not involve knowledge acquisition but is rather the act of contemplating or reflecting upon knowledge already acquired and in its "divine" form, upon *noūs*, which is translated as "mind" or "intellect."[24] *Theōria* is in its purest form thought thinking itself, and according to Aristotle, it is the highest form of human life.[25] It is, he says, "what is most pleasant and best."[26] It is theoretical wisdom, or *sophia*.

This understanding of philosophy as thought thinking itself, as pure self-reflection, would seem to put Aristotle in the category of hermit. Two points, however, prevent us from drawing this conclusion. First, despite *theōria* being by and large disengaged from particular contexts and conditions, it retains a practical *interest*, albeit often unacknowledged.[27] As Jürgen Habermas writes of theory in Aristotle's time, it "had an impact on life because it was thought to have discovered in the cosmic order an ideal world structure, including the prototype for the order of the human world."[28] The classical or Aristotelian notion of theory was reflection upon the law-like structure of the eternal cosmos so that it could be replicated (*mimesis*) or serve as a guide in the contingent and finite human world. While theory or contemplation was said to be the highest form of philosophical life, it was not done for theory's sake alone. This is an important point to keep in mind as we move through different historical periods of philosophy, for unacknowledged interests are often at work and support practical relations of domination.

The second point is that while Aristotle finds thought thinking itself most pleasurable, he identifies other important forms of knowing. These include knowledge of universals (*epistēmē*), practical knowledge (*phronēsis*), and productive or technical knowledge (*poiēsis*). First, *epistēmē* is the kind of (scientific) knowledge that, according to Aristotle, has universality and necessity through its deduction from first principles (e.g., rather than being inductively derived from experimentation). In other words, *epistēmē* is knowledge of things that do not change and thus things that have necessity and universality.[29] Knowledge of geometry and mathematics would be good candidates. Second, there is *phronēsis,* or practical wisdom, understood as the political extension of ethics—a knowledge of doing. In this form of knowledge, communal life is viewed as the means by which the individual cultivates and realizes virtue (*aretê,* or excellence of character), which assists one in making good judgments in particular situations. "That [*phronēsis*] is not [*epistēmē*] is evident," writes Aristotle, "for it is, as has been said, concerned with the ultimate particular fact, since the thing to be done is of this nature."[30] We cannot have *epistēmē* about politics or ethics, because these are historical and contingent rather than universal concerns, so we must cultivate the kind of practical knowledge necessary to make good, ethical judgments in contingent circumstances. Politics is therefore a matter of ethically informed action (*praxis*) informed by practical wisdom (the *prudentia* of Cicero), and contributes to the good life, which for Aristotle includes contemplation or *theōria*. For Aristotle, *phronēsis* concerns the deliberate decisions (*prohaeresis*) or right actions (*praxeis*) of the individual in cultivating the good life. It does not include changing the material and structural conditions of social life, which will be taken up in radical philosophy.

Poiēsis is the third form of knowing and involves the technical skill or knowledge necessary to successfully complete tasks with tools or to produce something using efficient means and proper tools—a knowledge of making. The role of *poiēsis* increasingly expands its intellectual territory in the history of philosophy and natural science, eventually becoming nearly synonymous with knowledge production in the modern period.[31]

The emergence of political *science* from political *philosophy* involves an important shift from *phronēsis* or practical knowledge, which informs political and ethical action, to a particular kind of *poiēsis* with its associated skills (*technē*) for making. This move marginalized concerns for self-development and community in the name of producing stable orders and technocratic administration. There was a parallel move in the sciences generally from *theōria* or theoretical knowledge to *poiēsis* or technical knowledge, insofar as universal knowledge was gained through creation (*poiēsis*) rather than reflection (*theōria*).[32] We have knowledge about only those things we produce, change, or create, be it through our mind's creation of the objects of our own experience, as Immanuel Kant argued in his *Critique of Pure Reason* (1781), or in practical work of the geneticist and fracking engineer.[33] Theory has gained, says Habermas, "a new criterion of its truth ... the certainty of the technician: we *know* an object insofar as we can make it."[34] That is to say, *poiēsis* is no longer just knowledge of the skills (*technē*) needed to accomplish a particular goal but is the only sure path to universal knowledge.

I raise these Aristotelian distinctions because they serve as helpful touchstones in tracing the historical evolution of what constitutes knowledge and philosophy in both their contemplative and practical forms. The important historical development for us to take note of is the transition from the Aristotelian or classical tradition to the modern scientific methodology, which still informs contemporary understandings of objectivity, truth, and the separation of theory from praxis. In political philosophy, for example, we find that the *phronēsis* or praxis of classical politics became marginalized by the influential and instrumental politics of power in Niccolo Machiavelli's *The Prince* (1513) and in the new political science found in *On the Citizen* (1647) and *Leviathan* (1651) by Thomas Hobbes

(1588–1679). Politics becomes the skillful construction (*poiēsis*) of a state or of maintaining the power of the sovereign and the stability of social relations. In Hobbes's work, the construction and maintenance of the state were based upon a natural, materialist science of individuals thought to behave with mechanistic and law-like regularity. "For seeing life is but a motion of Limbs, the beginning whereof is in some principall part within; why may we not say, that all *Automata* (Engines that move themselves by springs and wheeles as doth a watch) have an artificiall life? For what is the *Heart*, but a *Spring*; and the *Nerves*, but so many *Strings*; and the *Joynts*, but so many *Wheeles*, giving motion to the whole Body, such as was intended by the Artificer."[35]

The polis (*civitas*) was for Aristotle the community through which the moral character of free individuals is cultivated, but it had become in Hobbes's work an objectified society (*societas*) to be constructed and administered the way the modern natural sciences seek to master nature.[36] The technocratic use of mathematics and the new natural sciences was deployed to regulate, manage, and dominate. Since the causes and effects of human action were considered known and predictable, individuals can be treated like any other body in motion. The state was like a clock, constituted by gears and springs set in motion through the passions and desires of human nature.[37] Thus, in addition to this new, scientific treatment of political relations, we find here a new concept of the *person* that assumes it to be knowable apart from and antecedent to social relations and thus socialization; this presumption is sometimes called *abstract individualism*, which became explicit in the social contract tradition of the seventeenth and eighteenth centuries and finds echoes today in rational choice theory and the contractualism of political liberalism.[38]

Scientific Revolution and Subject Formation

This move from polity (*civitas*) to society (*societas*), which objectifies and analytically detaches individuals from their defining social relations, entails a shift in methodology signaled above by the move from praxis (*phronēsis*) to technical production and control (*poiēsis*). This is the emergence of the *scientific method*, which quickly rose to prominence in the period we now call the Enlightenment. Through the work of Galileo Galilei (1564–1642), Francis Bacon (1561–1626), Johannes Kepler (1571–1630), and René Descartes (1596–1650), there was a rapid and widespread acceptance of empirical observation and experimentation, which produced amazing technological innovation and was eminently useful in the mastery over natural and social forces. Each of these thinkers subscribed to the general mechanistic view that with the help of mathematical laws, all change could be explained by reference to the motion, size, and shape of matter.[39]

The groundwork for both inductive scientific reasoning and the relation of the modern sciences to nature was laid with Francis Bacon's *The New Organon* (1620). Bacon argued that knowledge is acquired through sense experience and the right inductive or empiricist rules (i.e., methods) to interpret it.[40] The natural sciences, he argued, contributed to enlightened autonomy and social utility, for they could "hand men their fortunes when their understanding is freed from tutelage and comes of age," and this results in "greater power over nature."[41] In other words, freedom for the rational subject comes through knowledge and, in particular, knowledge that is the power to rule over nature. "Enlightenment, understood in the widest sense as the advance of thought," write Max Horkheimer and Theodor Adorno, "has always aimed at liberating human beings from fear and installing them as master."[42]

Descartes, like Bacon, was a mechanistic philosopher, yet he advocated a rationalist and deductive method in his *Discourse on Method* (1637). He set out to secure the grounds of universal knowledge, to establish a foundational, self-evident belief in order to prevent infinite regression and defend against the challenges of skepticism. In doing so, Descartes constructed the famous distinction between mind (*cogitans*) and matter (*extensa*), in which matter was demystified, considered to be little more than the spatial extension of a body and open to mathematical and mechanistic explanation. He then sought to identify through introspection the foundation of a rational methodology for studying this matter. He arrived at *cogito ergo sum*—"I think therefore I am"—which seemed impervious to skepticism and thus suitable grounds upon which to build a rational and universally applicable scientific methodology.[43] The goal was nothing less than "universal wisdom," made possible by disenchanting the world in order to reveal its laws.[44] When self and world are taken to be as fundamentally distinct and discrete as they are in this Cartesian dualism, *objective* truth requires the elimination of *subjective* interpretations, interests, and values, which are viewed as a corrupting influence. Subjective experience, he thought, was too mired in the particularities of experience, tradition, and the materiality of the body, which made it a hurdle to achieving necessary and universal knowledge. Like the slaves of Plato's cave, the subjective perspective—trapped in the particularity of the body in the here and now—could only grasp appearances, whereas objective science sought to grasp the universality of the thing behind those appearances.

These developments in inductive and deductive methods, mechanistic theory, and universal methodology that contained an absolute division between mind and matter, constituted a scientific revolution. Indeed, it was *the* scientific revolution, and it contributed to technological advancements, economic growth, the technical administration of large states, and the domination of nature. It also represented a paradigm shift in how we think about the subject and its relationship to the natural world and to the social world. Indeed, what was truly revolutionary about the scientific discourse and universal methods of the Enlightenment was how they produced new subjects. The new mechanistic and universalistic thinking colonized spheres of life, displacing social, historical, and religious forms of knowledge and, as a consequence, the social, historical, and religious subjects they helped produce. Consider, for example, the rise of discourses about rights, contracts, and universal legal personhood in the seventeenth and eighteenth centuries. At first they concerned private property relations (e.g., land, tools, a house, and so on), then political states (i.e., constitutions), and finally they had insinuated themselves into almost all forms of social relations. By the late eighteenth century, Kant would conceive of marriage as a contract representing "the union of two persons of different sexes for lifelong possession of each other's sexual attributes."[45]

The scientific revolution thus involved a double movement: the objectification of subjects and their relations within the polity, which in turn allowed for them to be studied like objects with universal properties by the social sciences.[46] The subjects about whom scientific theories speak, and claim to have knowledge about, are in part constituted by the ideas and concepts informing those very same scientific theories. Such ideas and concepts originate in particular social relations and material conditions, such as those necessary for capitalism and European colonialism. We can see how this relates to the rise of political science in the modern period, which was more concerned about techniques for extracting wealth and maintaining political power (*poiēsis*) than about the normative concerns of practical knowledge (*phronēsis*). For Hobbes to be able to conceptualize the political state as a clock, for example, he had to conceptualize the citizens as replaceable parts that have similar qualities and interact in law-like ways. In addition to his mechanistic psychology (for which our "passions" are like gears and springs), the philosophical discourse of rights, legal personhood, and contracts were a means of managing a population at the state level. Legal personhood creates a universal quality in each person that can "bear rights," and such rights are said to be universal insofar as they are the same for everyone (deemed worthy, of course), a universal dimension created within the particularity of life, much like Descartes had done by abstracting mind from the contingencies of all matter.

The social interactions of these universal, rights-bearing entities are then coordinated with the help of laws, contracts, a judiciary, and the police to enforce contracts and protect property. This juridical discourse in political science creates an interchangeable subject position (e.g., citizen or legal subject) that can be occupied by a multitude of people with unique qualities, needs, and desires. It is a process by which one "makes dissimilar things comparable by reducing them to abstract quantities," write Max Horkheimer and Theodor Adorno.[47] This juridical construction of the person, so central to political liberalism, also dialectically entails the construction of a sphere of extra-juridical "nature." The latter is the space of violence, and we will find that it plays a constitutive, albeit often concealed, role in the construction of social identities and relations of domination.

In Hobbes's *Leviathan*, this process of rounding off the edges of idiosyncratic individuality and of untying the social ties that bind them in order to create the legal subject begins by a collective act of subjugation. We become subjects through our submission or *subjection* to the law of the sovereign. Hobbes famously writes that people need a "power able to over-awe them all" in order to "keep them in quiet."[48] Before sovereign power is created, we are said to live in a state of nature, defined by its lack of universality (i.e., law) and marked by relations of coercion (a condition that will be practically incorporated within civil society, yet juridically fall outside it). "Where there is no common power, there is no law," he says.[49] If there is no law, there is no justice, because justice is acting according to the law, which, says Hobbes, is determined by the sovereign. Becoming a subject is simultaneously empowering and limiting: one gains agency and protection as a political subject, but this position is only made possible by subordination. One gives up the liberty to do whatever one wants, transferring that liberty to the sovereign—voluntarily or involuntarily. More accurately, the giving up of one's liberty is the mechanism by which the sovereign is created. This relation was hinted at in Bacon's connection of individual freedom to the subjugation of nature: we become sovereign when we gain knowledge of nature's secrets and turn them against nature.[50] Since we, too, are nature, our rational sovereignty is won by mastery (*dominium*) over our own subjective and affective nature. As Judith Butler writes, "A subject is not only formed in subordination, but ... this subordination provides the subject's continuing condition of possibility."[51] This relation of subordination to subject formation will be important for understanding not only the citizen-subject as a juridical-political construct, but also the subject positions in economic, gender, sexual, and race relations discussed in subsequent chapters.

The rise of political science coincided with and facilitated the rise of stable nation-states and a capitalist mode of production and distribution dependent upon both strong private property rights and the means for calculation. Management of otherwise unique individuals and groups in economic production and political institutions required social and political knowledge, which was the impetus for the modern university system and a majority of its disciplines. Consistent to their purpose, these disciplines by and large embraced the concept of the individual as independent, rational, rights-bearing, and free, antecedent to any social relations. Once individuals were abstracted from their social relations and traditions by an objectifying scientific discourse, a universal logic (of identity) could then be applied to their relations. The methods of the scientific revolution, writes Friedrich Engels, "left us as legacy the habit of observing natural objects and processes in isolation, apart from their connection with the vast whole; of observing them in repose, not in motion; as constants, not as essentially variables; in their death, not in their life. And when this way of looking at things was transferred by Bacon and Locke from natural science to philosophy, it begot the narrow metaphysical mode of thought peculiar to the last century"—philosophy as postmortem.[52]

Even when these lifeless objects of study (i.e., abstract individuals) were set in motion, they were like billiard balls on a pool table, isolated and independent, acting and reacting as if to have only external, physical relations to each other. However, the methodology appropriated from the natural sciences needed this kind of atomistic conception in order to establish law-like relations and establish rule. If one could identify laws (*nomoi*) in the populations under study and make law-like (*nomological*) claims to knowledge about social relations, one could presumably predict, dominate, and manage them.[53] This was Bacon's idea: master the laws in order to bend nature to one's will. The three main social sciences emerging in the nineteenth century—sociology, political science, and economics—all claimed to be *nomothetic,* or law-based, disciplines that could identify laws in the social realm. As Immanuel Wallerstein writes,

Most nomothetic social sciences stressed first what differentiated them from the historical discipline: an interest in arriving at general laws that were presumed to govern human behavior, a readiness to perceive the phenomena to be studied as cases (not individualities), the need to segmentalize human reality in order

> to analyze it, the possibility and desirability of strict scientific methods (such as theory-related formulation of hypotheses to be tested against evidence via strict, and if possible quantitative, procedures), a preference for systematically produced evidence (e.g., survey data) and controlled observations over received texts and other residuals.[54]

This tendency culminated in a nineteenth-century form of *positivism* or the methodological commitment that true knowledge can only be derived from (and verified by) the empirical sciences, guided by mathematical laws. Positivist methods were widely considered applicable to the natural and social worlds alike. As we have seen, when such methods are employed in the social sciences, they objectify human activity into "facts" and marginalize problems of interpretation, questions of social justice, and generally isolate theory from lived, subjective experience. "The first characteristic of the positive philosophy is that it regards all phenomena as subjected to invariable natural *laws*," wrote Auguste Comte (1798–1857), founder of modern positivism and, arguably, of sociology as well. "Our business is—seeing how vain is any research into what are called *causes*, whether first or final—to pursue an accurate discovery of these laws, with a view to reducing them to the smallest possible number."[55] This reductive and objectifying approach, which Comte explicitly referred to as a "social physics," was thought to increase the researcher's claim to objectivity and thus scientific validity. For him, the value of scientific theory is derived from its factual basis rather than any normative concerns or concerns about what *ought* to be. This nineteenth-century positivism in social science echoed the seventeenth-century credo of the natural sciences: objectivity is ensured to the extent that subjectivity (with its values, interpretations, and interests) is prohibited from factoring into the equation of knowledge production.

The emergence of new empirical methods in the natural sciences, the identification of knowledge with science, and the transference of these empirical methods to social sciences, had a powerful impact on philosophy. Facing increased marginalization, the discipline of philosophy relinquished most normative, historical, and practical concerns and more or less adopted the analytic or scientific model, which echoed the positivism or "scientism" of the social sciences.[56] This model, claims Bertrand Russell (1872–1970), is "able, in regard to certain problems, to achieve definite answers, which have the quality of science rather than of philosophy. . . . Its methods, in this respect, resemble those of science. I have no doubt that, in so far as philosophical knowledge is possible, it is by such methods that it must be sought."[57] Russell concluded that this understanding of philosophy excludes questions about the good life (Aristotle), because this involved ethical or normative concerns about how we should live, individually and collectively. Analytic philosophy therefore became dominant in Anglo-American circles, pursuing narrow investigations that sought conceptual clarity and logical analysis of natural language claims or what the influential analytical philosopher Willard V. O. Quine called "regimentation."[58] This left social and political philosophy little space if any within the discipline.[59]

Analytic investigations were informed by and intended to contribute to the sciences, steering clear of questions related to ethical values and practical knowledge. Like the modern method of political science found in Hobbes, the normative sphere of praxis was sacrificed for the rigor and objectivity said to constitute disinterested and universal science. "In general," writes Scott Soames, "philosophy done in the analytic tradition aims at truth and knowledge, as opposed to moral or spiritual improvement. There is very little in the way of practical or inspirational guides in the art of living to be found, and very much in the way of philosophical theories that purport to reveal the truth about a given domain of inquiry. In general, the goal in analytic philosophy is to discover what is true, not to provide a useful recipe for living one's life."[60]

The same could be said of both the natural and the social sciences, which were supposed to deal with facts rather than normative concerns, and continually argued that the motives and products of their research were interest-free.[61] Their self-described goal was to produce scientific knowledge about the natural and social world, which could be used by leaders and policy makers for the supposedly neutral tasks of increasing economic productivity, efficiently extracting resources, controlling nature, and rationalizing social institutions. Even prominent counter-traditions in philosophy and the social sciences that rejected the nomothetic scientific model and endorsed *reflexive* methods acknowledging subjectivity and the researcher's position in a shared symbolic world still claimed to be neutral or interest-free, and largely endorsed a categorical distinction between theory and practice, empirical and normative theory. This includes the interpretive and phenomenological traditions in social theory that resisted positivism, from Max Weber (1864–1920) to Edmund Husserl (1859–1938) and Alfred Schütz (1899–1959). Weber, for example, famously argued for an interpretive (*verstehende*) method in sociology, attentive to subjective meanings and intentions in social action: "We can accomplish something which is never attainable in the natural sciences," wrote Weber, "namely the subjective understanding of the action of the component individuals."[62] That is to say, we would no longer be merely billiard balls on a pool table. Yet, Weber simultaneously argued that social science should remain *wertfrei* or value-free, and Alfred Schütz plainly asserted, "Scientific theorizing does not serve any practical purpose."[63] Although developed as alternatives to positivism and logical empiricism, these approaches still claimed to be value-free or disinterested and sought to avoid theory's relation to praxis.[64]

Radical Philosophy, Praxis, and Conflict

The intellectual history sketched above emerged from a practical context of conflict and struggle in divided and unjust societies. The production and distribution of knowledge had material constraints determined in large part by the purse strings of private or public patronage. The rise and institutionalization of disciplines such as political economy, international law, and anthropology at universities—held to be the only legitimate centers of knowledge production—reflected and facilitated processes of imperial conquest, colonization, war, and slavery, as well as the appropriation of natural resources. The marshaling of the natural sciences for economic exploitation of nature and labor, the increase of economic productivity, and the development of military technology were imperatives of the state. Meanwhile, sociology, political science, and economics as well as the biological sciences were often employed to defend ideologies and practices of white supremacy, patriarchy, ableism, and heteronormativity. These sciences created new subjects, objectified social relations, and marginalized ethical concerns. They universalized the interests and values of dominant groups, rendering others as partial, deviant, subhuman, and justifiably subjugated or destroyed. Decisions about what kind of knowledge was sought and who was sanctioned to pursue it were not neutral but reflected interests that in practice constituted and reinforced domination and inequality. Little could be more powerful than when supposedly disinterested and objective sciences conceal the interests of wealthy, powerful, or privileged groups as universal interests that serve the public good.[65]

Radical philosophies push back against these tendencies, historicizing subjects and social relations, uncovering the interests and relations of power operating in the politics of truth, and challenging the methods, discourses, practices, and structures of oppression and domination.[66] They make explicit the forces constraining and enabling various structural positions and social groups by incorporating historical, reflexive, and dialectical elements into their projects. Although radical philosophies cannot escape relations of power—even in their critiques and acts of resistance—they remain vigilant about not reproducing unjust or oppressive power relations. As Judith Butler writes, "To operate within the matrix of power is not the same as to replicate uncritically relations of domination."[67]

The question of how this is accomplished brings us back to the issue of emancipatory praxis and the realization of radical philosophical projects. If social relations of domination or oppression actively play a role in constituting different forms of subjectivity, supported by various cultural norms and structural conditions, then emancipatory praxis must also take up processes of subject formation and work to dismantle oppressive forms of consciousness and habituated privilege. "For we have, built into all of us," writes Audre Lorde, "old blueprints of expectation and response, old structures of oppression, and these must be altered at the same time as we alter the living conditions which are a result of those structures. For the master's tools will never dismantle the master's house."[68] Central to this project is self-critique, which is instigated through our engagements with others. Indeed, it is others (often in the midst of practical struggles) who guide us, who demonstrate what is possible, and who share with us the theoretical tools we need to facilitate our critique. This is the social process by which we cultivate new ethical and political virtues (*aretê*) and oppositional knowledge, which inform the development of practical wisdom (*phronēsis*). It is through others that we come to question our implicit commitments and unreflective judgments, confront internalized oppression, recognize our privilege vis-à-vis others, and develop accountability—all of which can be difficult work.[69] This is what Hegel would call the "labor of the negative," a transformative process that negates what exists to make possible something new, which in this case are our own commitments, behaviors, and identity.

Although I opened this introduction with a discussion of the potential insights gained through anger at injustice, there is no place for it in this interactive process of self-critique, for it only serves to defend the house that needs to be rebuilt, to use Lorde's metaphor. Overlooking this distinction (between anger at oppression and self-critical openness to others in a struggle) is perilous in resistance movements. The identity of an oppositional group is often at first only constituted through (or mediated by) its relation to what it opposes, rather than preexisting shared values or cooperative relations. This is a precarious condition and will remain so as long as the political struggle doesn't do the work of capacitating the resistance with practical knowledge related to mutual respect, ethical dialogue, and decision-making procedures that don't reproduce relations of domination. Anger often arises from those whose privilege typically reigns in such contexts and is therefore contested, and this anger is one of the most corrosive elements in movement building, for it weakens precisely the social relations that need to be strengthened.[70]

In addition to resisting the manifestations of privilege and domination at the level of our lived experience and relationships within struggles and producing livable alternatives, for long-term projects of social transformation it is also important to be able to scale up our theory and practice. A social theory able to critically assess the institutionalization of social structures such as gender, race, class, and sexuality, and grasp the logic operating in economic, environmental, political, educational, cultural, and international systems is therefore also necessary. "The practices and meanings that are intelligible to me are ontologically grounded in group interactions, which are themselves structured by political economies of social structures," writes Linda Martín Alcoff.[71] Such structures facilitate the distribution of opportunities, risks, and material resources at the level of institutional rules, cultural norms, and even physical design. They operate at a macro-level and are relatively stable, but they are neither necessary nor universal, for they are the result of human activity. This is similar to what sociologist Pierre Bourdieu calls *habitus*, namely, a set of "acquired dispositions" integrated into habituated conduct, embodying norms of behavior and the categories of perception and evaluation.[72] It is, he says, "society written into the body, into the biological individual."[73] However, habitus or a social structure can only be reproduced by social adherence to norms—enforced by coercive measures and material resources—so it is always contested.

Gender, race, class, and other social structures exhibit a dialectical logic, because they are relations of power and, more specifically, structured hierarchies of domination. The positions in this dialectic are internally related and interdependent insofar as they *result* from the same conditions and relations of domination. Consequently, they can exist neither apart nor as equals, and in this way structural groups differ from cultural groups. Particular individuals may also experience privilege in one structure and oppression in another (e.g., one may be gendered in a subordinate position but raced in a dominant one), but the dialectical relation of domination persists even within a plurality, because one group is positioned as dominant. Throughout this book, we will find that social relations of domination are supported by the legal constitution of populations vulnerable to exploitation and violence. Creating the conditions for such violence and exploitation facilitates the reproduction of patriarchy, white supremacy, heterosexuality, and capitalism as social structures of rule.

It is important to note that these structures do not depend on the conscious intentions of individuals occupying them. Once the structure exists, the causes of oppression, as Iris Marion Young notes, "are embedded in unquestioned norms, habits, and symbols, in the assumptions underlying institutionalized rules and the collective consequences of following those rules."[74] We must therefore develop a phenomenological critique of our (unconscious) embodiment of these norms and habits, as well as a social critique of institutionalized forms of oppression. Neither of these forms of critique narrowly focuses on an individual's conscious beliefs. This is not to say that an individual's racist beliefs, for example, should not be criticized, but rather that structural forms of racism exist whether a politician, doctor, mortgage broker, or police officer is intentionally racist or believes that they or their institution is "color-blind."

This understanding of social structures and their institutionalization is a form of *conflict theory*, since it holds that structures and the specific institutional forms they generate are best explained by social conflicts, rather than internal functions of the institutions themselves (i.e., functionalism). While attention must be paid to the empirical configurations of specific social structures, practices, and material conditions, the social theoretical framework is one of conflict. Marxist and anarchist analyses of the capitalist class interests of state institutions, Michael Omi and Howard Winant's racial formation theory, Foucault's notion of war as a "grid of intelligibility" for social relations, and Angela Davis's critique of prisons are all examples of conflict theory. In order to effectively resist the structures of oppression operative in our subjectivities, bodies, norms, institutions, and built environments, multiple forms of struggle are necessary—from acts of disobedience and political resistance, to educational projects in social history, social theory, and self-critique, and the development of alternative relations, practices, and institutions. This is difficult work, but as Frederick Douglass reminds us, "If there is no struggle there is no progress. Those who profess to favor freedom and yet depreciate agitation . . . want crops without plowing up the ground, they want rain without thunder and lightning. They want the ocean without the awful roar of its many waters. This struggle may be a moral one, or it may be a physical one, and it may be both moral and physical, but it must be a struggle. Power concedes nothing without a demand. It never did and it never will."[75]

CHAPTER I
CRITICAL METHODOLOGY

Just as theories, epistemologies, and facts produced by any group of individuals represent the standpoints and interests of their creators, the very definition of who is legitimated to do intellectual work is not only politically contested, but is changing.
—*Patricia Hill Collins,* Black Feminist Thought[1]

Care for human existence and its truth makes philosophy a "practical science" in the deepest sense, and it also leads philosophy—and this is the crucial point—into the concrete distress of human existence.
—*Herbert Marcuse, "On Concrete Philosophy"*[2]

We are as much "bundles of habits" (William James) as we are an "ensemble of social relations" (Karl Marx), which is to say that we often *unknowingly* follow rules and use concepts within the everyday social relations that define us.[3] Most of our actions and judgments are neither consciously intended nor accidental but are, rather, entrenched and habitual ways of navigating our social world. Habits have been a target of criticism in the history of philosophy, because they are thought to bypass freedom or prejudice reason. Habit "deprives even good actions of their moral worth because it impairs the freedom of the mind," asserted Immanuel Kant.[4]

However, there is nothing inherently problematic about habits. Indeed, habit plays an important role in social cooperation, education, ethical behavior, and even the way we perceive and evaluate the world and ourselves.[5] We *inhabit* a body, a culture, and a way of life. Yet, as John Dewey reminds us, "habit does not, of itself, know, for it does not of itself stop to think, observe or remember."[6] This means that unchecked habits can also, unbeknownst to us, reproduce oppressive behaviors, self-understandings, social structures, as well as various forms of power and privilege. In order to cultivate alternative habits, we need to recognize and scrutinize existing ones, which means making our habitual judgments and behavior explicit. Self-awareness makes self-critique of our problematic habits possible, and self-critique is essential to any radical philosophy.

Consider the "epic theater" of playwright Bertolt Brecht (1898–1956), which incorporated a self-reflective distancing or "estrangement effect" (*Verfremdungseffekt*) into its performance. In Brecht's play *Mother Courage and Her Children* (1939), for example, performers change their costumes and characters onstage as well as hold up signs describing the scene's events. The spectator "is prevented from feeling his way into the characters," Brecht writes. "Acceptance or rejection of the characters' words is thus placed in the conscious realm, not, as hitherto, in the spectator's subconscious."[7] Brecht referred to this reflexive experience as "dialectical theater," because it drew traditionally passive spectators into an active, participatory role, making them self-aware and self-critical.[8] One could not suspend disbelief or lose oneself in spectatorship.[9] As Theodor Adorno once wrote, the "consequence of the self-critique of logic is the dialectic," and we can see how the logic of Brecht's dialectical theater is a consequence of the self-critique of traditional spectatorship—a logic it shares with supposedly disinterested philosophy.[10]

Although this process of self-reflection and critique is never complete—we can never become fully transparent to ourselves for reasons relating to nonidentity and embodiment—it helps us to identify habits of oppression and the possibilities for new practices. It is in this sense that Marx described critical philosophy as the self-clarification of its time, the clarification of "the meaning of its own struggle and its own desires."[11] This holds true for those producing theory and for the content of the theory they produce. As theorists with a particular social location that engenders bias, we can carry out this self-critique of privilege and oppression personally and include it in the theory we develop about social action and social structures. Radical philosophy must, however, still do more. It needs to make explicit the potential for social transformation in existing social relations. This is sometimes called the *dialectic of immanence and transcendence,* for it is a process of identifying and developing emancipatory possibilities immanent to existing conditions in order to enliven them.

When we move from reflecting on *what* we think to *how* we think, we enter the realm of methodology, which is the theoretical account or *logos* of the methods of an inquiry. Having a methodology means not only pointing out which methods are used in an inquiry, but also having reasons for why they were chosen. Our theorizing always employs methods (i.e., procedures and practices) but often lacks a methodological account explaining their roles, limitations, and application. Because radical philosophical projects move back and forth between theory and practice, their methodology encompasses more than reflections on the methods of theory; it includes reflections on the methods of praxis as well. As with practical experimentation in the sciences, methodology informs and helps explain strategic and tactical choices in social struggles.

While it is important to develop an awareness of methodology, this does not guarantee certainty or precision, particularly when we are engaged in open-ended projects to understand and transform social conditions and relations. But this is not evidence of failure. As Aristotle remarked in his *Nicomachean Ethics,* "Our discussion will be adequate if its degree of clarity fits the subject-matter; for we should not seek the same degree of exactness in all sorts of arguments alike, any more than in the products of different crafts."[12] Efforts to understand and transform social relations and ourselves require practical knowledge, which does not lend itself to mathematical inference or clearly predictable outcomes (i.e., *epistēmē*). The contexts and projects of understanding and transforming human relations are always indeterminate insofar as they involve ongoing interpretations and unknown outcomes, but this does not render them any less important. These projects are both necessary and necessarily unending, and the unavoidable lack of certainty associated with them only elevates the importance of practical knowledge (*phronēsis*) for making good judgments. As Hans-Georg Gadamer (1900–2002) writes,

> The final confusion that dominates methodology of the sciences is the degeneration of the concept of practice. This concept lost its legitimacy in the age of science with its ideal of certainty. . . . One of the most important lessons the history of philosophy offers for this current problem consists in the role played in Aristotelian ethics and politics by practice and the knowledge that enlightens and leads it, the practical acuteness or wisdom that Aristotle called phronesis.[13]

One aspect of practical knowledge in this context is making judgments about method selection. Although there is no one single method employed in all radical philosophical projects, there is a set of overlapping reflexive, historical, and dialectical methods, which we can subsume under the general heading "critical methodology." Grouping these practices together in this way is an example of what Ludwig Wittgenstein called "family resemblance," or the definition of a group by its overlapping affinities or characteristics rather than any single shared characteristic or essence.[14] Together with its emancipatory interest, critical methodology is what generally sets radical philosophical projects apart and allows us to give them a family name. However, not all philosophies, radical or otherwise, make explicit their reasoning for choosing particular methods. It is thus useful to outline some representative examples here, which will allow us to (1) relate subsequent chapters to this historically influential methodological tradition; (2) identify the shared and overlapping methods employed in various projects (i.e., their family resemblance, described in subsequent discussions); and (3) see how these projects differ from other forms of philosophy and social theory, particularly the *nomothetic* or law-based models of *explanation* sketched in the Introduction.

A methodology encompasses several methods, chosen because they support the epistemological and metaphysical assumptions of the methodology and reflect the values and interests of the practitioners. As Georg Lukács writes, "Facts can only become facts within the framework of a system—which will vary with the knowledge desired."[15] Epistemology is the study of knowledge and so by *epistemological* assumptions I mean assumptions about belief, certainty, truth, and justification that follow from the method used to acquire knowledge. For example, a common definition in epistemology, going back to Plato, is that descriptive (or propositional) knowledge is a *true* belief that is *justified* by empirical observation and testing.[16] Metaphysics is the study of causes and concepts that are not empirically observable.[17] Thus, by *metaphysical* assumptions, I refer to assumptions about how to distinguish and relate concepts such as subject and object or universal and particular. Although these distinctions might at first appear inconsequential for radical social theory and practice, they make themselves felt in both mundane and revolutionary contexts. Finally, by *interests* I am referring to the motivating factor of the inquiry or investigation (i.e., practical, technical, material, or emancipatory interests), and by *values* I mean the commitments that shape those interests, such as various forms of equality, mutual aid, or social justice.

In the following sections, I outline some reflexive, historical, and dialectical methods employed within radical philosophical projects through a reconstruction of them that is itself historical and dialectical. These include hermeneutical, standpoint, phenomenological, dialectical, and materialist methods. Although not exhaustive of the possible constituent parts of a critical methodology, they do provide us with an important and influential set of approaches that can serve as touchstones for subsequent discussions.

Hermeneutics and Standpoint

The term *hermeneutics* comes from the Greek word *hermeneuō,* which means to translate or interpret and was associated with the Greek messenger-god Hermes. Each of us learns through a process of interpretation, which derives or constitutes meaning, and it is thus through a process of interpretation that we make sense of our world and our selves. All social and political struggles are engaged in creating new meanings, in developing new self-understandings, in critiquing oppression, and in articulating alternative forms of life from within a world (and a language) already marked and structured by oppression.[18] Hermeneutics helps us to identify the conditions that enable or foreclose the possibility for different kinds of interpretation and knowledge production in light of those struggles, while acknowledging that the language we use is never entirely our own.[19] No one can exit language, escape power, or bring an end, in one fell swoop, to the dominant interpretations circulating within the systems in which we find ourselves. Yet radical philosophies cannot fail to reveal the interests, structures, and relations of power reflected in these ways of understanding the world, or fail to engage in interpretive resistance and the process of creating alternatives. Hermeneutics is thus an essential part of a critical methodology, for interpretation is an important site of struggle.

The history of hermeneutics reveals concerns for the ways in which languages and practices are interpreted and for the processes of determining who is authorized to engage in meaning making. The Protestant Reformation, for example, represented a struggle to wrest the authority to interpret religious texts away from the leadership of the Catholic Church and redistribute it downward.[20] Around the time of the Reformation, we also witness the development of interpretive methods in philology (the historical study of language) and jurisprudence (the study of law) with the retrieval, interpretation, and incorporation of Roman law and classical texts into Renaissance culture and legal thought.[21] These interpretative methods arose in response to the problems with translating texts from another language, another time, or both—often the result of war and colonialism.

Over time there was an expansion of the *objects* of interpretation—from texts to experiences, traditions, and even the self—which led to an expansion of hermeneutics from a particular method to a general characteristic of all understanding. This shift from limited methods for interpreting texts to philosophical methods for understanding subjects and social relations more generally did not leave the struggles and conflicts over authority and exclusion behind.

The philosophical practice of hermeneutics emerged in opposition to the scientific model of the Enlightenment and its epistemological assumption of a rational, self-aware, and transcendental subject.[22] By uprooting the subject from what was thought to be the irrationalism of subjective and historical traditions as well as the corrupting influence of emotional life and the body, this independent subject could produce universal knowledge. These are two sides of the same coin: a universal rational subject abstracted from particular conditions, which makes possible universal knowledge unscathed by historical contingency. This tendency culminated in Immanuel Kant's *Critique of Pure Reason* (1781), in which experience is said to be possible only when mediated through certain universal properties of the transcendental subject's cognitive faculty (i.e., the categories of the understanding). These categories, together with the institutions of time and space, actively constitute the objects of its experience, making them congruent with our reason. Everything we can know about an object is only knowable because its representation is the result of the subject's understanding, because the necessity and universality of (truth) claims are only made possible by the subject.[23]

With the elevation of an abstract conception of the disembodied and rational subject by Enlightenment philosophers like Kant, the epistemic significance of one's lived and historical existence in the world was denigrated. "No real blood runs in the veins of the cognitive subject that Locke, Hume, and Kant constructed," writes Wilhelm Dilthey (1833–1911).[24] In response, we find a countermovement in the nineteenth century seeking to revive the role of experience in historical traditions and the role of the "spirit" of nations in constituting subjects and meaning. For example, Friedrich Ast (1778–1841) argued that the interpretation of ancient texts required explication of the "letter, meaning, and spirit."[25] By *spirit* (or *Geist*), he referred to a comprehensive and dynamic social condition that informs actions and texts but cannot be reduced to any individual act, text, or person. Recognition of the reciprocally constituting relation between an individual work, its author, and the social context of both has become known as the *hermeneutic circle*. "The basic principle of all understanding and knowledge is to find in the particular the spirit of the whole, and to comprehend the particular through the whole," writes Ast.[26]

The goal of hermeneutics is understanding meaning, rather than explaining natural events. Accordingly, interpreting the artifacts of human creativity—the results of human praxis—is qualitatively different from describing the physical properties of objects and explaining their law-like causal relations. "We explain nature, we understand mental life," writes Dilthey. Such understanding requires a self-reflective dimension that incorporates the actuality of our praxis in the world, historically and in the present, which is not possible with positivist (scientific) methods.[27] Dilthey argues that hermeneutics should serve as the methodological foundation of the humanities (*Geisteswissenschaften*), the main purpose of which is securing the objective validity of historical knowledge due to its dialectical relation with self-knowledge.[28] "The first condition for the possibility of a science of history," he writes, "consists in the fact that I myself am an historical being, that he who researches in to history is the same as he who makes it."[29] Hermeneutics had thus become reflexive, viewing the interpreter and the object of interpretation as products of social and linguistic traditions, while the constitution of meaning was recognized as a social and dialectical process (i.e., the hermeneutic circle); this set it apart from dominant positivistic methods.

Twentieth-century hermeneutics was deeply influenced by Martin Heidegger (1889–1976) and Gadamer. Heidegger focused on the way we human beings—which he refers to as *Dasein* or *being there*—understand the world in a pretheoretical fashion, habitually negotiating and acting without propositional knowledge or conscious interpretation.[30] As *Dasein*, we have a *practical* comportment that precedes our interpretive or *theoretical* understanding. Prior to any reflection upon it, this practical way of being fundamentally structures the way we exist, act, and know the world. The structure of this *practical understanding*, which defines our fundamental mode of being, is what Heidegger calls "care" or "concern" (*Sorge*).[31] All of our interpretations of the world, Heidegger argues, are derived from this pretheoretical and practical mode of understanding that situates and directs us toward things that matter for us. The role of interpretation is to elucidate this "forestructure" or "preunderstanding" of our theoretical knowledge.

Gadamer was also interested in our pretheoretical and situated forms of understanding. He asserted that we are already habituated in social practices, relations, discourses, and identities before we systematically reflect and become aware of the nature of these relations. "Long before we understand ourselves through the process of self-examination," he wrote, "we understand ourselves in a self-evident way in the family, society, and state in which we live. . . . *That is why the prejudices of the individual, far more than his judgments, constitute the historical reality of his being.*"[32] Prejudices or prejudgments (*Vorurteile*) for Gadamer do not have a negative connotation, as in the case of an unfair bias. They refer rather to those preexisting judgments or presuppositions that follow from having a particular vantage point and necessarily structure our thoughts and perceptions—what he calls "historically effected consciousness." They are in this way similar to Heidegger's notion of the forestructure of understanding. According to Gadamer, such prejudices are the essence of *tradition*—particularly as it relates to language—and constitute the historical and situated reality of our being. They are the standpoints that ground all of our practical knowledge. The hermeneutic task is to make explicit how our contemporary concerns and projects are mediated by tradition, a process that Gadamer calls a *fusion of horizons.*[33] Understanding is, then, "an event of transmission in which past and present are constantly mediated."[34] Such fusion of past and present perspectives is *dialogical* or dialectical insofar as it has the structure of the back-and-forth of a dialogue in which each side is changed through the encounter.[35]

Unfortunately, neither Gadamer nor Heidegger accounts for social structures of domination that differentially situate people in this dialogue, authorizing only a very few to participate and excluding or devaluing others.[36] Thus, while their hermeneutical methods and theories provide rich resources for our understanding of the historically situated and limiting condition of interpreters (us) and the importance of habit and pretheoretical practical life for practical knowledge (*phronēsis*), they fail to take up a critical stance. Critical hermeneutics must identify the normative possibilities within traditions of oppression in order to challenge the justificatory meanings they produce. As Jürgen Habermas writes, "Language is *also* a medium for domination and social power . . . language is *also* ideological."[37] To gain traction for a critique of ideological language, or interpretations that support relations of domination, Habermas combines hermeneutical methods with a critical social theory, which draws upon the immanent normative potential in language itself.[38] He argues that language users necessarily presuppose an *ideal speech situation* with which to judge actual claims and dialogues.[39] When we enter into dialogue, for example, the normative expectation is that our interlocutor will be sincere, will be motivated to come to an understanding, and will not engage in coercive tactics. Now, these expectations are often violated, but Habermas's point is that these are expectations inherent to language use and we can thus use them to justifiably critique those violations—an ability Gadamer's hermeneutics lacked. This normative resource in language, which Habermas connects to an emancipatory interest, is not constrained by cultural or linguistic tradition. This, he argues, enables his critical theory to identify when language is a medium of domination or when "communicative action" is replaced by "strategic action" in an attempt to coerce compliance.[40]

Linda Martín Alcoff also develops Gadamer's notion of an *interpretive horizon,* because it captures the "framing assumptions" and "congealed experiences" that orient our perceptions and interpretations of race and gender. However, since Gadamerian hermeneutics lacks a necessary account of the body (as does Habermas's critical hermeneutics), it is insufficient for a critical theory of race and gender, and she thus incorporates phenomenological methods as well.[41] Such methods allow a critical hermeneutical theory to be more attentive to the epistemic consequences of one's embodied experience and location in particular social structures. Because our bodies enact tacit knowledge, which varies depending on one's social identity (particularly the "visible" identities of race and gender), bodies and their location in social structures matter.[42] Concerning location, Alcoff uses the example of a servant who has an entirely different experience of the various rooms, passageways, and functions of a queen's castle than the queen has. Acknowledging these "perspectival knowledges," however, does not result in "dysfunctional relativism." On the contrary, while the queen's and servant's perspectives or horizons will each have limitations, we can determine which one is epistemically advantageous depending on the nature of our project. "For emancipatory and egalitarian projects," she writes, "clearly the servant's horizon will be the most valuable."[43]

This is an example of the standpoint method, which is a procedure for assessing the social limitations and conditions of knowledge production, and thus falls within what is called *social epistemology.* Social epistemology employs normative standards of evaluation (e.g., the servant's perspective is most *valuable*), although in making value judgments, it relies on situated experience within social structures rather than any essentialist identity categories. Gadamer's notion of prejudices that constitute the horizons or perspectives of cultural groups is therefore adapted to the dialectical logic of social structures of domination.[44] We live in a stratified society with social relations and bodily knowledge shaped by the social structures of race, class, and gender, and thus group-determined perspectives are shaped by and reflective of these hierarchical and antagonistic social relations. These conditions produce what Donna Haraway calls "situated knowledges."[45] An epistemic goal of radical philosophy is the recognition, generation, and cultivation of situated and oppositional knowledges from below.[46]

As we have seen, traditional approaches to epistemology or the study of knowledge often assume a disinterested and universal perspective—a God's-eye view of sorts—that is supposed to insulate knowledge claims (and the theorists making them) from the evaluative biases or limitations that follow from taking a particular perspective. Standpoint rejects this view, because claims to universality have masked the interests and values of privileged groups. To return to the castle example, it isn't that the queen and the servant would disagree about, for example, the physical existence of the castle, the numbers of rooms it has, or existing monarchical rule. The problem arises when monarchy (or capitalism, white supremacy, heterosexuality, patriarchy, and imperialism) is taken to be the neutral or value-free beginning assumption of a social science that produces a theory of its workings and reproduction, while viewing resistance to it as biased and problematically destabilizing. All such knowledge and assessment of knowledge is situated, informed by values, and thus perspectival—everyone has a standpoint, which is shaped by their social identity. The history of anthropology and the medical sciences on the topics of race and sex differences is a clear example of how incredible discourses of superiority and inferiority are constructed by naturalizing (or rendering biological) the social structures most beneficial to the social location of the theorists.[47]

The normative dimension of standpoint is to give greater weight to the perspectives of marginalized or oppressed groups, for they reflect experiences that are most often excluded in dominant discourses and knowledge production. More importantly, these situated knowledges are often the most important for resisting systems of oppression and developing practical wisdom for the construction of alternatives. The "distinction between knowledge and wisdom, and the use of experience as the cutting edge dividing them, has been key to Black women's survival. In the context of intersecting oppressions, the distinction is essential. Knowledge without wisdom is adequate for the powerful, but wisdom is essential to the survival of the subordinate."[48]

Early standpoint feminists, such as Dorothy E. Smith and Nancy Hartsock, were clearly informed by historical materialism and, more specifically, the Marxist analysis of class formation and class consciousness. As Sandra Harding writes, "Feminist standpoint theory revives, improves, and disseminates an important Marxian project."[49] This Marxian project concerned the epistemic privileging of the standpoint of the proletariat in capitalism, while also developing a sustained critique of the science of economics whose evaluative standards made exploitation and efficient capital accumulation its neutral starting point.[50]

Although standpoint does evaluate situated knowledges differently, it does not grant automatic epistemic privilege to oppressed or marginalized social locations, for while the possibility for perspectival insights objectively exists, they are not always realized. The "vision available to the oppressed group must be struggled for and represents an achievement which requires both science to see beneath the surface of the social relations in which all are forced to participate, and the education which can only grow from struggle to change those relations," writes Hartsock.[51] Theoretical insights are won through practical struggles.

Phenomenology

Phenomenology is a descriptive analysis of lived experience and, like herme- neutics, seeks to situate knowledge production in the lives of historical subjects who come to self-awareness and produce theory within linguistic and cultural traditions. More specifically, phenomenology makes the habitual practices of the body an essential mode of experience and thus of knowledge, which alters the way we understand human consciousness. The term *phenomenology* is derived from a combination of the Greek words *logos* and *phainomenon* ("appearance") and is therefore the study of that which appears to consciousness. Although the term and even method of phenomenology are found to some degree in the works of Immanuel Kant, Johann Gottlieb Fichte, and Georg Wilhelm Friedrich Hegel, it was Edmund Husserl who rigorously defined the project and method of modern phenomenology in his *Logical Investigations* (1900–1901).[52] We can speak of his work as a form of transcendental phenomenology, whereas many of his successors pursued a form of existential phenomenology.[53]

For Husserl, phenomenology is foundational to all philosophical thought: "All philosophical disciplines are rooted in pure phenomenology, through whose development ... they obtain their proper force."[54] Husserl believed phenomenol- ogy to be a new science "inferior in methodological rigor to none of the modern sciences." To achieve scientific rigor and establish objective knowledge meant a turn away from precisely the kind of historicism that Dilthey championed (see the section on hermeneutics above). Historicism, Husserl argued, "carries over into extreme skeptical subjectivism. The ideas of truth, theory, and science would then, like all ideas, lose their absolute validity."[55] A rigorous phenomenological method and a better understanding of consciousness are the only ways to ensure such validity.

Consciousness is, Husserl argued, always conscious *of* something, like an object, a person, an experience remembered, or a mathematical term, and is thus directed. Our awareness is invariably directed and relational, since subject and object are mutually constituted within experience. Everything appearing to consciousness is inherently connected to the *intentionality* of consciousness. Hence, there is no appearance of things without intentionality. This model of experience complicates the traditional metaphysical distinction between subject and object, which in the Cartesian tradition becomes a distinction between an internal mind and an external body that, in turn, supports an epistemological distinction between essence and appearance. The mind in the dualism model is said to produce representational copies (i.e., appearances or pictures) of objects it encounters in the world outside of itself (i.e., essences or things in themselves). Phenomenology's notion that appearance is a *dynamic relation* of consciousness—stretching to incorporate and unify the two poles of subject and object—undermines this inside/outside model and calls metaphysical categories central to modern philosophy into question.

In order to comprehend what appears to consciousness, Husserl employs a method of detached and completely disinterested description, moving from the factual reality of our experience to its essential structure. Husserl calls this detachment or suspension of judgment the *epochē*. Its generalization into a method is called *phenomenological reduction*. Such reduction is the suspension of all empirical interests that—while essential to the initial experience, since we are always interested—must now be neutralized to facilitate a pure form of contemplation. We must withhold "questions of being, questions of value, practical questions, questions about being or not-being, about being valuable, being useful, being beautiful, being good, etc. All natural interests are put out of play."[56] To put these interests "out of play" does not discount them or our everyday world of prescientific experience. Indeed, it elevates the epistemic status of our experience and everyday empirical interests that orient us in the world; appearances are no longer merely secondary qualities that conceal the real or true world but are the matter of truth and knowledge. "From what rests on the surface," says Husserl, "one is led into the depths," but to descend we need to interrupt the flow of things.[57] When phenomenological reduction is done correctly, it is as if, says Husserl, "I stand above the world."[58] It is only by "bracketing" or suspending the natural interests involved that phenomenology can become transcendental.[59]

Although Husserl ultimately desired pure theory and objective knowledge, we can see here that his phenomenology, like hermeneutics, sought to defend the value of lived experience against a common enemy: a dominant and positivistic scientific methodology. "Galileo," he wrote, "abstracts from the subjects as persons leading a personal life; he abstracts from all that is in any way spiritual, from all cultural properties which are attached to things in human praxis."[60] For Husserl, it is only through the unscientific life of human praxis that we can "overcome the philosophical naiveté which lies in the [supposedly] 'scientific' character of traditional objectivistic philosophy."[61] That is to say, it is not by getting rid of our everyday experiences that we come to a universal condition for "pure theory," but by working through such experiences. In short, praxis enables theory. Everyday experiences and perceptions are the foundation of knowledge, and all so-called scientific knowledge is (and must always be) rooted in what Husserl calls the prescientific life-world (Lebenswelt). This is the "world in which we are always already living and which furnishes the ground for all cognitive performance and all scientific determination."[62] It is the taken-for-granted "substrate" of possible judgments and acts as a "horizon of typical familiarity." This world is shared; we belong to it and navigate it through "communication, education, and tradition."[63]

An important consequence of this understanding of a life-world is that the objective determinations of science are predicated on the intersubjective conditions—the "we-subjectivity" as Husserl calls it—of our world of experience, interests, and meaning.[64] Objectivity is then the objectification or rationalization of a primary and pregiven intersubjective existence: The rationalization of the world of science is invariably situated within the sphere of intersubjective meaning. The intersubjective dimension of this life-world is always already there and enables other forms of thinking it, as in the natural and social sciences. Our perception in this life-world to which Husserl calls for us to return is not that of a disembodied self but is experienced in a bodily or corporal (*leiblich*) way that orients us. Indeed, it is the only way we can be oriented, have interests, and make our way. Our "living body," says Husserl, is "never absent from the perceptual field."[65] This body exists within a historical tradition, has interests that orient and guide it, and accrues habits.

It was this dimension of Husserl's phenomenology—namely, the role of the life-world and the body in experience—together with his critique of consciousness that most influenced the early to mid-twentieth-century existentialist phenomenological tradition. Heidegger's *Being and Time* (1927), Jean-Paul

Sartre's *Being and Nothingness* (1943), Maurice Merleau-Ponty's *Phenomenology of Perception* (1945), and Simone de Beauvoir's *The Second Sex* (1949) are leading works in this tradition. Merleau-Ponty's and Beauvoir's phenomenologies of the body have been particularly influential in queer, disability, postcolonial, race, and feminist works in critical phenomenology today. Utilizing the phenomenological method in the female body's felt experience of sexism, Iris Marion Young writes, "An essential part of the situation of being a woman is that of living the ever-present possibility that one will be gazed upon as a mere body, as shape and flesh that presents itself as the potential object of another subject's intentions and manipulations, rather than as a living manifestation of action and intention."[66] Kevin Paterson and Bill Hughs give expression to similar experiences of alienation when navigating disabling environments that create "a vivid, but unwanted consciousness of one's impaired body." In this disabling context, "one's impaired body 'dys-appears'—is made present as a thematic focus of attention" and the body is "stunned into its own recognition by its presence-as-alien-being-in-the-world."[67]

Frantz Fanon's description of his experiences as having a black body under colonial rule combines this alienated sense of being-for-another with the objectifying gaze Young describes. With the white gaze, an "unfamiliar weight burdened me," he writes. "In the white world the man of color faces difficulties in the elaboration of his bodily schema."[68] This is a qualitatively different experience than when "the black man is among his own," where he "will have no occasion, except in minor internal conflicts, to experience his being through others."[69] Judith Butler's queer phenomenology asserts that gender is "instituted through the stylization of the body and, hence, must be understood as the mundane way in which bodily gestures, movements, and enactments of various kinds constitute the illusion of an abiding gendered self."[70]

Dialectics

As a method, dialectics (*dialektikē tekhnē*) emerged in ancient Greek philosophy, where it meant roughly the "art of dialogue" or a form of discourse. Plato's dialogues, particularly the *Parmenides,* popularized a dialectical approach, which through his work came to be known as the *Socratic method.*[71] Contemporary dialectics originated with Hegel, who combined this ancient Greek tradition with a phenomenological method, but with a very important twist—one that does not fit into the oft-repeated but decidedly misleading "thesis-antithesis-synthesis" formula. Forgoing Descartes's dream of an unmoving Archimedean point upon which knowledge could be built, Hegel opted instead for the metaphor of a circle, later to become known as the *hermeneutic circle*. The circle represents unity, but also change and return. We often speak of the "circle of life" that involves the cycle of birth, growth, and death—ashes to ashes, dust to dust. "It is the process of its own becoming," Hegel writes, "the circle that presupposes its end as its goal, having its end also as its beginning; and only by being worked out to its end, is it actual."[72]

Hegel sees the dialectic as an expression of rationality (*logos*) in natural and human development, declaring that it is "the one and only true method,"[73] because "this method is not something distinct from its subject matter and content."[74] Method (thought) and subject matter (natural and social world) are not "distinct," says Hegel, because both are dialectically structured, which is to say that they have the structure of reason. The objective rationality of the world and the subjective rationality of thought are, he argues, two sides of the same concept (*Begriff*), which actualizes itself through the intellectual and practical activity of human communities over time—a tragic story recounted in his *Phenomenology of Spirit* (1807). To adequately explain Hegel's claim in all of its dimensions would take us far beyond the bounds of this book, so I limit my discussion to the dialectic operating in Hegel's phenomenological method, particularly as it concerns social relations.[75]

Generally speaking, we can think of the dialectic development as starting with growth or alteration (negation) that produces out of itself opposing forces (contradiction), which, if successful, reconcile (through the negation of the negation) in a new unity. This new unity is a sublation (*Aufhebung*) or absolute reconciliation, which involves a mediated and thus transformative process. Perhaps the most well-known example of this dialectical logic is Marx's analysis of class formation and conflict, in which two classes emerge from the same process (capitalism), come into conflict (class struggle), and then find a mediated reconciliation (communism). The concepts and movement of this process are difficult to comprehend at first. Indeed, the most challenging aspect of Hegel's dialectical method is grasping the moments of nonidentity, mediation, negation, and contradiction that characterize the movement within this circle. I explain these in the context of the two particularly important ways in which Hegel's dialectical method is taken up in radical philosophies. The first concerns the social condition of individual freedom, which involves the dialectic of *mutual recognition,* while the second concerns the relation of theory and praxis, or the *dialectic of immanence and transcendence.* I begin with the role of nonidentity in Hegel's dialectic of social recognition.

Adorno wrote that "dialectics is the consistent sense of nonidentity," and to understand nonidentity, we must see it as a critical response to the first law of classical logic, namely, the law of identity.[76] This law asserts that each thing is identical with itself and different from another (or A is A and not ~A).[77] I am myself and not you, while you are yourself and not me. That's the claim of the law of identity and it sounds plausible. Hegel contests this claim because he regards identity logic as a kind of "picture-thinking." This was his term for the positivism or scientism we encountered in the Introduction—a representational view of the world in which there are seemingly only extrinsic relations and forces at work between discrete entities.[78] Applying the law of identity to humans would be like attempting to capture the identity of an individual by taking a picture of them and recording their physical measurements, as if something like a driver's license could capture the nature of that person's identity. This notion of identity would provide no insights into human action, conflict, social norms, or cultural traditions and thus be of no use in a critical social theory.

At the core of Hegel's *nonidentity* thinking is the notion that the identity of one entity is dynamically *mediated* or conditioned by another: what it *is* to be entity A includes its *relation* to entity B and vice versa.[79] A is only itself through its relation to B. An obvious example would be a parent's relation to a child and vice versa, but Hegel wants to delve deeper into the mediating relations necessary for anyone to develop as a self-conscious human being as such. In his *Phenomenology of Spirit* (1807), Hegel speaks of "a *becoming-other* that has to be taken back, or is a mediation."[80] The Latin root of mediation is *mediatio,* meaning "middle point" or "middle division," and mediation in the original German of Hegel's text is *Vermittlung,* the root of which is *Mitte* or "middle." Hegel says, "Each is for the other the middle term, through which each mediates itself with itself and unites with itself."[81]

In the context of Hegel's "becoming-other" idea, I could say that the other is the middle point in the circular process of my own development: I recognize myself in the other (mediation), and this recognition is then "taken back," as Hegel put it, in my act of comprehension. What I (and they) take from the encounter is the recognition that I am an instance of something larger, a concept of the *human being* that is not located within me but with which I (and others) identify. Recognition is a form of reflection, not introspection. It relies on our reflection on something that exists for us in the world—it must involve something that is not us, or said another way, is an *other* to consciousness. To see myself in the other and for the other to see themselves in me is to *mutually recognize* that we are the same in a fundamental sense—namely, as free human beings—yet different instances of this sameness: "*Self-consciousness achieves its satisfaction only in another self-consciousness.*"[82] Recognition (*Anerkennung*) is, then, more than merely taking notice of the other. It is rather the practical affirmation of the other as an equal much the way nation-states might recognize other nation-states as sovereign and potential members of a federation, trade agreement, or subject of international law.

What one "takes back" from the practical experience of mutual recognition is a new self-understanding that grasps, Hegel says, the "I which is a We, and the We which is an I."[83] Through my encounter with the other I recognize something that I share with the other, and thus my identity is in some way *nonidentical,* as it involves my identification with something that exceeds my individuality—the "We that is an I" or the concept of the human species (consciousness). When I self-identify as a human being, I'm invoking a general concept, which mediates my particular self, and so the particular "I" that I am is defined by my identification with a concept (the I that is a We). Although this example emphasizes a form of conscious unity, mediation is also a process of establishing difference. "Because each is for itself insofar as *it is not the other,*" writes Hegel, "each *shines* in the other and is only insofar as the other is."[84] That is to say, one is only individuated through the other. My development as a unique self is made possible through the recognition that I am a free human being: "the supersession of individual existence is equally the production of it."[85]

According to Hegel's account, individual freedom can be neither independence in the sense of a lack of dependency on others—a popular conception in political liberalism—nor freedom as supremacy achieved through the domination of others (thereby ensuring that others, rather than you, are dependent). In short, in the dialectical development of individual freedom, there must exist a social condition of interdependency, but not domination. Hegel illustrates the logic of this relation using the example of two potential self-consciousnesses engaged in conflict, trying to force the other to recognize them as independent.[86] This is referred to as the "struggle for recognition" or the "master-slave dialectic," and reflects the desire of human beings to be free.[87] One of the lessons learned in this battle is that the desire for freedom cannot be satisfied by forcing another to recognize you as free, because the other's freedom is what you need to see in yourself. If I am to take myself as free, I must take the other to be free. Seeking to *force* someone to recognize me as free is therefore contradictory and self-defeating, because I would only see subjugation in the other and, in turn, in myself.[88]

Force is in this context a form of *negation*. To negate is to alter, transform, or determine something or someone, be it the apple I negate by eating it, my self-understanding I negate by transforming it, or my attempt to negate or determine another's will. Hegel describes subjects as "pure negativity," because they (we) have the power of negation. Two forms of negation operative in Hegel's dialectic of recognition are of particular note. First, in his story of the failed experiment in using domination as a means to freedom, the lord forces the bondsman to do the manual labor necessary to satisfy the lord's desires. While this forced division between labor and consumption, or between labor and desire's satisfaction, involves the determination of the bondsman's will, this process also entails an opening: the bondsman comes to see his will in the world upon which he has labored (rather than in the freely given recognition of another subject), and thus begins to develop a sense of self, and thereby an inkling of freedom.[89] This notion of recognizing oneself in the objects one alters through one's own labor and the idea of domination as a division of labor and consumption are central to Marx's dialectical theory of class consciousness, class conflict, and alienation.

The second form of negation is subtler and often overlooked but is essential to Hegel's idea of freedom and important for radical philosophical projects. This is a form of *self-negation*. The solution to the question of mutual recognition is to negate our own desire to negate or dominate the other, because we discover that attempting to satisfy our desire for freedom through domination leads us into a contradiction. Dewey says that habit does not "stop to think" and desire or "impulse" does not "of itself engage in reflection or contemplation." We can think of Hegel's notion of self-negation as an intentional check on a habituated form of desire satisfaction—a moment of stopping and reflecting.

The story Hegel tells in the *Phenomenology*—a parable of dialectical development of self-consciousness—is one of a conscious being habitually negating the form or existence of the objects around it, eating, drinking, building, and transforming whatever it wants and thus demonstrating that the world is there to satisfy its desire and not vice versa. The struggle for recognition begins when it encounters another conscious being like itself that has the same habit. The existence of each appears to the other as just another object in the world to negate in the satisfaction of its own desire, which is the essence of slavery (and in the context of states, the essence of colonialism and imperialism). As we have seen, a relation of domination does not provide freedom for either the lord or the bondsman, since the recognition necessary for freedom cannot be coerced. The only possibility for exiting this condition is a mutual act of self-negation, of checking the pursuit of one's desires out of respect for the other—the original privilege check. This is the constitutive moment of the development of freedom (and "spirit" or *Geist,* for Hegel).[90]

Self-negation is negativity turning back upon itself—the closing of a dialectical circle. This self-reflexive movement engenders subjectivity insofar as it is the inaugural moment of a self-conscious subject that is other-regarding insofar as it takes the needs of the other into consideration of its own actions. This newfound faculty is that of self-determination—the self-negation of our own desire in light of the other. Mutual recognition is the result of a simultaneous act of self-negation, and it is this (negated) self that we see in the other—the self that *our* self-negation brings into being and that we experience in the other. This is the social condition of individual freedom, which involves mutual recognition and respect.

We can think of this negation as a form of *self-critique,* and according to Hegel, it is necessary in order to disrupt a social relation of domination (i.e., a social structure). Applying this critical self-relation beyond the scope of Hegel's text—moving from self-consciousness as such to various social identities—we can see the importance of self-critique as self-negation for white-supremacist, patriarchal, colonialist, ableist, and homophobic subjects that are habituated to certain forms of privilege or unchecked desire satisfaction vis-à-vis the objectification of or violence toward the other. These forms of subjectivity are committed to a self-defeating notion of freedom insofar as they attempt to shore up their own identities through the domination or destruction of others. Yet, these attempts to satisfy this desire for freedom through domination only reproduce or exacerbate instability and resistance, which, in turn, induces fear. No matter how forceful their domination, they remain vulnerable and dependent upon the other.[91] Even when there is a successful revolt against the dominant group—and it is likely that the Haitian slave revolt of 1791 to 1804 against the French colonizers in Haiti was the inspiration for Hegel's dialectic of lordship and bondage—self-negation is still necessary for the development of new horizontal forms of subjectivity.[92] This is certainly not to say that practical struggles against formalized inequality and domination are unnecessary, but rather that until self-negation is by and large accomplished, the contradiction will most likely morph yet persist, regardless of any achieved formalized equality. For example, the outlawing of slavery and Jim Crow segregation in the United States did not eliminate white supremacy.

In a way, Hegel was the original conflict theorist, but he drew conservative and contradictory conclusions from his own social and dialectical model of freedom. He historicized everything, except those social structures that secured his (white, European, heterosexual, and male) privilege by essentializing gender in a way that made women unfit for public life, promoting a racist and colonialist philosophy of history, and endorsing monarchy as the most rational form of political organization. It was therefore left to others to develop a dialectical critique of Hegel's philosophy, and the social structures it naturalized, using his own method. Marx's analysis of class alienation and class conflict, Sartre's critique of anti-Semitism, Simone de Beauvoir's feminist critique of patriarchy, Butler's queer and feminist critique of heteronormativity, and Fanon's and Aimé Césaire's critiques of colonialism and white supremacy are just a few examples of the influence of Hegel's dialectical method and its evolution.[93] Finally, despite the fact that Hegel was a conflict theorist, he assumed a totalizing model of critique in which difference persists *within* a unity—namely, a positive reconciliation through the negation of the negation or "determinate negation"—but a unity that was absolute, rational, and left nothing other than itself remaining. The circle was closed and complete. Hegel conceived of the nation-state, for example, as potentially such an ethical, political, and economic unity that realized the concept of freedom. The circle drew upward from the abstract personhood of the rights-bearing individual and moved through several social structures of domination until reaching the concrete personhood of the sovereign and then moving back down again.[94] Since the mid-twentieth century, there have been several detotalizing responses to Hegel's work, some of which are mentioned above.[95] This is the context of Adorno's claim about dialectics never relinquishing the tensions and remainders of nonidentity.[96] Adorno's critique of Hegel's closed or positive dialectical method—namely, that through the negation of the negation there would be no remainder—produced a *negative dialectics* or an open dialectical method that does not sacrifice nonidentity thinking in critical and materialist theorizing. Since Marx largely appropriated the totalizing nature of Hegel's dialectical method, this critique and alternative apply to early Marxism as well.

The second significant way in which radical philosophies have incorporated Hegel's dialectical method concerns the identification of potentials for change within relations of domination and injustice. Generally speaking, dialectical thought views social reality as filled with tension, marked by conflict, and populated by interdependent identities in a continual process of change. The "radical potential" of dialectical critique, writes Nancy Fraser, "achieves traction only insofar as it discloses tensions and possibilities that are in some sense immanent to the configuration at hand."[97] Axel Honneth refers to such possibility as a "normative potential" immanent within present social and material conditions but that "points beyond all given forms of social organization," indicating a possibility for transcendence or fundamental transformation.[98] This was Marx's understanding as well: "We do not anticipate the world dogmatically," he wrote, "but rather wish to find the new world through criticism of the old."[99] For Marx, in his time, this potential for a new world was located in the emancipatory interests of the working class, which was emerging in class struggle. The role of theory was to facilitate this emergence through the development of a critical class consciousness: theory, as Georg Lukács put it, was "essentially the intellectual expression of the revolutionary process itself."[100] In this dialectic of immanence and transcendence it is always by way of human praxis that the immanent potential for transcending conditions of oppression is revealed.

Materialism

In the study of social change, the materialist method gives explanatory primacy to practical activity, particularly as it relates to economic production and exchange, asserting that the "*ultimately* determining element in history is the production and reproduction of real life."[101] This method evolved in tandem with the *historical materialist* methodology of Marx and Friedrich Engels (1820–1895), which combines materialist, historical, and dialectical methods with an emancipatory interest in the liberation of the laboring classes. New material conditions demand new theory, and thus materialist critiques remain historically specific and continuously open to revision. These critiques serve the primary aim of critical resistance—namely, the transformation of the forms of practical relations that define us. "All social life is essentially *practical*," writes Marx. "All mysteries which lead theory to mysticism find their rational solution in human practice and in the comprehension of this practice."[102]

Historical materialism operates as a situated and oppositional knowledge in class struggle; it is a pedagogy of the oppressed, to use Paulo Freire's phrase.[103] "The history of all hitherto existing society is the history of class struggles," begins the *Communist Manifesto* (1848).[104] Within capitalist societies, the expansion of wealth entails the growth of the working class, because the value and thus wealth accumulated by the capitalists derives from workers' labor (see Chapter 2). These classes arise from the same process and are intrinsically related, yet confront each other antagonistically like Hegel's lord and bondsman. The most basic social structure of capitalism is thus inherently dialectical and antagonistic. "What the bourgeoisie ... produces, above all, is its own grave-diggers."[105] Historical materialism is therefore intended to empower a movement of critical resistance against class-based oppression by identifying the possibilities immanent in the material conditions of the time.[106] Its function does not "lie in the elucidation of pure scientific knowledge," writes Lukács, "but in the field of action. Historical materialism ... existed so that the proletariat could understand a situation and so that, armed with this knowledge, it could act accordingly."[107] Although the oppressed have not willed their own situation, by coming to understand their condition and the logic of the relations of power structuring their lives, they can empower themselves to bring about change.

In the beginning of historical materialism's development, the emancipatory interest motivating oppositional knowledge production was decidedly class-based—particularly a white, male, industrial working class—and the primary institutions targeted for transformation were overtly economic in nature. However, over time and through critique, the appropriation of historical materialism by other resistance movements—and its incorporation into an intersectionalist methodology—both strengthened its foundations with a more sophisticated analysis of power and interrelated structures of domination and broadened its applicability in postcolonial, critical race, queer, and feminist projects.[108] For example, contemporary feminist philosopher Chandra Talpade Mohanty advocates a "revised race-and-gender-conscious historical materialism."[109]

Materialism identifies how the *relations of production,* such as the social structures of race, gender, and class, are shaped by the *forces of production,* or the means of production in labor power, technology, tools, buildings raw materials, and land. The *mode of production* is the term Marx and Engels use to represent the totality or combination of the forces and relations of production, and thus they speak of a capitalist or feudalist or hunter-and-gatherer mode of production. As Marx writes in the third volume of *Capital,* "For the totality of these relationships which the bearers of this production have toward nature and one another, the relationships in which they produce, is precisely society, viewed according to its economic structure. Like all its forerunners, the capitalist production process proceeds under specific material conditions, which are however also the bearers of specific relations which the individual enters into in the process of reproducing their life."[110] Marx and Engels are thus arguing that the forces of production ultimately determine all social relations, norms, practices, political and economic institutions, and forms of consciousness—expressed in everyday beliefs and values, as well as systematically in, for example, theology and philosophy. "In general, such ways of life resulted from the repetition and accumulation of the humblest actions of practical life," writes Henri Lefebvre.[111] We could even include our bodies within this process. As we saw in the discussion of phenomenology, the materiality and practices of the body are essential for understanding our identities and subjectivity, and they are shaped by social structures, worked over and resignified in light of historical norms. In industrial capitalism, the bodies of wage-laborers, for example, become "appendages of machines," says Marx.

Therefore, capitalism produces not only the material means for commodity production, but it also reproduces the subjects—both physically and mentally— that are necessary to labor in or support this production process. This involves producing particular kinds of raced and gendered subjectivities to "fit" and reproduce existing divisions of labor. For example, there is a traditional gendered division of labor existing between those who labor for a wage and those who labor for the reproduction of the wage-laborer (through domestic work, child rearing, etc.). Both types of labor contribute to the production of surplus value or profit necessary to reproduce the capitalist class and its form of domination. (Generally speaking, we could say that unpaid reproductive labor produces use-values and wage-labor produces exchange-values—a distinction discussed at greater length in Chapter 2.) The capitalist reproduction of subjectivities also entails ensuring that the most pervasive relations, theories, values, images, and norms—the ones with the most "purchasing power" in colloquial and scientific discourses—are also those that support the capitalist mode of production.[112] Freedom, for instance, is commonly understood to be the capacity of an independent individual to exercise their rational (i.e., selfish) choices in the use of their private property, which is facilitated by individual rights thought to be natural rather than political.[113] This conception of freedom is a good fit for capitalist relations, in which the rich can privately own the means of production, while the workers "own" their labor power that they can "freely" contractually exchange for a wage. Women and people of color were, for most of capitalism's history, not even believed to own their own labor, so this abstract conception is not so abstract as to transcend existing social structures of domination. Democracy and capitalism are also popularly presented as complementary systems, and the contract and the market are the habitual explanatory models for all human relations (including the "marketplace of ideas"). Every value, relation, and self-understanding, write Marx and Engels, is abstracted from its social context and drowned "in the icy water of egotistical calculation."[114]

According to the materialist method, if production changes, so do the social relations and forms of consciousness that support it. An example of this, which began in the early 1970s in the United States, is the shift from Fordism to what is now called neoliberalism. Fordism takes its name from Henry Ford of Ford Motors, who personified a period of standardized, assembly-line mass production that contributed to a relatively stable labor force, new forms of management, and corporate stabilization of the economy with help from organized labor. Unions secured livable wages, job security, and health and retirement benefits for large parts of the paid labor force. Cities were built and rebuilt around these large-scale sites of production, affecting patterns of transportation, consumption, housing, and leisure. This hierarchical rationalization, centralization, and administration—greatly assisted externally by American imperialism—brought about an entirely new form of American "middle-class" life after World War II.[115] Antonio Gramsci wrote that the rationalization represented by Fordism was the "biggest collective effort to date to create, with unprecedented speed, and with a consciousness of purpose unmatched in history, a new type of worker and of man."[116] Ford also instituted the five-dollar wage for male wage-laborers, often called a "family wage," because it was enough to sustain the gendered division of labor, with women generally doing unpaid domestic work (although women of color were often hyper-exploited, having to take on both paid and unpaid labor). This effectively stabilized the patriarchal economy of the family, for the time being, and allowed some of the workforce to afford to buy the products they produced.

An oil embargo (OPEC, 1973), increasing global competition, and declining profits led capitalists to withdraw from the grand compromise with labor, aggressively reduce wages and benefits, and move to post-Fordist forms of production that entailed a flexible workforce (i.e., part-time and precarious work) and a form of "flexible accumulation," as David Harvey calls it.[117] This was the beginning of the period of deregulation and "globalization," or deindustrialization in the United States and the shifting of production to low-wage and non-unionized labor forces abroad. These changes affect consumption patterns, family structure, immigration patterns, urban design, and forms of resistance, from the international and local operations of the alter-globalization movements, to the

Zapatista Rebellion in Chiapas, Mexico, launched by the Zapatista National Liberation Army (EZLN) the day the North American Free Trade Agreement went into effect on January 1, 1994.

In this period, we also witness the deregulation of the financial sector, a rise in personal credit and debt, intensifying global flows of capital, and a rise in cognitive and affective labor, all facilitated by new forms of transportation, organization, and communication.[118] We also witness the rise of postmodern philosophy, theology, art, and methodology, replacing the "grand narratives" of modernism. With the decentralization of production and increase of precarious labor that brought an end to stable, hierarchically rationalized and managed production (with tightly integrated related institutions, such as schools), came the theorization of the fragmentation of the subject, demise of the rational metanarrative, rejection of totalizing theory, and the emergence of deconstruction, networks, signs without referents, flows, deterritorialization, and talk of schizophrenia.[119] However, as Fredric Jameson writes, "postmodernism is not the cultural dominant of a wholly new social order ... but only the reflex and the concomitant of yet another systemic modification of capitalism itself."[120] The materialist method analyzes the production of these forms of (postmodern) knowledge within the context of the contemporary economic production in a way that "does not lose sight of the fact that the basic rules of a capitalist mode of production continue to operate as invariant shaping forces in historical-geographical development."[121] This includes remaining cognizant of the global rise of industrial production and corporate colonialist rule beyond the centers of finance and service, which are more modern than postmodern in their material conditions and social relations.

One example of how the materialist method can contribute to situated and oppositional knowledge today—in the wake of the 2008 financial crash, global economic recession, and foreclosure crisis (which began earlier in communities of color)—concerns the intensification and disciplinary function of debt relations and the forms of subjectivity they cultivate. Long used as a means of imposing capital-friendly restructuring and austerity internationally, through the World Bank and International Monetary Fund, debt discipline has grown domestically in the United States with an increasingly credit-fueled economy and the insinuation of financialization mechanisms into every facet of life.

An increasing portion of the population today has their lives structured around debt repayment (or their lives destroyed by default, bankruptcy, and foreclosure). As a result, the values and norms necessary to ensure repayment have risen in prominence as have resistance to them.[122] As Maurizio Lazzarato writes, the creditor-debtor relation is "one of the most important and universal of modern-day capitalism. Credit or debt and their creditor-debtor relationship constitute specific relations of power that entails specific forms of production and control of subjectivity—a particular form of *homo economicus,* the 'indebted man.'" Debt, he argues, "produces a specific 'morality.'"[123] There are resistance movements around the globe organizing against financialization, austerity, and debtor subjectivity. Within the United States, the rise of foreclosure resistance groups and debt strikes across the country has drawn energy and organizing strength from Occupy Wall Street activists and oppositional knowledge in, for example, the *Debt Resisters' Operations Manual,* compiled by Strike Debt, whose motto is, "You are not a loan."[124]

CHAPTER 2
MARXISM AND CLASS CRITIQUE

Bourgeois liberal theory takes into account only ... the realm of "peaceful competition," the marvels of technology and pure commodity exchange; it separates it strictly from the other aspect: the realm of capital's blustering violence which is regarded as more or less incidental to foreign policy and quite independent of the economic sphere of capital.
—*Rosa Luxemburg,* The Accumulation of Capital[1]

The philosophers have only interpreted the world in various ways; the point is to change it.
—*Karl Marx, "Eleventh Thesis on Feuerbach"*[2]

It was about 8:00 a.m. on March 17, 2010, when seventeen-year-old Tian Yu jumped from the fourth-floor dormitory for assembly workers at the Foxconn factory in Shenzhen, China. She survived but was paralyzed from the waist down. "I was born into a farming family in February 1993 in a village near Laohekou City, Hubei Province, central China," Yu told an interviewer from her hospital bed. "My grandmother brought me up while my parents were earning money as factory workers far away from home."[3] Tian and her parents' move from farming to industrial labor is part of the largest rural to urban migration in history, involving hundreds of millions of people over the past few decades of industrialization in China.[4]

Tian Yu's time in the electronics factory in Shenzhen was short-lived. After a month of long, monotonous work on the assembly line, Foxconn did not pay her wages due to a technical error, her supervisors claimed.[5] "I was so desperate that my mind went blank," Tian said of her psychological state before her jump. She is now back in her village and weaves slippers to try to make ends meet. Seventeen other employees at Foxconn, a Taiwanese corporation specializing in the assembly of smart phones and tablets, also attempted suicide that year, fourteen of them dying. The company—which has posters on its walls reading "Value efficiency every minute, every second," "Growth, thy name is suffering," and "Achieve goals or the sun will no longer rise"—responded to worker desperation by installing suicide nets around their facilities and making employees sign an "antisuicide pledge." The pledge didn't actually make them promise they wouldn't commit suicide, but rather that their families couldn't hold the company legally responsible if they tried.[6]

Although assembly line manufacturing and labor-intensive agricultural production still exist in the United States, a rise in service sectors has accompanied a traumatizing process of deindustrialization over the last few decades.[7] A large portion of service sector work is affective labor, which "produces or manipulates affects such as a feeling of ease, well-being, satisfaction, excitement, or passion," write Michael Hardt and Antonio Negri. "One can recognize affective labor, for example, in the work of legal assistants, flight attendants, and fast food workers (service with a smile)."[8] Indeed, one of the early studies on affective labor was *The Managed Heart* (1983) by Arlie Hochschild, who participated in a Delta flight attendant training program, where smiles and cheerfulness are workers' "biggest 'asset.'"[9]

C. Wright Mills, who influenced Hochschild's work, studied the rise of a "personality market" in his groundbreaking work *White Collar* (1953). In the "great shift from manual skills to the art of 'handling,' selling, and servicing people, personal or even intimate traits of the employee are drawn into the sphere of exchange," writes Mills.[10] In this market you'll find people selling confidence in cars, cappuccinos, and mortgage-backed securities. For many, manipulative tactics and affective management become a "'genuine' aspect of oneself," insofar as one tells "little lies about one's feelings, until one is emptied of such feelings."[11] Mills rightly notes here how work upon one's personality is similar to manual labor that transforms raw materials, contributing to what we now call *subject formation*.[12] The mask you wear and the affects you feign come to mediate your interactions, on the clock and off. Affective labor is a productive practice that shapes both the actions of our bodies and our subjectivity and, like manual labor, produces alienation. We become estranged from each other on yet another level as "each secretly tries to make an instrument of the other," and in the process, one makes an instrument of oneself.[13] After years of working in the service industry, I could feel a particular smile and higher-pitched intonation in my voice that crept into my everyday interactions, as if I might expect a tip from whomever I set at ease with my habituated pleasantries.

The commodification of affect in the service and entertainment industries, the long history of gendered and unpaid affective labor in the domestic sphere of reproductive labor, as well as the production of physical commodities in manufacturing, such as Tian Yu's labor in the Foxconn factory, all produce *value* in a capitalist system. Although capitalism is often considered just an *economic* system of production, exchange, and distribution, Marx took a more comprehensive and radical view. He argued that the material conditions of economic life are the key to understanding our present practical lives and forms of consciousness, our social structures and political and legal systems, as well as our relation to nature. Capitalism produces subjects, concepts, and values as much as it produces and distributes objects and services. It generates antagonistic classes and inscribes itself into our politics, laws, rural and urban landscapes, and even our history— not just by influencing what will become history, but by revising the history that has already come, making capitalism seem like a much older system than it is. It has moved entire populations (as is rapidly happening in China today), created new ecosystems, privatized water, reengineered nature's seeds, and dug deep into our DNA and claimed a property right to it. In short, capitalism transforms everything it comes in contact with into conditions for its own reproduction and, more specifically, for the accumulation of capital. Capitalism emerges under conditions of great inequality, and it can survive only by reproducing such inequality—and not just in terms of wealth or class.

We can speak of societies as capitalist when, as E. P. Thompson writes, "the logic of capitalist process has found expression within all the activities of a society, and exerted a determining pressure upon its development and form."[14] It reproduces sexism and racism to its advantage by dividing and driving down the cost of labor; it stokes the fires of chauvinism to justify colonization and expropriation of others' resources and labor (also eased by racism), and it decimates any cultural traditions incompatible with capital accumulation. It engenders deprivation, insecurity, and instability in order to then profit from their overcoming; lengthening the distance between social needs and their satisfaction, capitalist relations insinuate themselves into the necessary means of their fulfillment, be it in fashion and beauty, or food, housing, education, and health care. It uproots, abstracts, and breaks apart, creating gaps and divisions to which it then makes a tantalizing offer to heal, rejoin, or satiate—at a cost.

The first step to understanding these different dimensions of capitalism is, according to Marx, to identify the form of value found in the commodity and employ what we might call a *value hermeneutics*. Value, says Marx, "transforms every product of labour into a social hieroglyphic. Later on, men try to decipher the hieroglyphic, to get behind the secret of their own social product: for the characteristic which objects of utility have of being values is as much men's social product as is their language."[15] This is the first project of Marx's three-volume work, *Capital: A Critique of Political Economy* (1867–1894) that reveals "the economic law of motion of modern society," beginning with an analysis of commodities, the labor theory of value, and the secret of surplus value.[16] Through the interpretation of value and the identification of its process of expansion, we can decipher the dialectic of class relations, as well as identify points of leverage for systematic change and even revolution. This is a critical task of Marxism: to reveal what can be *known* and discern what can be *done*; to produce "a particular kind of knowledge uniquely capable of illuminating the principles of historical movement and, at least implicitly, the points at which political action could most effectively intervene."[17] This is the practical knowledge (*phronēsis*) that informs our praxis.

Marx's theories and historical materialist methodology—his unique combination of *praxis* and *poiēsis*—continue to inform critiques of capitalism and the practical strategies of emancipatory social movements today. In this chapter, I discuss Marx's phenomenology of labor or practical activity and his hermeneutics of value, which deal with alienation and commodity fetishism, before turning to the concepts of use-value, exchange-value, and surplus-value. These concepts will provide us with the building blocks of Marx's larger theory of capitalism, in which labor is the source of value and at the root of the dialectical formation of class and class conflict. This inevitable social antagonism between classes means, Marx argued, that the only path to emancipation is the revolutionary overturning of the conditions of capitalism in its entirety. Only this can transcend the dialectical opposition defining the social structure of class and thus dissolve class exploitation. The standpoint of the oppressed in this relation is said to be insightful and universal in its interests. The universal interest here is emancipatory, but emancipation is more than merely taking power or turning the tables on the dominant class. Rather, it is doing away with systems of domination altogether, reorganizing production within a post-capitalist order in a way that cultivates the social conditions of freedom, promotes fulfilling practical activity, and satisfies human needs—for everyone.

Alienation and the Phenomenology of Labor

In capitalism, people are alienated from the products of their labor, the laboring process, their coworkers, and even their own nature, and only class struggle and a revolutionary change in the way we produce to satisfy our needs can end this alienation. This is the claim of Marx's unfinished essay "Estranged Labour" (1844), which remained unpublished until 1932.[18] Despite the fragmentary condition of the text, the concept of alienation the essay develops has been very influential in feminist, queer, critical race, and anti-capitalist theory, and continues to resonate with the experiences of workers (paid and unpaid), the marginalized, and the unemployed.

The concept of alienation, as well as those of externalization and self-realization, was also central to Hegel's *Phenomenology of Spirit* (1807), which greatly influenced Marx. He was particularly impressed by Hegel's idea that "the dialectic of negativity" was the moving principle of history and that Hegel clearly associated this dialectic with the practical activity of human beings. Hegel, he says, "conceives objectification as loss of the object, as alienation and as transcendence of this alienation; that he thus grasps the essence of *labour* and comprehends objective man—true, because real man—as the outcome of man's *own labour*."[19] That is to say, Hegel believed that human development involved externalizing ourselves in the social and natural worlds in the objects of our creation. It is only through this externalization, that is, the externalization of our practical activity or our praxis, that we can reflect upon and thus comprehend ourselves, which is part of the process of our development. My writing of this book, for example, is a process of (developmental) externalization that reflects and changes me in the process. "The *real*, active orientation of man to himself as a species being (i.e., as a human being)," continues Marx, "is only possible by his really bringing out of himself all the *powers* that are his as the *species* man."[20] What and how we externalize reflects our free and productive nature—it is the nature of the species to create itself—and thus what we find expressed in the world is not just our individual will but something more universal. We see our human nature or what Marx called our species-being in the products of our labor—even if they are not commodities. Indeed, particularly if they are *not* commodities.

Although Marx rejects Hegel's notion of philosophy (opting for historical materialism instead), it is clear that he finds Hegel's dialectical and phenomenological methods, as well as his emphasis on praxis and alienation, useful and illuminating. The narrative of Hegel's *Phenomenology* is the autobiography of human consciousness—its entire historical coming-to-be from infancy to maturity, at which point it can reflectively appropriate all that came before it as its own story or narrative.[21] Hegel's book thus chronicles the experience of human externalization through praxis, of estrangement vis-à-vis the results of its praxis and, ultimately, of our reconciliation with our past praxis (i.e., the recognition of ourselves in the objects, practices, institutions, ideas, and norms we have produced). Until such reconciliation allows objectivity to reflect subjectivity and vice versa—or, as Hegel says, until "Substance shows itself to be essentially Subject"—there is a condition of alienation.[22] For Hegel, reconciliation is ultimately an act of rational comprehension in which we recognize ourselves in the world of our collective creation. Marx will speak of the value that labor creates in commodities as the "social substance" that laborers (subjects) are prevented from recognizing as their own practical activity under capitalism.[23] He will argue that the class version of Hegel's notion of rational comprehension is *true class consciousness* and that the material parallel to Hegel's notion of the reconciliation of subjectivity and objectivity is *communism*. For Marx, those who produce must come to see themselves reflected in the world created by their own activity without alienation. This is, he argues, a condition of everyone's freedom—it is the realization of true praxis.

Marx's phenomenological critique of capitalism here is not a critique of poverty or economic inequality, but a critique of existential alienation that produces *unfreedom*. When the process of reconciliation is thwarted, so is our freedom, because freedom, we find, is dependent upon social recognition and material conditions. As human beings that self-create, each of us, says Marx, has to "confirm and manifest himself as such both in his being and in his knowing."[24] That is to say, *learning* who we are is a part of a dialectical process that produces and reproduces our subjectivity, and this is only possible through the production and reproduction of the material conditions of our freedom. It is through external reflection, rather than introspection, that we develop self-knowledge, and it is through the externalization of ourselves in our practical activity that such reflection is made possible. Marx focuses on this process as it operates in economic production, but it is true of our practical activity more generally. Our development is mediated by the practical activities of, for example, our speech, labor, friendships, political activism, and our collective production of social norms, which shape the world around us.

This circle of practical externalization and reflective internalization is what constitutes the subject, and both moments of this cycle are socially mediated— by labor and practical cooperation in the former (practical externalization) and by shared concepts and discourses in the latter (reflective internalization). The *self* of self-consciousness is produced by this circle or reflexive turn back into the subject; the interiority of our subjectivity is, we might say, made possible by our production of the exteriority in which we find ourselves.[25] Externalization through practical activity is more than just individual self-realization; it is us manifesting our *species-being,* or what defines us as a human being and is thus important for us all. Our nature as a species, writes Marx, is to be self-creating and, what is more, to incrementally develop the material and social conditions of our freedom: "free, conscious activity is man's species character," says Marx, and that freedom can become actualized or realized in the world with the right material conditions.[26]

In addition to a dynamic and practical concept of the human being, this understanding of praxis changes how a world in which nearly everything is the result of human practical activity appears to us. In the first of his "Theses on Feuerbach," Marx writes, "The chief defect of all previous materialism ... is that things, reality, sensuousness, are conceived only in the form of the *object, or of contemplation,* but not as *sensuous human activity, practice,* not subjectively."[27] That is to say, what we contemplate or encounter in the world (i.e., what appears to consciousness) is *actualized human practice.* As we saw in our earlier discussion of phenomenology (Chapter 1), Edmund Husserl sought objective knowledge through phenomenological reduction, a process by which we suspend our natural interests and contemplate our experiences as disinterested observers standing above them. The achievement of objectivity in theory, says Husserl, is only possible via the intersubjective horizon of shared meanings and traditions in the life-world. Marx would probably agree to this social conception of individual consciousness, but what we stand apart from, the appearances we contemplate, result from human praxis. Transcendence in this case is achieved through praxis, not contemplation, and the objectivity we achieve is a practical objectivity through the objectification of our labor. "The product of labour," writes Marx, "is labour which has been congealed in an object, which has become material; it is the *objectification* of labor."[28] What is more, my activity reveals the social nature of my needs as well as the social nature of their satisfaction insofar as my practical activity, which is a process of externalization and is enabled by my cooperation with others. Husserl spoke of a "we-subjectivity," but with Marx we must also speak of a *we-objectivity* that emerges through the objectification of social or cooperative labor. I produce for others and the satisfaction of my needs is, in turn, accomplished through the labor of others. The self that is revealed in my labor is thus a social self: "man's relation to himself only becomes *objective* and *real* for him through his relation to the other man," writes Marx.[29] In capitalism, however, we are separated from these objectifications and the circle of recognition is broken. Our means of externalization have been privatized or are mediated through capital, thus subordinating and fragmenting our activity within a relation of social domination. Although externalization is necessary for our development, alienation is what fuels the capitalist system, and thus as capitalism grows, the prospects for freedom diminish.

This alienation goes unmentioned in the scientific discourse of political economy, or what we now call economics. Concepts such as private property, wages, profit, competition, and economic laws circulate, says Marx, as if they are universal or objective, rather than the historical products of alienated human praxis. These concepts are only intelligible in a condition of social alienation, yet their origin and necessary condition are concealed by the positivist discourse of economics. "Political economy proceeds from the fact of private property, but it does not explain it to us," Marx writes. "It expresses in general, abstract formulae the *material* process through which private property actually passes, and these formulae it then takes for *laws*. It does not *comprehend* these laws."[30] By "comprehend," Marx means grasping the nature of something dialectically— that is, to see *how it came to be and how it relates to other things,* or to "grasp the connection within the movement."[31] In this case, it means recognizing how the mediating and dynamic process of human labor brought these economic concepts into being and, conversely, how a different organization of human labor would empty them of any meaning.[32]

One important dimension of Marx's concept of alienation that I haven't yet discussed, and that also has its origins in Hegel's philosophy, concerns the idea of opposition or contradiction. The process of dialectical development involves self-differentiation, so when we think about the separate moments of the dialectic, we must remember that they share a common origin and will have an antagonistic relation until their form in a structure of domination is dissolved. In this sense, a car crash is not a dialectical opposition and a rock slide is not an instance of alienation. They are examples of opposition and separation, but without a shared origin or relation of interdependency. A dialectical example would be our relationship to our own bodies. Maurice Merleau-Ponty wrote, "The subject that I am, understood concretely, is inseparable from this particular body and from the particular world."[33] We as reflective subjects are necessarily embodied, yet we experience alienation from our bodies due to sexual and racial objectification, disabling conditions, or through their commodification and instrumentalization of our labor power—affective, manual, or unpaid. As much as we are alienated from our bodies, we are still fundamentally bound to them, which is why alienated bodies haunt us, weigh us down, and often engender feelings of shame. We develop an antagonistic relationship with our own bodies, sometimes hurting them, hiding them, and starving them. Until we have a positive self-relation that reincorporates them, until we recognize ourselves in our bodies not as objects but as subjects, we stand apart and in conflict.

Marx thinks we have a similar relationship with nature and the world that we make of it. He says, "The object which labour produces ... confronts it as *something alien,* as a *power independent* of the producer." Just as with our bodies whose objective dimension is necessary for our survival, subjective experience, self-understanding, and social relations, the realization of our selves in the objective world is a necessary part of our development as free subjects. Again, this does not mean we must create objects in the world, but that the objective world reflects our activity. The problem isn't our realization or externalization per se; the problem is alienation. "In the conditions dealt with by political economy," writes Marx, "this realization of labour appears as a *loss of reality* for the worker; objectification as *loss of the object* and *object-bondage*; appropriation as *estrangement,* as *alienation.*"[34]

When Marx writes of the conditions dealt with by political economy, he is speaking of the conditions of capitalism, under which workers do not have control over what and how they produce. In capitalism, laboring for another is not voluntary (when you can't afford to own the means of production), and what and how we produce is determined by profit motives rather than social needs. The demands of capital have insinuated themselves into our practical activity and subordinated that activity to its interests. "In tearing away from man the object of his production, therefore, estranged labor tears from him his *species life,* his real species objectivity, and transforms his advantage over animals into the disadvantage that his inorganic body, nature, is taken from him."[35] In short, says Marx, our human nature as free, self-creating beings has been turned into a means for mere survival, rather than an end toward which we willingly strive. In the process, our bodies (and our relation to them) have become broken and exhausted—fragmented into the "appendages of machines" or colonized in the service of affective labor.[36] Our highest potential as well as our psychological and physical health are squandered in a system engineered to benefit only a few, and even in our unemployment, which compounds our experience of alienation, our very existence generates a downward pressure on wages for those who are employed. The alienation described here is a class phenomenon insofar as the loss of reality, of one's objectified activity, is not a mere vanishing or disappearance. It goes somewhere and is accumulated.[37] It goes to those who own the means of production—such as the factories and refineries, retail shops and restaurants, oilrigs and mines, commercial buildings and land, tools and patents, and the means of transportation and communication—and they claim ownership of what we produce using these means and in effect privatize the process of social reproduction.[38]

Fetishism and the Hermeneutics of Value

Marx's critique of capitalism begins with a critique of the economic theories that take the social relations and economic conditions of their time as simply given, without history, and unrelated to the practical activity of human beings. The basic unit of his analysis is the commodity, since capitalism is a system of commodity production and because what is most basic is also what is most mystified, says Marx. "A commodity appears at first sight an extremely obvious, trivial thing. But its analysis brings out that it is a very strange thing, abounding in metaphysical subtleties and theological niceties."[39] The failure to interpret the commodity in a way that reveals the strangeness of its apparent autonomy, as well as the division of labor and social production that constitute it, contributes to some very flawed economic theory among Marx's contemporaries (and our own). This economic theory, still nearly ubiquitous today, gives us a severely constrained and constraining account of the social relations of production; it rationalizes existing conditions of exploitation and inequality, while treating capital as if it magically expands on its own and portraying the private ownership of the means of production as a natural condition and thus unquestionable. The "function of these unmediated concepts that have been derived from the festishistic forms of objectivity," writes Georg Lukács, "is to make the phenomena of capitalist society appear as suprahistorical essences."[40] In such economic theory, another world is simply *not* possible.

Marx explains the fetish character of commodities as the result of a fundamental inversion, which is similar to the character of religious fetishism, to the extent that one attributes magical powers to an entity as a form of projection. Although commodities are produced by cooperative or social labor and their value is the result of this labor, commodities confront us as if they have independent powers, agency, and intrinsic value—that is, this phenomenon is related to alienation insofar as the value of the commodity is the alienated labor of the producer now circulating on a market. The constitution of the commodity is the result of alienation, but fetishism occurs when we do not recognize the value of commodities as the alienated labor of producers, instead attributing fantastical qualities to them. In short, we are not just *estranged* or separated from the products of our labor (i.e., alienation), but these products appear to us as *strange,* as not recognizable results of our own doing. Commodities become the avatars of producers, appearing to actively do things while we passively observe.[41] There is no perceptible link between the value of the commodity and the social character of labor, which disempowers us. "Doing (human activity) disappears further and further from sight," writes John Holloway. "Things rule."[42]

This fetish character is perfected in finance capital (i.e., capital in money form). Value seems to expand as if by magic: It is lent out and, abracadabra, returns in greater volume. Investment bankers and hedge fund managers are referred to as *wealth creators,* as if wealth increases by simply flowing through their hands, rather than through the labor of others. Bankers and investors don't actually create wealth; they've just figured out a way to appropriate the wealth others have produced, and not just in the past, but also into the future in the form of interest. The term Marx uses for the expansion of value through the labor process is *valorization* (*Verwertung*). Although there is value found in natural materials, Marx believes that value *creation* comes from labor, and the creation of new values is the lifeblood of capitalism—a point I'll discuss at greater length in a moment. The fetish, then, is to see growth without human practical activity, to see the value of capital magically give birth to new value by immaculate conception. "In the form of interest-bearing capital, capital appears," writes Marx, "... unmediated by the production and circulation processes. Capital appears as a mysterious and self-creating source of interest, of its own increase. . . . The result of the overall reproduction process appears as a property devolving on a thing in itself."[43] The fact that the creation (capital) appears as the creator and the true creator (the worker) becomes a spectator is not due to a simple confusion that can be cleared by a good critique; it is a structural result of capitalist production that fragments human praxis into spectatorship and a detached process of production. In other words, from a historical materialist perspective, the root cause of the fetish character of commodities and capital is rooted in a particular form of socioeconomic organization—namely, the social structure of class. (On the fetish character of white subjectivity, see Chapter 4.)

One important aspect of this form of organization is the division of labor, not just at a site of production or company office but across entire countries and, now more than ever, globally. As capitalism has spread across the globe and the population has steadily grown, the interrelations of production and distribution within global markets have become amazingly complex. Today it is difficult to trace the production and assembly history of even the simplest of commodities available to us at a local store. This contributes to commodity fetishism, because we can't associate the commodity with its producers, while also creating an aggregate phenomenon that contributes to the seemingly magical powers of commodities. To quote Marx,

> Objects of utility become commodities only because they are the products of labor of private individuals who work independently of each other. The sum total of the labor of all these private individuals forms the aggregate labor of society. Since the producers do not come into social contact until they exchange the products of their labor, the specific social characteristics of their private labors appear only within this exchange. In other words, the labor of the private individual manifests itself as an element of the total labor of society only through the relations which the act of exchange establishes between the products, and, through their mediation, between the producers.[44]

The commodity displays the social qualities of our own labor in a production process too dispersed to comprehend through empirical experience. A division of labor that corresponds to the production of different use-values—one factory produces shoes and another produces shoelaces—means that exchanges need to be made. If you lived your entire life on a self-sufficient farm, making your own clothes, furniture, and so on, then there would be no need for a market or exchange and commodity fetishism would not arise. A large division of labor, however, necessitates exchange, and in a global capitalist system, no individual can experience the entirety of the production process the way one could on a small self-sufficient farm. Although it may seem like just an abstract idea—like the number of grains of sand in the entire world—it has, Marx argues, real and material repercussions in our daily lives. "In the midst of the accidental and ever-fluctuating exchange relations between the products, the labour-time socially necessary to produce them asserts itself as a regulative law of nature."[45] This is a difficult idea to grasp at first, but by developing the basic concepts of Marx's dialectical social theory, we can reveal the functioning of these relations and interpret the different forms of value circulating in them the way meaning circulates in a language. It is to these forms of value that we now turn, before taking up the revolutionary solution to the mystifying powers of capital in the subsequent section.

The first basic form of value is *utility*, or what Marx calls *use-value*. A bicycle has utility as a mode of transportation. Something does not have to be created by human labor to have a use-value. Water, for example, has utility and thus value to the extent that it can quench our thirst. Regardless of its origin, the utility of an object is connected to its physical qualities, be they qualities that satisfy our hunger or thirst, keep us warm or dry, or move us from one place to another. Use-value cannot be separated from the physical qualities or characteristics of an object and its value materializes only in the use of the object—the use-value of my glass of water is realized when I drink it. It's important to note, however, that use-value isn't limited to the satisfaction of "natural" needs, like food and shelter. If a particular brand of car is needed to achieve a particular social status, for instance, then it has real use-value—"needs" can be culturally specific. "The nature of these needs," writes Marx, "whether they arise, for example, from the stomach or the imagination, makes no difference."[46]

The second basic form of value is *exchange-value*. Unlike use-value, which manifests in the consumption or use of an object, exchange-value only appears in the process of exchange. Such value is *quantitative* and proportional rather than qualitative (as with use-value). "Exchange-value appears first of all as the quantitative relation, the proportion," writes Marx, "in which use-values of one kind exchange for use-values of another kind."[47] Although bikes and computers have different use-values, we are able to determine that, for example, two particular bikes are equivalent in value to one computer. Thus, despite their different physical properties (e.g., a bike's properties that can transport us to the post office, while a computer's properties can send an e-mail to a friend), the bikes and the computer share something in common that allows an *equivalency* to be found. Before turning to the shared substance that allows us to find an equivalency among qualitatively different objects, there is one other characteristic to note about exchange value: it is always tied to a use-value insofar as what is being exchanged are commodities with different use-values. Marx describes the properties of an object that give it use-value as the "material bearers" of exchange value.[48] If something has exchange-value, it must also have use-value, but not vice versa. An apple picked from an apple tree in a food forest—cultivated on city lands for public foraging—has use-value but not exchange-value. A bicycle given to me by a friend or used as part of a free bike-share program has use-value but not exchange-value. Another way of saying this is that the apple I pick from the apple tree and the bike given to me by a friend are not commodities. Both could come to have exchange-values, and thus become commodities, if I sold them or exchanged them for something else.

A *commodity* has both use-value and exchange-value, and in capitalism, the goal of private producers or capitalists is to create commodities at the lowest cost with the highest exchange-value or price. Unless there is a monopoly, capitalists must compete with other capitalists, creating an objective incentive to produce profit or surplus value (a topic I return to shortly)—it is a system imperative rather than a subjective preference. Companies do not produce things to use but to sell, and their profit is made regardless of whether the product's use-value is eventually realized. The same goal of producing surplus value holds in the service industry, although their use-values are almost always immediately realized.[49] Whereas bread, for example, is first baked and then later sold and eaten, service work by a plumber to fix a sink is use-value realized, right then and there, in the labor.

This brings us back to the question about what allows us to find a value equivalency between qualitatively different commodities. In short, what determines the price of the bike as $500 and of the computer as $1,000, giving them a 2:1 exchange-value ratio? The "substance" both commodities share and that allows us to determine an equivalency is the value of *labor*. This is a third form of value analyzed in *Capital*. The first form is *use-value*, or the utility of something; the second is *exchange-value*, or the relational value of use-values; and the third form is simply *value*, or what Marx has called "congealed labor time."[50] It is this third form that allows us to find an equivalency between qualitatively and quantitatively different things or groups of things. It is this value that is created by—but alienated from—workers.

The idea that human labor is the source of economic value was not original to Marx. John Locke (1632–1704) and Benjamin Franklin (1706–1790) wrote about a labor theory of value, and major classical economists such as Adam Smith (1723–1790) and David Ricardo (1772–1823) subscribed to some version of it. Marx's original contribution to this general theory was the concept of *socially necessary abstract labor time* (generalized as a "law of value"). Moreover, he identified the ways in which the labor theory of value explained class formation and class conflict, specifically through the production and distribution of surplus value. To appreciate Marx's innovations, we need to understand his distinction between *concrete* and *abstract* labor.

Concrete labor is the labor of a particular person in the production of particular commodities or the performance of services. For example, I once worked on an assembly line that shrink-wrapped and packaged notepads. The labor that others and I did each workday was what Marx calls "concrete labor," and the commodities we produced were shipped to retailers. Our concrete labor was solely responsible for the creation of *use-value* in these commodities, for concrete labor alone makes *qualitative* changes to things. The exchange value or price of these commodities, however, is determined by what Marx calls "socially necessary abstract labor," rather than by the concrete labor of those of us on the assembly line. What "exclusively determines the magnitude of the value of any article is . . . the amount of labor socially necessary, or the labor-time socially necessary for its production," writes Marx.[51] This abstract labor represents the average time necessary to produce a notepad at the global level, and it is this average that determines its price, even in a retail store across the street from our factory. How can this be the case, if we rule out magic?

Consider the example of two different notebook factories, which organize their production process, and therefore the workers, in different ways. One factory, Factory A, has each worker doing each part of production from start to finish, from hauling, bleaching, and cutting to gluing and packaging. Five workers each produce six finished notebooks in a ten-hour shift, or thirty notebooks in a day. In Factory B, there is a division of labor, so each of the five workers completes only one of the tasks in production—for example, one worker is the hauler, another the cutter, and so forth, and they all become very good—specialized—at their particular job. This turns out to be a much more efficient way to mass-produce commodities, and at the end of a ten-hour shift they have completed 150 notebooks in total. "The greatest improvements in the productive powers of labour, and the greater part of the skill, dexterity, and judgment, with which it is anywhere directed, or applied, seem to have been the effects of the division of labour," writes Smith in *The Wealth of Nations* (1776).[52] Each notebook is similar, so each has the same *use-value* regardless of which factory and thus which concrete labor produced it, but the factory with the division of labor (Factory B) puts less necessary labor into making each notebook. If the rent, electricity, raw material, labor costs, and so on, are similar for both factories, Factory B can sell notebooks for much cheaper than Factory A, because the costs of producing them are only one-fifth of Factory A's costs. Until Factory A figures out a way to cut its costs, particularly its labor costs, Factory B will have the competitive advantage and eventually put Factory A out of business. Factory A could perhaps stay competitive by outsourcing production to a cheaper labor force (the globalization strategy) or by instituting a more efficient division of labor, as in Factory B, or by introducing machinery that speeds up the production process in Factory B even more. Indeed, the process of mechanization is made possible by first dividing up the laboring process into pieces so monotonous that machines can replicate them.

What Factory B has demonstrated in this example is that the *concrete labor time* of those working in Factory A is more than the *socially necessary labor time* for notebook production in the market as a whole.[53] Due to the downward pressure of capitalist competition, each company is trying to make its concrete labor produce more efficiently than the abstract average of socially necessary labor, which determines the market price. If production can be made more efficient or labor costs slashed somehow, it might give that particular factory a competitive advantage until another factory is able to mimic their processes. This phenomenon contributes to constant innovation in production. This is why, according to Marx, the "bourgeoisie cannot exist without constantly revolutionizing the instruments of production"—it is a condition of their survival dictated by competition in the form of socially necessary labor time.[54] Given that changes in the production process affect social forms of life in a multitude of ways (see Chapter 1), the profit motive has a perpetually and accelerating destabilizing effect on our lives. "The unceasing improvement of machinery, ever more rapidly developing, makes their livelihood more and more precarious."[55] New technologies in communication and transportation developing in the race for profit within a context of global competition accelerate changes in social life, but also present new means for resistance. Even in 1848, Marx and Engels write that worker organizing "is helped on by the improved means of communication that are created by modern industry and that place the workers of different localities in contact with one another."[56] The more integrated the markets, the faster the rate of change; we experience a compression of both time and space as people, things, and information all over the globe are integrated into the networks of capitalism.[57]

The immensely complex division of labor in capitalism, facilitated by the compression of time and space, means that "individuals are now ruled by abstractions, whereas earlier they depended on one another."[58] That is, labor has been integrated into a system so expansive that we have lost contact with other producers almost entirely and from the "total labor of society" has emerged an abstract force in the form of social necessary labor time applying downward pressure on workers everywhere. This force arises from the social relations of commodity production and comes back to face concrete social relations as an alien entity. The socially necessary labor time (or law of value) is, in short, what regulates exchange-value in capitalist production.[59] Smith famously called it the "invisible hand," but mistakenly attributed it to the relation of supply and demand. This abstract law of value becomes apparent when capitalists squeeze the maximum amount of productivity out of the workers. It "becomes manifest as the desire of the individual capitalist who," writes Marx, "in his wish to render this law ineffectual, or to *outwit it* and turn it to his own advantage, reduces the *individual* value of his product to a point where it falls *below* its socially determined value."[60] Each individual capitalist seeks to escape the law, but with every effort to do so, they contribute to the downward spiral in socially necessary labor time for which workers pay dearly.

Surplus Value and Class Conflict

Class conflict results from an antagonism that is internal rather than external to class relations, since such relations emerge out of a dialectical relation. Classes are defined by this dialectical relation, regardless of the moral commitments or personalities of individuals within them.[61] Marx's analysis of the dialectical nature of class conflict was in a context of a growing and rather clearly defined industrial working class and the unpaid domestic labor that contributed to their physical reproduction. Thus, Marx's application of historical materialism in his time produced theories concerning the conflict of two powerful and antagonistic classes. Indeed, it was the existence of these conflicting classes that clarified for him (and Engels) the very nature of the class structure. That said, he did not claim that there are only two classes or that classes are stable, but that large-scale class conflict creates major historical change. In his time, this was the emerging outright conflict between industrial capitalists and an industrial working class. "Society as a whole is more and more splitting up into two great hostile camps, into two great classes directly facing each other," Marx and Engels famously wrote in the *Communist Manifesto* (1848).[62] With the decline of the nebulous "middle class" in the United States today, there is a sense in which class conflict (which is always happening) is taking shape on a grand scale, yet capitalism has changed since Marx's day, as has class structure; therefore, a materialist class analysis remains attentive to these changes. The middle class in the United States was largely created in the mid-twentieth century through New Deal legislation, public works, the GI Bill, strong unions, and an imperial force that coercively influenced global markets, currency, and even the political and economic leadership of other states. With the shrinking of the middle class—related to global competition, destruction of unions, flexible production (post-Fordism), and financialization (see Chapter 1)—we have again an increasing clarification and conflict, but it is not defined by the industrial class as it was in Marx's day. With the decentralization of value production, an amalgam of manual, service, affective, care, and unpaid laborers—be they unemployed, underemployed, homeless, landless, or deeply indebted—constitutes a growing opposition to capital.[63] Although they are more socially fragmented than the industrial working class of Marx's time, their existence is still mediated by capital and thus subject to exploitation and appropriation; they all exist in an antagonistic relationship with capital. Occupy Wall Street captured the spirit of recent times with its "We are the 99 percent" slogan, which articulates a division and confrontation with the 1 percent—that is, capital.

Work has become more precarious, production decentralized, and the ratio of finance to industrial capital is changing, but the logic of capital is the same. Classes arise out of the process of the production and reproduction of capitalism, thus the definition of a class is not derived from social status or wealth. Wealth only becomes capital when it is invested in production for the purpose of creating surplus value, and it is the struggle over this surplus that is at the heart of class conflict. Extracting surplus value (i.e., profit) is the goal of capitalists, the mechanism of capital accumulation, and the basis of exploitation. The only way to expand value is through the use of labor, and according to Marx, the secret of surplus value is therefore the "appropriation of unpaid labour."[64] In terms of ownership, capitalists own the means of production used to make commodities or sell services, whereas most workers only possess their ability to labor and, if they're fortunate, perhaps a place to live and a means of transportation. Owning a house or apartment not used in a process of production or rented out to tenants does not make one a capitalist, nor does possessing a car or clothes or a computer. When Marx speaks of abolishing private property, he is referring to the private ownership of the means of production (i.e., capital) and not to one's private items for personal use.[65] Capitalism is only possible when a small minority of people own the means of producing the necessities of life, because capitalism survives only through the production of surplus value. Surplus value is created by workers who must labor for others—be it for a wage or unpaid in the home, which reproduces the conditions of the wage-laborer—only because they have to, because they don't have their own means of production. This inequality, in terms of the control over the means of production, is not natural; it is created through coercion—a point I return to after developing the notion of surplus value.[66]

It is important to note that Marx's analysis is centered on the relation of wage-labor to capital, thus excluding all of the unpaid care, domestic, and reproductive labor traditionally done by women. Although aware of this essential component of value production, Marx tended to ignore it. Engels wrote *The Origin of the Family, Private Property and the State* (1884), drawing on Marx's notes, and it is a trenchant materialist analysis of patriarchy, family structure, and the exploitation of women, but nevertheless the central role of women's unpaid labor was excluded from Marx's major works.[67] I discuss feminist critiques of this exclusion and the analysis of domestic labor in Chapter 3.

In order to explain the circulation of value in capitalism, Marx provides two different formulas to track changes in the form value takes. The first formula is the one that the majority of people recognize in their everyday life: Commodity-Money-Commodity or C-M-C. Marx calls this the simple form of commodity circulation. You exchange your *labor power* (Commodity), measured in units of time for wages or a salary (Money), which you then use to purchase the commodities you need for personal use, such as food or a shirt (Commodity). Money serves as a universal value equivalent in the circulation process. This process is short-lived, however. After we have used up or consumed the second C in the formula—namely, food or a shirt—the circulation comes to an end. Value has been converted into money and back again into a commodity, but value has not been added. I took ten dollars from my wages to buy ten dollars' worth of food: $10 = 10$. We are "selling in order to buy," says Marx, which means the goal is use-value or the satisfaction of a need.

Marx's second formula is Money-Commodity-Money or M-C-M, which is "buying in order to sell." It is the inversion of C-M-C and thus the *general formula of capital.* Money (M) is used to purchase your labor power (C), which produces other commodities, such as food or a shirt that can then be sold and converted back into money (M). The goal of this form of circulation is exchange-value, not use-value. It is money circulating as capital.[68] If it is capital, then this form of circulation must facilitate the expansion of value or *valorization,* not just its change in form. Thus, an investment of $10 in wages might generate an output of $20 worth of food products, a few dollars of which goes into other expenses (from raw materials to the electricity bill), and the rest is pocketed as profit by the owner. To indicate this quantitative increase in the second M, or money form of the formula, Marx uses M-prime or M', thus M-C-M'. The difference between M and M' is the *surplus value.*[69] Value has not only circulated, but it has also grown. "The simple circulation of commodities—selling in order to buy—is a means to a final goal which lies outside circulation, namely the appropriation of use-values, the satisfaction of needs. As against this, the circulation of money as capital is an end in itself, for the valorization of value takes place only within this constantly renewed movement. The movement of capital is therefore limitless."[70]

The secret to this growth is labor power, "a commodity whose use-value possesses the peculiar property of being a source of value, whose actual consumption is therefore itself an objectification of labour, hence a creation of value."[71] The output from the objectification of our labor is worth more than the input of money for payment of our time. This is the case, because we are a force of negativity that transforms our environment, making qualitative changes that create use-value. This activity/negativity translates into quantitative increases of exchange value (i.e., profit for the capitalist). This basic relationship is the source of conflict in two ways. First, the condition in which one group controls the means of production must be created and continually reproduced, through coercion and violence.[72] This is the production of inequality by *extra-economic* means. Second, there is conflict over surplus value, which is produced by cooperative or social labor, yet privately appropriated by capital. This is the production of inequality by *economic* means. I discuss both of these sites of conflict in turn.

The most important step in producing surplus value is having a labor market in which labor power is exchangeable for wages. This presupposes two conditions: first, that there are workers whose "labor power" has been objectified, allowing them to sell their labor as a commodity. This involves the development of a new kind of *self-owning* subject who considers their own powers and capabilities to be private property that can be contractually exchanged (i.e., in the form of wage labor).[73] C. B. Macpherson calls this "possessive individualism," and its emergence in political discourse, law, and philosophy tracks the rise of modern capitalist development.[74] The second condition is material insofar as workers have no other way to support themselves.[75] The most common way to create this fundamental condition is to dispossess people of their means of production and thus self-sufficiency. Domestically (in Europe), this meant dispossessing small farmers through *enclosure* (i.e., the privatization of common lands) or through legal and economic policies that render self-sufficiency impossible—a process called *primitive accumulation*. Take the land away from the farmers and they have no choice but to turn to laboring for another. "Primitive accumulation cut through traditional lifeways like scissors," writes Michael Perelman. "The first blade served to undermine the ability of people to provide for themselves. The other blade was a system of stern measures required to keep people from finding alternative survival strategies outside the system of wage labor."[76] Karl Polanyi, author of an excellent study of the history of enclosures in England at the turn of the seventeenth century, calls enclosures "a revolution of the rich against the poor."[77] In *Capital,* Marx examines the history of forcible evictions and enclosures in the early stages of capitalism and how they gave way to legal means in later centuries. By the eighteenth century, he writes, "the law itself now becomes the instrument by which the people's land is stolen," thereby "'setting free' the agricultural population as a proletariat for the needs of industry."[78] Not everyone was equally "set free," of course, for women and people of color were long denied property rights and thus forced into relations of dependency even more severe than those of white male wage-laborers. These ideological and juridical exclusions were also naturalized as conditions of natural inferiority.

Internationally, primitive accumulation's predominant methods are, writes Rosa Luxemburg (1871–1919), "colonial policy, an international loan system . . . and war. Force, fraud, oppression, looting are openly displayed."[79] Rather than tell mythical tales of historical accumulation through hard work and thrift, or write philosophical treatises about imaginary states of nature, these historical studies recount the bloody story of original usurpation and violence. These were the *extra-economic* means of kick-starting the *economic* form of capital accumulation—namely, various forms of appropriating the means of production and creating dependency. "In actual history," writes Marx of primitive accumulation, "it is a notorious fact that conquest, enslavement, robbery, murder, in short, force, play the great part."[80]

Although the violent undermining of self-sufficiency has been described as primitive or original (*ursprünglich*) to illustrate how capitalism's foundational conditions were painfully cultivated centuries ago—the "pre-history of capital"—it is a process that continues today. David Harvey's name for this process, which Luxemburg had identified, is *accumulation by dispossession*.[81] This happens domestically, by private capital and state institutions within their own territorial jurisdiction, but also globally through neo-colonial regimes of international property rights and military imperialism. In China's continuing process of industrialization today, for example, we find enclosure practices very much like those of seventeenth-century England, which are dislocating tens of millions of rural farmers and sending them looking for wage labor in the growing cities.[82] This was the context of Tian Yu's migration to Shenzhen, where she became a wage-laborer in the Foxconn factory. Wherever agribusiness wields political and economic clout, it dispossesses small farmers and appropriates other means of agricultural production, such as seeds. Through the patenting of seeds, corporations like Monsanto can privatize a natural process harnessed for centuries and force farmers to pay annually for their use. This is often called *biopiracy* and is a popular practice by global corporations that also frequently exploit the medicinal knowledge of indigenous peoples around the globe with the help of international trade agreements. "The land, the forests, the rivers, the oceans, and the atmosphere have all been colonized, eroded, and polluted," writes Vandana Shiva. "Capital now has to look for new colonies to invade and exploit for its further accumulation—the interior spaces of the bodies of women, plants, and animals."[83]

Contemporary imperialism is little different from centuries past in this regard: military supremacy translates into political and legislative power that immediately seeks to transform economic conditions to the advantage of the invading powers. This typically involves the rapid privatization of public resources before any domestic resistance can successfully take root. Naomi Klein has called such a strategic exploitation of crisis—be it natural, political, or economic—"radical economic shock therapy."[84] The US-led invasion of Iraq is a contemporary example. The first official act of Paul Bremer, the American head of the occupying Coalition Provisional Authority in Iraq in 2003, was to privatize all state resources—most importantly the state's oil resources—and give preferential treatment to the private oil companies of the invading countries. Iraq, he said, was now "open for business."[85] Another example is the continued existence of forced labor within the United States, growing out of a tradition of slave labor that produced so much wealth for the white slaveholders in American history. Prison labor is big business in the United States, made possible by the Thirteenth

Amendment (1865) to the US Constitution, which abolished slavery and indentured servitude "except as a punishment for crime"[86] (see Chapter 4).

As mentioned, the second site of contention, or the terrain upon which the dialectic of class conflict plays itself out, is the surplus value created by labor. The relationship between workers (of all kinds) and capitalists is inherently antagonistic because it is dialectical. Capital cannot expand without the employment of labor, because labor produces the value that capital accumulates, which allows capital to employ more labor and reproduce itself. *Labor, not machinery, makes capital.* This is more than simple dependency, for it was capital that called the working class as a class into being and it is in turn the working class that sustains the capitalists. The dependency is mutual and existential, which is what Marx and Engels are referring to when they say in the *Communist Manifesto* that capitalism produces its own gravediggers. That is to say, the most powerful opposition to capital is created precisely by the realization of its necessary condition. "The essential condition for the existence, and for the sway of the bourgeois class," writes Marx, "is the formation and augmentation of capital; the condition for capital is wage-labour."[87]

Far from digging any graves, organized labor has historically won a larger cut of surplus value for its members through higher wages, health benefits, and pensions. The redistribution of more value to workers cuts into capital accumulation and is thus a compromise made only if the owners of capital fear the alternative, such as production disruptions or even revolutionary transformation. Better wages and benefits can temporarily tilt the balance of power, but they can neither reverse the antagonistic relation of domination from which these class relations are born, nor resolve the problems of alienation, commodity fetishism, unpaid reproductive labor, or environmental destruction. Franklin D. Roosevelt supported New Deal reforms in the 1930s, not because they benefited laborers, which they did, but because he thought they would prevent the revolutionary anti-capitalist tendencies sweeping the globe from coming to fruition in the United States. It succeeded for a time, but we have witnessed organized labor attacked by capital and state forces, and their compromises systematically undermined since the 1970s, and with great fervor since the 1990s. This has led to renewed class conflict and the growth of a plurality of critical resistance movements today.

In the context of capitalist class relations, the general forms of subjectivities produced reflect the material and social conditions necessary to facilitate capital accumulation, such as abstract legal personhood, private property rights, the commodificaton of labor power (i.e., life), and self-ownership or "possessive individualism" of laborers who work for a wage or salary. Marx argues that this notion of individuality, the laws and rights associated with it, as well as the constitutionalist (i.e., social contract) and representational forms of government derived from it, merely mimic and thereby serve to reproduce the contractual forms of social relations and ownership necessary to capitalism. Subjects structured around these mostly juridical notions, together with the values of efficiency, hard work, honesty (i.e., debt repayment), and self-sufficiency—rendered synonymous with the dignity and success of an individual—are structured to support capitalist social relations. This concept of the subject and its associated values are so deeply entrenched in the social norms, laws, moral theories, and cultural products of capitalist societies that they appear universal rather than class-specific and historically constituted.[88]

The class dimension of the values associated with this form of subjectivity becomes clearer when we reflect on the means of economic and extra-economic capital accumulation discussed above. Despite overwhelming evidence of systematic theft, dishonesty, unearned wealth (both inherited and through uncompensated surplus value), unpaid debts, broken promises, and constant attacks on collective bargaining by the capitalist class, these values continue to garner widespread public acceptance as "American" values. The degree of one's passionate commitment to them, however, typically tracks one's position in other structures of domination, such as patriarchy and white supremacy. The poorest white worker will more often identify with the white mine owner or CEO, and believe that they're both hardworking and honest, if the worker is a little bit better off than the poor black or Latino worker down the road. The racial differences in economic well-being resulting from the unearned benefits of structural racism or white supremacy can then be explained in moral terms (e.g., hard work and honesty)—what W. E. B. Du Bois called the "psychological wage" of white privilege.[89] "Racial solidarity, particularly the solidarity of whiteness," writes bell hooks, "has historically always been used to obscure class, to make the white poor see their interests as one with the world of white privilege."[90]

The abstract, rights-centric, autonomous subject—the core of American rugged individualism—emerged in the context of European colonialism, has roots in white supremacist popular sovereignty, and supports a masculine myth and thus patriarchal power, concealing its dependency on unpaid reproductive labor, the cooperative nature of labor itself, and the intersubjective conditions of freedom (see Chapter 4).[91] This is, indeed, such an *inhuman* concept of the person that it has come to literally *personify* capital in corporate personhood, which has Constitutional rights, such as the freedom of speech (i.e., money) and religion (i.e., the ability to exercise sexist and heteronormative discrimination on religious grounds), but no responsibilities for which it is held accountable.[92]

Post-Capitalism, Communism, and Autonomism

As an inherently antagonistic relation of exploitation, Marx argues that class relations can only be transcended through a fundamental negation of their origin in the private ownership of the means of production. This transformation of property relations undermines the material conditions of class-based domination and opens up the possibility for worker-managed production that focuses on needs (use-values) rather than private profit (exchange-values): "from each according to his ability, to each according to his needs."[93] Democratizing production, and not just distribution (as in liberal theories of economic justice), is essential. This is not, however, sufficient. A society without economic classes does not guarantee the realization of human praxis, social recognition, mutual aid, the free and creative development of individuals, or ecologically sustainable forms of social life. There are forms of domination embedded in the social infrastructure of contemporary life—such as patriarchy, white supremacy, compulsory heterosexuality, nationalism, and ableism—which, despite their deep ties to capitalism's productive and reproductive imperatives, operate with their own distinctive logics. Like class, these social relations configure cultural traditions and state institutions as well as forms of subjectivity, and they, too, must be engaged, transformed, or dismantled.[94] Anti-capitalism is therefore not synonymous with communism; our abilities and our needs are more than economic in nature, and their realization and fulfillment require more than a classless society.[95]

But what would a communist society look like? It's an important question, but simultaneously unanswerable, at least in the way that any question about future and radically different forms of social organization is unanswerable.[96] There was certainly no feudal theorist who told us what capitalist society would look like.[97] Rather than provide a blueprint for communist society, Marx and Engels focused instead on the historical conditions, social critiques, and human praxis transforming oppressive conditions. Communism, they wrote, "is for us not a *state of affairs* which is to be established, an *ideal* to which reality [will] have to adjust itself. We call communism the *real* movement which abolishes the present state of things."[98] Committed to a historical materialist method of analysis, their notion of communism is *historical* insofar as it is identified as a concrete possibility within existing conditions, and *materialist* insofar as the actualization of communism necessitates changes in material conditions and practical social relations. This is an example of the dialectic of immanence and transcendence described in Chapter 1. Through rigorous historical analysis and social critique, the origins and logic of existing relations of domination, exploitation, and alienation are identified. Each of these relations is inherently unstable, because each invariably involves resistance. Identifying the points of resistance and their potential development is a central task of radical social theory. The immanent potential is the form of practical resistance inherent to the social structure—however small or large in scale—which, if expanded, could negate and thereby transcend the social structure itself. Resistance gives rise to its theorization, which in turn empowers resistance to overcome the conditions of oppression. This is a historical and dialectical *movement* opening up and realizing possibilities, which although aided by theory, cannot be foretold by it.

The immanent potential within capitalist class relations, identified by Marx and Engels in their time, was a growing and increasingly revolutionary industrial working class. Indeed, they penned the *Communist Manifesto* just months before insurrections broke out in Europe in 1848, and when ordinary people began to actualize communist social relations in the Paris Commune of 1871, they saw glimmers of the future. The Commune, wrote Marx, was "essentially a working-class government, the produce of the struggle of the producing against the appropriating class, the political form at last discovered under which to work out the economic emancipation of labor."[99] The communards disbanded the military, dissolved the police as a separate body, instituted universal suffrage, and began socializing church property and the means of production. They didn't have "ready-made utopias," but rather knew that for real emancipation "they will have to pass through long struggles, through a series of historic processes transforming circumstance and men."[100] They were defeated, but their achievements represented "the glorious harbinger of a new society," according to Marx.[101]

Critics of communism often conflate totalitarian political states with Marx's notion of communism, which has freedom and the democratization of practical life at its core, a form of association "in which the free development of each is the condition for the free development of all."[102] Indeed, Marx advocated abolishing the state entirely, since it served the interests of capitalist domination and reflected and alienated political life that undermined the conditions of human freedom. Engels described the state as "essentially a capitalist machine, the state of the capitalists, the ideal personification of the total national capital."[103] There are, however, historical and theoretical reasons for the popular association of Marxist communism with dictatorship. The former Soviet Union proclaimed itself a Marxist state and its most famous early leaders, such as Vladimir Lenin (1870–1924) and Leon Trotsky (1879–1940), were erudite Marxist theorists. The 1917 revolution in the Russian Empire began as a large-scale movement initiated by ordinary men and women who organized themselves in worker councils (or soviets) to manage their own production, but were eclipsed by a growing state behemoth that fought and competed with capitalist state powers. Although the means of production were socialized, they were state-owned and controlled by the political party said to represent the people, thus reproducing relations of domination and dissolving the creative praxis that brought about the revolution in the first place. Joseph Stalin completed the counter-revolution in the 1930s with a murderous purge of political "enemies"—executing approximately 1 million people, including most of the Bolsheviks involved with the 1917 revolution, such as Trotsky. A similar state-centric approach with similar effects was taken in the People's Republic of China under Mao Zedong (1893–1976).

The theoretical origins of the association of communism with dictatorship lie in the infamous concept of the "dictatorship of the proletariat," which referred to the transitional phase of worker control of state institutions in which production would be socialized and the revolution defended against capitalist counter-measures in the process. "Between capitalist and communist society lies the period of the revolutionary transformation of the one into the other. There corresponds to this also a political transition period in which the state can be nothing but the *revolutionary dictatorship of the proletariat*."[104] It was thought that undermining the proprietary basis and class structure of the state would make the state "wither away" over time.[105] "The state is not 'abolished,'" wrote Engels. "*It dies out.*"[106] This was a tactical and theoretical point of contention between orthodox Marxism and anarchism, insofar as anarchists viewed state power as incapable of being harnessed, however temporarily it was intended, to realize the conditions of freedom. Instead, anarchists like Mikhail Bakunin (1814–1876) advocated direct economic struggle, rather than seizure of the institutions of political rule.[107] Anarchist warnings about the potential for an authoritarian state power in the name of the working class proved correct (although many anarchists still had a problematic non-social and unhistorical understanding of freedom). Disempowering capital did not itself lead, directly or over time, to communism, for the means by which it was won—namely, by a vanguard party taking state power—undermined the very social relations and forms of praxis that needed to be cultivated.[108]

There were many Marxists who criticized the Leninist party and state-centered approach, including, most importantly, Luxemburg.[109] The historical experience of the failures of Leninism gave rise to alternative forms of Marxist theory and praxis, from Frankfurt School critical theory to various forms of ecosocialism, autonomism (*operaismo* or "workerism" in its Italian variant), and Open Marxism, which favors economic and anti-authoritarian forms of organization and resistance.[110] Autonomist feminists, such as Maria Dalla Costa and Silvia Federici, broadened the Marxist critique of labor beyond its traditional ("productivist") focus on wage labor, and developed critiques and forms of resistance specific to the "unwaged" reproductive labor traditionally done by women.[111]

Retained throughout these contemporary schools of Marxism is a *social* form of freedom grounded in mutual recognition and concrete social relations that facilitate agency and self-development. "Only within the community has each individual the means of cultivating his gifts in all directions; hence personal freedom becomes possible only within the community," write Marx and Engels.[112] This freedom, and the community relations that inhibit or give rise to it, are more than mere economic relations. Abolishing the "present state of things" involves abolishing other forms of social domination as well. As the history of anti-capitalist movements has made evident, without an intersectionalist critique of capitalism, as well as prefigurative, anti-oppression work within the movements themselves, relations of domination and exploitation are reproduced under post-capitalist conditions. Horizontal or nonhierarchical social relations free from sexism, racism, and new forms of subjectivity congruent with them must therefore be actively cultivated as well—"the production on a mass scale of ... communist consciousness," reaching beyond social relations free from class domination.[113] Horizontalism is the dissolution of social structures insofar as such structures are formed through a relation of domination that makes the subordinate group dependent upon the dominant group for their survival.[114] The term *horizontalism* comes from the Spanish *horizontalidad* and was popularized by its use in characterizing the directly democratic and nonhierarchical forms of political resistance in Argentina in 2001. Horizontalism rejects representational forms of politics, using general assemblies and consensus-based decision-making as are found in the Zapatista movement: the alter-globalization movement (which had its origins in the

Zapatista movement); Occupy Wall Street; as well as in resistance movements in, for example, Argentina, Chile, Spain, Venezuela, and Greece today.[115] Marx would describe these horizontalist social and self-relations as communist, but we can call them anarchist as well.

CHAPTER 3
FEMINISM AND QUEER THEORY

One is not born, but rather becomes, woman. No biological, psychic, or economic destiny defines the figure that the human female takes on in society. . . . Only the mediation of another can constitute an individual as an *Other*.
—*Simone de Beauvoir*, The Second Sex[1]

Tension grips the inhabitants of the borderlands like a virus. Ambivalence and unrest reside there and death is no stranger.
—*Gloria Anzaldúa*, Borderlands/La Frontera[2]

In 1851, Sojourner Truth (1797–1883) stood before a white crowd at the Women's Convention in Akron, Ohio, to speak about women's suffrage and her own experience as it related to the suffragist debate at the time. She was a black woman, former slave, feminist, and abolitionist who dropped her slave name and took the free name Sojourner Truth. Her short speech that day in 1851 challenged the white and essentialist notions of gender and sexuality operating in the debate, such as the belief that while women's exclusion from political and economic self-determination was justified by natural weakness, their delicate nature was rewarded with chivalrous attention by men, that this subordination was rewarded with privileges and men's desires:

That man over there says that women need to be helped into carriages, and lifted over ditches, and to have the best place everywhere. Nobody ever helps me into carriages, or over mud puddles, or gives me any best place! And ain't I a woman? Look at me! Look at my arm! I have ploughed and planted, and gathered into barns, and no man could head me! And ain't I a woman? I could work as much and eat as much as a man—when I could get it—and bear the lash as well! And ain't I a woman?[3]

The lived experience of Sojourner Truth undermined the binary and hierarchical gender and sexuality categories at work in the arguments against women's suffrage, while also shedding light on their racial makeup. These were not complementary differences, but the mechanisms of domination. The oppression of black women like Truth involved brutal physical toil as well as physical, psychological, and sexual violence, which demanded tremendous courage and strength to persevere. The fact that Truth not only survived in this dehumanizing white supremacist and patriarchal society, but also organized resistance devastated claims about women's essential weakness. "Black women had already proven their inherent strengths—both physical and psychological," writes Paula Giddings. "They had undergone a baptism of fire and emerged intact."[4] Truth inserted herself and her standpoint into this white, patriarchal, and heteronormative discourse as living proof of its contradictions and exploded it from within. She was neither weak nor treated with chivalry, and she was present at the Women's Convention as someone with agency, not the servant of another, and men's heterosexual desires would not protect her. She was challenging the social roles of women described that day as irrelevant, unjustified, or unwanted.

Truth's speech touches upon several important commitments within the radical feminist and queer projects that challenge cultural and institutional forms of patriarchy and heteronormativity. First, her testimony speaks to the *intersectionality of oppression and privilege* insofar as it draws attention to the multiplicity of our social identities operating within our lived experience. These identities are often separated out in our theoretical analyses (to analyze means to break apart, to dismember), although gender, race, class, ability, ethnicity, and sexuality are all lived simultaneously and each is made possible by, and thus inseparable from, the others.[5] Different contexts will inevitably foreground or background different parts of our identity, with different forms of oppression or privilege manifesting in different experiences, and while individuals are unequally oppressed, there is "no hierarchy of oppression," as Audre Lorde succinctly put it.[6] Racism is not inherently worse than sexism, and class domination is not more oppressive than ableism or the persecution of LGBT (lesbian, gay, bisexual, and transgender) people, although they affect different people to greater or lesser degrees. Unfortunately, there is a long history of hierarchical thinking about oppression, in claims, for example, that all forms of oppression are derivative of class domination or that gender oppression is the oldest injustice and thus takes precedence in theory and praxis.[7] Arguing for a hierarchy of oppression or reducing one form of oppression to a symptom or epiphenomenon of another is not only problematic theory, but also leads to divisive and exclusive forms of praxis that reproduce oppressive hierarchies within resistance movements.[8] Feminist theory in the United States has traditionally been the product of white, middle-class, and straight women, which led to the exclusion of the experiences of women of color and working class and lesbian women.[9] Such exclusions from the production of theory led to exclusive forms of collective action and goals incompatible with the social, political, and psychological needs of other women.[10]

Intersectionalist theory and postcolonial feminism and queer theory arose in part as responses to these exclusions. They provided dynamic anti-oppression frameworks that account for the interests, experiences, and projects of a plurality of subjects and groups struggling against various systems of oppression. Not every feminist and queer project can (or, tactically, even should) encompass all interests or oppose all forms of oppression, but the lack of a reflexive, intersectionalist understanding of their relations perpetuates intragroup oppression and marginalization, undermines standpoint insights and oppositional knowledge, and inhibits pluralist cooperation and allyship in particular struggles.[11]

The second commitment of radical feminist and queer projects that Truth's speech highlighted is a critical hermeneutics, which reveals the *historical* and *socially constructed* nature of gender and sexual identities. Given that the social structures of gender and sexuality are historically constituted and culturally configured, they and the relations of oppression and privilege they reflect can be reformulated or abolished. What is more, if neither gender nor sexuality is a natural category, we can decouple them to some degree and develop a vocabulary to talk about queer sexuality and gender fluid or nonconforming identities.[12] To have a gender, writes Judith Butler, "does not presuppose that one engages sexual practice in a particular way ... and to engage in a given sexual practice ... does not presuppose that one is given a gender."[13] In tandem with transgressive gender and sexual practices, theorizing this difference is a necessary step in the dialectical development of norms or even the dissolution of the social structures of gender and sexuality as we know them. The creation of alternatives is crucial to sustain critical resistance and make life livable for those nonconforming to dominant social structures.[14]

The supposedly neutral position within mainstream discourses about gender and sexuality, the unstated "we" that centers the norm, tends to reflect the characteristics and interests of privileged groups. It generalizes their particular social position into a horizon of universality and makes their standpoint the only legitimate grounds for evaluation. This is a process of what Pierre Bourdieu calls "symbolic violence."[15] As Truth discovered, this can also happen within social movements that actively challenge one social structure (gender), yet intentionally or unintentionally reproduce others (race and sexuality). How one is accounted for or excluded is an expression of power that produces and then normalizes and polices the boundaries of the acceptable and inacceptable.[16] The precarious borders of social hierarchies always demand the most policing, for it is at the border where acquiescence and internalized oppression no longer hold sway, lines are challenged, and revolts simmer. There is ambivalence, unrest, and death along what Gloria Anzaldúa calls the *borderland,* for the privileged employ militant rhetoric and violence and encourage self-hatred in the other to defend their position.

In this chapter I use the term *queer* in the context of radical philosophy, rather than LGBTQ (lesbian, gay, bisexual, transgender, and queer). The term *queer* was reclaimed not long ago from its traditional heteronormative use as a shaming slur and signifier of pathologized sexuality.[17] Its resignification by individuals and political groups challenged the terms of the heteronormative binary, or what Adrienne Rich calls "compulsory heterosexuality," and resisted their institutionalization and deadly effects.[18] The political group Queer Nation, for example, was founded in 1990 at a meeting held at the Lesbian, Gay, Bisexual, and Transgender Community Service Center in New York City by activists from the group ACT UP (AIDS Coalition to Unleash Power), itself founded in 1987 at the Lesbian and Gay Community Services Center, as it was then called. The Queer Nation Manifesto, "Queers Read This" (1990), reads in part, "Being queer . . . means everyday fighting oppression; homophobia, racism, misogyny, the bigotry of religious hypocrites and our own self-hatred. . . . Being queer means leading a different sort of life. It's not about the mainstream, profit-margins, patriotism, patriarchy or being assimilated. It's not about executive directors, privilege and elitism. It's about being on the margins, defining ourselves."[19] This intersectionalist notion of queer politics is similar to that of radical feminism.

While they both have roots in gender and sexual practices and politics, they are projects of resistance, oppositional forms of knowledge, and to the extent that gender and sexuality are "inextricable from one another ... in that each can only be expressed in terms of the other," their related political projects are deeply connected.[20] These terms are, and always should be, open to contestation and change; for the purposes of this chapter I use *queer* to signify a political project rather than a term of self-identification. Queer and feminist projects are radical philosophies in that they focus on particular social relations, structures, and institutions; employ a critical methodology that is historical, dialectical, reflexive, and materialist; develop practical and oppositional forms of knowledge motivated by an emancipatory interest; and engage in collective forms of praxis.[21]

I begin with a phenomenological discussion of the production of meaning and the construction, policing, and transgression of boundaries in performance and bodily habits. These give rise to the historical sedimentation of law-like social structures—becoming both codified and naturalized—that segregate and regulate the desire, labor, and practices of freedom in gender and sexual identities through violence and coercion. Violence is constitutive of identity construction and facilitated by laws that create vulnerable populations in which violence *beyond the law* can be exercised. I conclude with a discussion of the legal and capitalist forces at play in the construction and naturalization of the patriarchal family, the production and regulation of sexuality, and the role of unwaged labor in value production.

Bodies, Performance, and Normalization

The body is the practical medium that situates and orients our gender and sexual practices. It is the materiality of the meanings produced in the social world and is therefore a site of communication, interpretation, and contestation. Our bodies exist in the world as objects, they have visibility and *facticity* or object-like qualities, yet they simultaneously situate and enable our subjectivity, or our reflexive condition as a subject who acts and desires. "If I find, while reflecting upon the essence of the body, that it is tied to the essence of the world," writes Maurice Merleau-Ponty, "this is because my existence as subjectivity is identical with my existence as a body and with the existence of the world, and because, ultimately, the subject that I am, understood concretely, is inseparable from this particular body and from the particular world."[22] Over long periods of time, our habitual practices constitute a generally stable and intelligible meaning of gender and sexuality—a process enabled and constrained by traditions and material conditions. Material conditions determine possibilities, and social norms enable or deny recognition in social action. Conventions accrue, building layer upon layer over time, taking hold in patterns, images, and built environments; they are infused with normalizing discourses that make social patterns and relations of domination seem like natural laws.

Thinking about bodies, gender, and sexuality in this way is rather new. For a long time, sex and gender were not differentiated; to have a particular body meant that one would (or was at least expected to) behave and desire in a certain way. A baby born with male anatomy and physiology was an indicator of future masculine behavior, and a baby born with female anatomy and physiology was an indicator of future feminine behavior—biological determinism. This is referred to as *gender assignment*. Once this correlation between anatomy and behavior was repudiated, sex and gender were explicitly differentiated—a development associated with the work of Simone de Beauvoir and second-wave feminism more generally. With this step, male and female *sexes* were considered the natural categories, whereas masculine and feminine *genders* were considered conventional.[23] The binary held in both cases, but whereas sex difference was still taken to be a natural category, gender was now understood to be a social category that is open to critique and transformation. "When the constructed status of gender is theorized as radically independent of sex," writes Butler, "gender itself becomes a free-floating artifice, with the consequence that *man* and *masculine* might just as easily signify a female body as a male one, and *woman* and *feminine* a male body as easily as a female one."[24]

It is often assumed that male and female categories of reproductive anatomy exhausted all possibilities, and this binary was normalized in the medical sciences. As a result of sustained political activism and critique, however, there has been a growing awareness of the diversity of *intersexed* bodies whose anatomy does not conform to binary distinctions. In addition to this natural nonconformity to social expectations, bodies are also surgically and hormonally modified. Historically, intersex infants have had their bodies surgically altered to normalize them (i.e., make them conform to the norm) as male or female, while transgender or queergender people—that is, those who do not identify with their socially assigned gender, as *cisgender* people do—can have voluntary sex reassignment surgery and hormone therapy.[25] Both of these forms of body modification, involuntary and voluntary, undermine the "natural" status of the body and sex determination. But if bodies are not conforming in these ways, how are we to interpret sex difference? Most of the interpretations and meanings of sex established by the medical sciences have been contested and undone. The traditional causal interpretation was that sex (biology/desire) determines gender (behavior/ performance), but then this link was broken and gender was acknowledged to be socially constructed within traditions of cultural practices.

The most powerful way to justify relations of domination is to naturalize the relation and universalize the norms that serve the interests of the dominant group—to deny their origins in such cultural traditions. We have seen how this happened in the case of gender, but it wasn't long before sexuality was to be claimed as a social construction as well. This is not to say that anatomical or hormonal differences in bodies are denied, or that "culture" or the "social" is not material (rather than merely linguistic, as some of Butler's formulations might make it seem), but rather that the value-laden categories and concrete practices used to order them, as well as the meanings then derived from them, are contested—somewhat similar to the categorization and meaning of race.[26] Sexed identities turn out to be *gendered* or socially constructed categories, rooted in and mediated by the practical relations and material conditions, thus reversing the direction of causation in the traditional narrative.[27] As Butler concludes,

> It would make no sense, then, to define gender as the cultural interpretation of sex, if sex itself is a gendered category. Gender ought not to be conceived merely as the cultural inscription of meaning on a pregiven sex (a juridical conception); gender must also designate the very apparatus of production whereby the sexes themselves are established. As a result, gender is not to culture as sex is to nature; gender is also the discursive/cultural means by which "sexed nature" or "a natural sex" is produced and established as "prediscursive," prior to culture, a politically neutral surface on which culture acts.[28]

Similar forms of "prediscursive" foundations are, for example, the practical relations of white supremacist social structures, which discursively write back into nature the supposed superiority of whites and biological inferiority of other races. The social relations and material inequality of white domination are then justified by appealing to the natural order of things, which has the additional ideological benefit of erasing the histories of conquest and resistance. Speaking similarly of class domination, Georg Lukács writes, because "every society tends to 'mythologize' the structure of its own system of production, projecting it back in to the past, this past—and even more *the future*—appear likewise to be determined and controlled by [its seemingly natural] laws. It is then forgotten that the *birth* and the triumph of this system of production is the fruit of the most barbaric, brutal and naked use of 'extra-economic' violence."[29] Butler's related critique is intended to reveal the relations of power operative in the prediscursive establishment of sex difference, and to identify its logic of concealment, which also characterizes other claims about the foundations of subjectivity.[30] That is, what we often assume to be the "I" or the "core self" of an individual, with all of its various attributes, is not timeless or purely transcendental, but constituted materially and discursively in concrete social relations and bodily practices. Gender and sexuality are forms of practical relations and cultural meanings, rather than the expression of a biologically determined or ahistorical transcendental self.[31]

Given that both gender and sex are invariably the result of the material conditions and traditional social relations, with no underlying essence, substance, or quality shared by all women and men, how do so many people come to fit these categories and enact their gender assignment (i.e., come to be cisgender)? Simone de Beauvoir famously wrote that one "is not born, but rather becomes, woman," by which she meant that gender ("woman") is an ensemble of behaviors, habits, interests, and desires to which one is materially and symbolically socialized, rather than an expression of biological sex difference.[32] Woman and man are positions acquired through "constituting acts" in the sense of bodily performance, rather than the expression of something that lies within.[33]

In her essay "Throwing Like a Girl," Iris Marion Young provides a phenomenological description of typical feminine bodily comportment, or the "modalities of feminine motility."[34] Following Merleau-Ponty, she locates intentionality in the body prior to any conscious reflection. Following Beauvoir, Young describes the meaning of gendered existence as it is constructed in bodily performances and, in particular, the act of throwing "like a girl." She concludes that the meaning of femininity as a category of gender is to exhibit "an *ambiguous transcendence, an inhibited intentionality,* and a *discontinuous unity* with its surroundings."[35] The body transcends by being oriented outward in its activity, always tending to apprehend and gesture. It is "an actively *orienting* force" that "escapes self-enclosure," writes Edward Casey. "To orient, after all, is to orient *to*—to something *other than* that which does the orienting itself."[36] This is not unlike Hegel's description of consciousness as *negativity* and Husserl's description of consciousness as always consciousness *of* something—a form of transcendence achieved through apprehending what is other to it (see Chapter 1).[37]

Bodies do things by their very nature, always interest-directed and projecting. To not be outwardly directed is to remain in "immanence," or to be passive, which can only be the result of a countervailing (social) force. By *ambiguous transcendence,* then, Young refers to something like inaction or a withholding, a constraint on the potential for projection and engagement. Throwing "like a girl" exhibits this ambiguity insofar as physical movement is largely limited to the wrist and arm, while the rest of the body is immobilized. This kind of comportment underestimates one's potential and thereby constricts one's intentions, which is what Young means by *inhibited intentionality.* It is a repressing of bodily possibility—a "self-imposed 'I cannot.'"[38] This leads to contradictory performances in which the withholding undermines the intention. "By projecting an aim toward which it moves, the body brings unity to and unites itself with its surroundings."[39] There is a natural concordance in the body's orientation toward an aim, having already taken up the objective into the action in a way similar to Husserl's description of the intentionality of consciousness. This unity in orientation is, however, disrupted in the case of feminine comportment, for parts of the body that would otherwise move in unison with the action are immobilized and thus out of sync—*discontinuous unity.*

Young's explanation for this disruption and, indeed, for the general pattern of bodily comportment called *feminine,* is that the girl is reflecting on her own action in the process of motion in order to regulate it. She has made an object of herself rather than of her objective or intended act. As Merleau-Ponty writes, "For us to be able to move our body toward an object, the object must first exist for it, and hence our body must not belong to the region of the 'in-itself.'"[40] In the phenomenological tradition influenced by Hegel, the "in-itself" is the (ontological) status of objects in the world, which are determined by external forces and lack both consciousness and the possibility of a self-relation or a "for-itself" relation, which is the status of subjects. Rather than be a subject reaching toward an object, the performance of femininity is to make oneself an object—"a thing that exists as *looked at and acted upon*" rather than someone who is looking and acting.[41] I return to the topic of looking and objectification in the following section.

To *con-form* to the conventional practices and images of a tradition is to form one's gendered or sexual behavior around norms, to meet the expectations directed toward us, which in turn renders our behavior intelligible to others and ourselves. "'Intelligible' genders are those which in some sense institute and maintain relations of coherence and continuity among sex, gender, sexual practice, and desire," writes Butler.[42] The conventional concepts and norms of a tradition indicate the available subject positions and the means of assimilating to them, which is how we situate ourselves within social groups and become recognizable. We learn to occupy the gendered positions of feminine or masculine, for example, by conforming our behavior to the social expectations and images associated with those positions. This is often not done willingly and thus coercion is often used to "straighten us out."

Gender and sexuality socialization in explicit and implicit forms operate continuously in ways both big and small. Schools, for example, communicate gender and sexuality norms to students in the content of the curriculum, and they regulate the social relations and bodily practices of students through institutional rules related to dress, bathrooms, dating, school dances, sports, and cheerleading. Other students, through jokes, bullying, and sexual harassment, police appearance and behavior. Classroom facilitation, at its worst, discourages assertive girls, tolerates disruptive boys, enables stereotype threat, reproduces gender and sexuality binaries in speech and assignments, and reflects permissive attitudes about sexist and homophobic speech. Such actions characterize space as gender-binary and heteronormative, where feminine bodies are constrained and queer bodies are "out of place" and *unfit*.

Space is often considered neutral, universal, and open, but this assumption of neutrality disregards how space is lived and how its normative borders and boundaries regulate who is authorized to project or extend themselves in it.[43] Some bodies and desires are *at home,* while others are excluded, unintelligible, or objectified. This creates a kind of transitional space or borderland, as Gloria Anzaldúa calls it, a "vague and undetermined place created by the emotional residue of an unnatural boundary." It is the lived place of liminal territory. "The prohibited and forbidden are its inhabitants," writes Anzaldúa. "*Los atravesados* live here: the squint-eyed, the perverse, the queer, the troublesome, the mongrel, the mulato, the half-breed, the half dead; in short, those who cross over, pass over, or go through the confines of the 'normal.'"[44] Norms inform the contours of the built environment, facilitating unreflective performance or forcing the self-awareness of bodily projection—the phenomenon referred to in Chapter 1 as the *dys-appearance* of the body in disabling spaces. These spaces are saturated with what Patricia Hill Collins calls "controlling images," making visible raced norms of gender and sexuality performance as well as their appropriate desires.[45] Desire is a modality of the body's transcendence toward others, and thus the management of desires is a disciplinary strategy to straighten out any migrating or deviant forms of transcendence. "Spaces and bodies become straight as an effect of repetition," writes Sara Ahmed.[46]

Not all forms of embodiment are about following norms, however. As Linda Martín Alcoff writes, "The possibility of pregnancy, childbirth, nursing, and in many societies, rape, are parts of females' horizons that we carry with us throughout childhood and much or all of our adult lives. The way these are figured, imagined, experienced, accepted, and so on, is as variable as culture. But these elements exist in the female horizon, and they exist there because of the ways in which we are embodied."[47] Young's analysis has demonstrated the qualities of gendered space and our extension in it. She remarks on the material constraints put on the bodies of girls and women, which limit their "free and open engagement with the world" through which they have the opportunity to develop skills.[48] Beauvoir makes a similar point in *The Second Sex*, where she describes how boys are socialized to have "free movement towards the outside world" and to practice "self-realization in concrete projects." It is, she says, "by *doing* that he creates his existence, both in one and the same action." By contrast, passivity is "the essential characteristic of the 'feminine,'" which "is in fact a destiny imposed upon her by her teachers and by society."[49] To take just one small example, consider traditionally masculine sports and athletic fields and the kinds of material resources necessary to sustain them (and exclude others). In 1972, after feminist organizing, the US government passed Title IX, a law that prohibited gender discrimination in educational institutions receiving federal funding. This included extracurricular athletics and greatly expanded the material conditions for women's participation in physical training and sports traditionally monopolized by men. Before 1972, women accounted for approximately 2 percent of all collegiate athletes, but by 2001 they accounted for approximately 43 percent, which has in turn resulted in the normalization of more muscular and powerful body images for female athletes.[50]

When our behavior is consistent with prevailing norms and thus intelligible to others, our performance has a place, even if it is one of subordination and insecurity. We work our way into structural relations; we mutually orient each other by quietly affirming each other's actions (or, when we transgress, being subjected to or subjecting others to coercive or violent regulation). "We could say that history 'happens' in the very repetition of gestures, which is what gives bodies their tendencies. We might note here that the labor of such repetition disappears through labor," writes Ahmed.[51] Norms reappear as an outside limit in acts of transgression. This is how we come to know them. Those who do not transgress, those habituated to straight and cisgender norms in their raced and classed inflections, do not experience them as perpetually operative or policed. "In a way," Ahmed explains, "we learn what home means, or how we occupy space at home and as home, when we leave home."[52] To make manifest our structuring habits and regulating spaces, it is good to leave home. When home is a space of violence, insecurity, or, as Beauvoir writes, "degradation of existence into 'in-itself,' of freedom into facticity," then it can be necessary to leave.[53]

Objectification, Praxis, and Masculinity

How our bodies are treated, looked upon, or imagined by others affects our subjectivity, our self-worth, and our material possibilities. Our bodies, writes Merleau-Ponty, are "at once an object for others and a subject for me."[54] Others experience our bodies differently than we do, thus making them sites of tension, conflicting interpretations, violence, and resistance. Many can only achieve a positive self-relation at the cost of perpetual vigilance and resistance to violence, dehumanizing objectification, and degrading representations. Even when we oppose how others perceive, interpret, and act upon our bodies, it can have alienating effects. Phenomenological descriptions of the performativity of gender and sexuality, and of the normative regulation of lived spaces, need therefore to be supplemented with a social theoretical account of their oppressive structure and the material conditions necessary to reproduce them.

When Beauvoir said that one becomes a woman rather than is born as one, she viewed this becoming within a dialectical relation: "She is determined and differentiated in relation to man, while he is not in relation to her; she is the inessential in front of the essential. He is the Subject, he is the Absolute—she is the Other."[55] Beauvoir is not claiming that man is not defined in relation to woman. Her point is to indicate rather the moment of concealment in this relation of domination. The dialectical structure of gender and sexuality is always hierarchical. "Gender here is a matter of dominance, not difference," writes Catharine MacKinnon, yet this is almost always obscured, because the privileged position in the social structure always naturalizes and thus conceals its malleability and dialectical dependency.[56] The law of the dominant insinuates particular interests into the form of universality and thereby naturalizes his rule. "I will put my law in their inward parts, and write it in their hearts; and will be their God, and they shall be my people" (Jeremiah 31:33). Abiding by the law is thus serving the dominant, who renders the interests and lives of subordinates as derivative—the way Eve was derived from the rib of Adam.

Young describes this ideological process as *cultural imperialism,* in which "the dominant meanings of a society render the particular perspective of one's own group invisible at the same time as they stereotype one's group and mark it out as the Other. Cultural imperialism involves the universalization of a dominant group's experience and culture, and its establishment as the norm."[57] Because we come to know ourselves through our practical experience, experiencing a world so deeply marked by the values, images, and norms of, say, masculinity and heterosexuality can be profoundly alienating. Such estrangement follows, on the one hand, from one not having a significant role in the creation of this normative and symbolic order and, on the other hand, from the fact that the dominant group's norms *necessarily* situate the subordinate group as inferior, not only as inversions or as difference.[58] Paulo Freire describes this condition as "antidialogue" insofar as the dominated group confronts a ready-made world, rather than one in which they can dialogically participate in constructing. It is an attempt to transform the logic of nonidentity into identity thinking—the logic of objectification, atomization, and alienation—which thereby naturalizes a normative order supporting the relations of domination. "In order to present for the consideration of the oppressed and subjugated a world of deceit designed to increase their alienation and passivity," writes Freire, "the oppressors develop a series of methods precluding any presentation of the world as a problem and showing it rather as a fixed entity, as something given—something to which people, as mere spectators, must adapt."[59]

This alienation from a simultaneously degrading and objectified social world is necessarily experienced within oneself, for the experience of ourselves is always already mediated by practical experience and values and perspectives embedded in what Gadamer called "historically effected consciousness" (see Chapter 1). The dominant culture's "stereotyped and inferiorized images of the group must be internalized by group members at least to the extent that they are forced to react to behavior of others influenced by those images," writes Young.[60] This is the context of W. E. B. Du Bois's notion (and experience) of "double consciousness," which arises precisely because being a member of a subordinate group does not make one passive or a mere spectator, despite disciplinary strategies that try to make it so. Alienation is experienced as a confrontation between two worlds, between two self-understandings. Experience in a white supremacist world, writes Du Bois, "yields him no true self-consciousness, but only lets him see himself through the revelation of the other world. It is a peculiar sensation, this double consciousness, this sense of always looking at one's self through the eyes of others, of measuring one's soul by the tape of a world that looks on in amused contempt and pity. One ever feels his two-ness ... two warring ideals in one dark body, whose dogged strength alone keeps it from being torn asunder."[61] The "dogged strength" Du Bois speaks of is sustained through countercultural norms, images, and values that make life livable, that make oppositional knowledge possible, and that enable critical resistance. Out of the doubling, a multidimensional knowledge can be developed, a situated knowledge unknown to dominant groups, which are more often than not captivated by their own self-serving mythologies. Black Americans are thus "gifted with second-sight in this American world," writes Du Bois, which is to say that the social location of black experience in a white supremacist society, while not fixed or limited to one form of identity (e.g., masculine, feminine, gay, trans), does open up the possibility of insights into the mechanisms of, in this instance, white supremacist domination and oppression.[62] The colonized, writes Chandra Talpade Mohanty, "must know themselves and the colonizer. This particular marginalized location makes the politics of knowledge and the power investments that go along with it visible so that we can then engage in work to transform the use and abuse of power."[63] Due to complexity of our lived identities and the interlocking social relations of domination we inhabit, in the spirit of Du Bois's model we can speak of multiple divisions—two-ness, three-ness, four-ness—each constituting a dimension of one's subjectivity and each making possible a different form of situated knowledge.

Despite the powerful tendency to think of dualities and dichotomies as *alongside* each other, as a relation of complementary difference, in lived space and practical experience we find that relations of domination and subordination dialectically animate these pairings. Within these relations, as Du Bois's notion of double consciousness illustrates, "there is no such thing as a neutral subject. We are all inevitably someone's adversary," writes Foucault.[64] Until we undermine the social structure, the adversarial stance will persist. A similar conclusion was drawn from Hegel's dialectic of lordship and bondage, wherein the lord attempted to achieve freedom through a relation of domination. However, freedom could not be had by denying one's dependency on the other (mediation) or by subordinating the other. Indeed, in the same paragraph that Beauvoir speaks of man as the Absolute, she writes, "These phenomena could not be understood if human reality were solely a *Mitsein* based on solidarity and friendship. On the contrary, they become clear if, following Hegel, a fundamental hostility to any other consciousness is found in consciousness itself; the subject posits itself only in opposition; it asserts itself as the essential and sets up the other as inessential, as the object."[65] The German term *Mitsein* translates as "being with" and refers to a fundamental kind of sociality—the social nature or socially mediated condition of our experiences, which does not entail hierarchy.

The process of *othering* someone is to render them object-like, for to not see the other as a subject is to take them to be something one does things to; they come to have an "in-itself" status like other objects in the world. This process occurs in all dialectical social structures: others become instrumentalized the way Hegel's lord reduced the bondsman to a mere means or instrument for satisfying his own desires. There is a subtle and pernicious dimension to this construction and reproduction of the social structures of identity as experienced in the strife of double consciousness discussed above—namely, that those in the subordinate position of the social structure must confront and struggle against taking up the perspective of the dominant. This is always a threat, because it is the perspective and interests of the dominant group that have been normalized, so when we seek to fulfill the norms regulating our social life, we are taking up the perspective of the dominant position. "The desire to persist in one's own being requires submitting to a world of others that is fundamentally not one's own," writes Butler. "Only by persisting in alterity does one persist in one's 'own' being. Vulnerable to terms that one never made, one persists always, to some degree, through categories, names, terms, and classifications that mark a primary and inaugurative alienation in sociality."[66]

Our bodies perform and signify or communicate in certain ways, and our desires are regulated to achieve recognition in particular subject positions or to avoid harm. This is how we render ourselves intelligible within the normative order structured by the dominant's interests. For example, dressing, disciplining, concealing, mutilating, or starving one's body are means by which one can literally *embody* a norm. Power is the particular concrete body being materially forged into a recognizable instance of the relevant (raced and classed) norms of gender and sexuality, through both coercion and consent. "Through the pursuit of an ever-changing, homogenizing, elusive ideal of femininity," writes Susan Bordo, "female bodies become docile bodies—bodies whose forces and energies are habituated to external regulation, subjection, transformation, 'improvement.'"[67] The law of the dominant writes itself into the flesh, from hair straightening, skin whitening, and implants to cosmetic surgery to widen eyes, narrow noses, and thin torsos.

This is a self-relation of objectification and is related to Young's description of femininity in her analysis of throwing "like a girl." In that case, the girl's self-relation is one of an observer (rather than a doer)—a condition of immanence. She takes on the perspective of the dominant and thereby others her own body. The lived experience of femininity is, Young argues, defined by this mode of objectifying self-disruption. "For feminine bodily existence," she writes, "the body is often lived as a thing that is other than it, a thing like other things in the world. To the extent that a woman lives her body as a thing, she remains rooted in immanence, is inhibited, and retains a distance from her body as transcending movement and from engagement in the world's possibilities."[68] Freedom becomes a dream of invisibility or of life without a body.

There is a connection here between dis-identification with another, treating the other as an object, and taking an objective epistemological stance—othering, objectification, and objectivity. "Objectivity is the epistemological stance of which objectification is the social process, of which male dominance is the politics, the acted-out social practice," writes MacKinnon.[69] The debilitating self-relation of objectification, having a self-relation of immanence, *is how power operates in social structures* of race, class, sexuality, and gender. It is a form of self-negation, but unlike the self-negation that generates moral consideration of another's freedom—as in Hegel's example of the dialectic of social recognition in Chapter 1—this self-negation is debilitating. "For the girl, erotic transcendence consists in making herself prey in order to make a catch," writes Beauvoir. "She becomes an object; and she grasps herself as object ... it seems to her that she has been doubled; instead of coinciding exactly with her self, here she is existing *outside* of her self."[70] The result of this self-relation is alienation from one's body, which is experienced as ultimately belonging to others, in both meaning and in the flesh.[71] As Frantz Fanon observes, "The image of one's body is solely negating. It's an image in the third person."[72]

This is not unlike the way Marx described alienated labor in capitalism: In the social structure of class, our practical activity and its results are for another rather than for ourselves. The harder we work to fulfill the expectations of our class position—in this case, productivity and efficiency in the production of surplus value—the more we empower the dominant class. What is more, this condition of alienation makes us take an objectifying stance toward our own activity. Georg Lukács describes the objectifying condition in which consciousness and social relations are stripped of their intersubjective and interdependent relations as *reification*, which is a result of commodity fetishism. "Its basis is that a relation between people takes on the character of a thing and thus acquires a 'phantom objectivity,' an autonomy that seems so strictly rational and all-embracing as to conceal every trace of its fundamental nature: the relation between people."[73] This condition favors the requirements of capital accumulation over the social conditions of freedom and human development. More importantly, it creates a disempowering form of consciousness that undermines resistance, as Freire described, because it dis-integrates our praxis and thereby produces deformed forms of both knowing and doing. On the one hand, we develop a contemplative and abstract perspective toward our practical activity. On the other hand, this practical activity from which we've disassociated ourselves comes to appear law-like, alien in origin, or identical to a process of production over which we have no control. This alienation instills resignation. "What is important is to recognize clearly that all human relations (viewed as the objects of social activity)," writes Lukács, "assume increasingly the objective forms of the abstract elements of the conceptual systems of natural science and of the abstract substrata of the laws of nature. And also, the subject of this 'action' likewise assumes increasingly the attitude of the pure observer of these—artificially abstract—processes."[74]

As evidenced by Young's analysis, taking the position of an observer in the process of one's own actions undermines those actions—disembodying reflection through the objectification of our material body. This reflective observation is not neutral, because it regulates the body according to norms that serve the interests of, in this case, patriarchy, but there are clear parallels with white supremacy. The objectifying stance produces an experience of alienation. Indeed, writes Sandra Bartky, "much of what is held out to us as 'femininity' is in fact alienation."[75] The most obvious parallel to Marx's analysis is the laborer's alienation from the *products* of their labor—a parallel I discuss in the next section; however, for the wage-labor relationship to even begin, the worker's body must already be objectified as *labor power* so that it can be exchanged as a commodity.[76] The worker's body is an instrument and each of its motions is subjected to scientific study (Taylorism) to render it as efficient as possible in the service of capital accumulation. Entire scientific discourses as well as regimes of surveillance and management are created around this alienated dimension of our activity. Foucault describes this as a form of *disciplinary power,* which emerged in the seventeenth century, "centered on the body as a machine: its disciplining, the optimization of its capabilities, the extortion of its forces, the parallel increase of its usefulness and its docility, its integration into systems of efficient and economic controls, all this was ensured by the procedures of power that characterized the *disciplines*:

the *anatomo-politics of the human body.*"[77] This is akin to forms of alienating sexual objectification, in which bodies are fragmented, observed, measured, and "reduced to the status of mere instruments," says Bartky.[78] As a result, many women (although not exclusively women) invest tremendous amounts of time, labor, and resources transforming their bodies in appearance and performance. This experience of alienation undermines feminist and queer political praxis insofar as subjects feel disempowered in the face of social structures that appear natural, law-like, and thus impossible to resist. Once human relations are objectified, they become seemingly disconnected from our own activity and are, in turn, naturalized.

However, this disciplinary form of power is coupled with another form of power that regulates desire and exercises control over reproduction. Foucault calls this *bio-power,* and it underlies state efforts to normalize, control, and indeed construct sexual identities and behavior. This power focuses on the body "as the basis of the biological process: propagation, births and mortality, the level of health, life expectancy and longevity."[79] Part of the exercise of this form of power, which is also motivated by capitalist economic interests, is the creation of discourses about sexuality that normalize and regulate certain social relations and bodily desires central to life and reproduction. In the nineteenth century, the "deployment of sexuality," writes Foucault, became one of the most important technologies of power and continues to operate in the construction of sexuality today.[80]

One dimension of radical feminist and queer projects is to denaturalize these alienating relations and identify and critique regulatory discourses in order to empower and cultivate the already existing forms of resistance—the immanent potential—within them. Queer and feminist projects have an emancipatory interest in not just overcoming the alienation and exploitation of subordinate and nonconforming identities, but in undoing the state-supported and pathological tendencies of the dominant masculine and straight subject positions. These positions, together with their associated norms and practices, are the true source of the problem of alienation and objectification; in the dialectic of immanence and transcendence (see Chapter 1), it is the social structure that supports them that must be transcended.

In 1872, John Stuart Mill published a significant analysis of the production of femininity, the pathologies of masculinity, the power of habit, and the despotism of the family structure. His book *The Subjection of Women* was a critique of gender oppression, which identified the affective dimension of domination and the social pathologies that result from oppression. He considered the family to be "the school of despotism," for it habituates children to the *practice* of patriarchal rule, which no *formal* education or theory can successfully counter.[81] All talk of equality and theorizing about freedom "remains merely on the surface, as long as the citadel of the enemy is not attacked," the citadel here being the social structure of patriarchy.[82] The "self-worship of the male," believing himself to be an "absolute master," is matched only by that of kings and feudal lords.[83] This megalomania, cultivated from birth, corrodes all other social relations:

> All the selfish propensities, the self-worship, the unjust self-preference, which exist among mankind, have their source and root in, and derive their principal nourishment from, the present constitution of the relation between men and women. Think what it is to a boy, to grow up to manhood in the belief that without any merit or any exertion of his own, though he may be the most frivolous and empty or the most ignorant and stolid of mankind, by the mere fact of being born a male he is by right the superior of all and every one of an entire half of the human race.[84]

While Mill's diagnosis of the social pathologies that result from social structures of domination is accurate, his reduction of their source to patriarchy alone is problematic. Mill had no problem with class oppression or heteronormativity and was an enthusiastic supporter of white supremacist colonialism, working his entire life for the East India Company and eventually leading it (as his father had done before him).[85] These striking omissions are only further evidence of the need for an intersectionalist analysis of oppression. Despite these shortcomings, Mill's identification of the learned habits of masculinity as an oppressive social relation for both men and women is insightful. He also provides a dialectical understanding of femininity that articulates the affective and consensual dimensions of domination, the objectification of women's bodies and emotional life, as well as the role of property ownership and thus class in coercing subordination.[86] Concerning affectivity and consent, Mill writes, "Men do not want solely the obedience of women, they want their sentiments ... not a forced slave but a willing one, not a slave merely, but a favorite."[87] Since this devotion does not follow naturally from physical domination, men "put everything in practice to enslave their minds," which includes "the whole force of education to effect their purpose." Girls are inculcated with a morality of women's duty to men and schooled in how "to make complete abnegation of themselves, and to have no life but in their affections."[88] Through an act of self-negation (or abnegation), women's praxis is reduced to reproductive and affective labor, which is done for the benefit of hetero-masculine desires. The so-called nature of women is, then, "an eminently artificial thing," he writes.[89] And yet there is resistance.

Mill is describing the operation of what Italian Marxist Antonio Gramsci calls *social hegemony*. Gramsci distinguished coercive forms of "direct domination or command" by state forces (police, military, judiciary, prisons, etc.), from schools and intellectuals that enable *consent* to rule through the production of hegemonic ideas and values—such as those associated with patriarchy.[90] Although Gramsci developed this distinction in an analysis of the mechanism of class domination through social and state institutions, it is applicable to gender and sexual relations, which are shaped by state forces (a point I return to in the following section) and discourses about gender and sexuality. When cultural hegemony fails to induce subordinate or subaltern groups to voluntarily reproduce existing relations of domination—namely, when a woman, to use Mill's example, no longer willingly accepts subordination or "slavery"—direct coercion or violence is used to force compliance and quell rebellion.[91]

Although Mill never explicitly critiques class oppression, his critique of gender oppression does include a class analysis at its core: The unpaid affective and domestic labor of women is the result of coercion insofar as patriarchal property relations give women no other choice. Given these material constraints, which make their husband the sole means of satisfying their own needs, it is no surprise that the most important goal of all "feminine education and formation of character" is that of being attractive to men—an object of desire.[92] The social structures of gender and sexuality are relatively stable, insofar as they are institutionally, linguistically, and practically embedded in particular societies. Because they are dialectical and hierarchical, however, they are always threatened with destabilization. "Where there is power, there is resistance," writes Foucault, "and yet, or rather consequently, this resistance is never in a position of exteriority in relation to power."[93] No amount of cultivated affections, class domination, or even violence can eclipse resistance.

The violence associated with masculinity and heterosexuality is physical, but it emanates from an anxiety associated with its own precariousness as a social relation. "Violence is often the single most evident marker of manhood," writes Michael Kimmel.[94] It is an attempt to perform identity in a world of nonidentity. In addition to actual violence, performing masculinity is in part due to the fear of being conquered, assaulted, objectified, or penetrated, since masculinity is a relational subject position that demands one conquer, assault, objectify, and penetrate others. (It wasn't until 2012 that the Federal Bureau of Investigation changed its definition of rape in its Uniform Crime Report to include the possibility that men could be raped.) These forms of domination must be exercised—against women or other men—or one is at risk of becoming an object, an *in-itself,* that other subjects do things to.[95] Kimmel argues that "homophobia, men's fear of other men, is the animating condition of the dominant definition of masculinity in America."[96] In order to sustain itself, masculinity produces pathological defense mechanisms and ritualistic affirmations of sexist, homophobic, and individualist norms. The prohibition of homosexual desire—compulsory heterosexuality—while itself oftentimes evidence of such desire, is a constitutive part of heterogendered relations.[97] The prohibition or othering of one form of desire is the naturalization of another and thus an integral moment in the construction of dominance. Homophobia is not an *irrational* fear, but rather a stabilizing form of discrimination and thus, in the logic of masculine domination, it is rational. "As supplementary 'other,'" notes Rosemary Hennessy, "homosexual identity is a product of this discourse even as it threatens to belie the naturalness of the heterogender systems."[98]

The demands of masculinity are never fulfilled or quieted. Like the capitalist that must continually innovate and reinvest capital to expand production in order to survive, masculinity must constantly exercise domination to reproduce itself. This entails the production of a subject population in a generally precarious condition, within which such violence can be routinely exercised. The production of such populations is typically a function of the state through law. Instability and fear are structural conditions of masculinity, because resistance is inevitable and gender boundaries shift for reasons beyond its control. No one, says Simone de Beauvoir, "is more arrogant toward women, more aggressive or more disdainful, than a man anxious about his own virility."[99] As I was completing this book, a young man in Santa Barbara, California, went on a shooting spree, targeting the women who, he said, "would have all rejected me and looked down on me as an inferior man," as well as the men who treated him "like a mouse." To the men, he said, he will soon be "like a god," and as for the women, they will regret the "injustice" of not having sex with him: "I will slaughter every single spoilt, stuck-up, blonde slut. . . . I'll take great pleasure in slaughtering all of you. You will finally see that I am, in truth, the superior one. The true alpha male."[100] The logic of the murderous violence here is clearly connected to the fear and entitlement associated with the (sought after) Absolute of masculinity. In a study of school shooters between 1982 and 2001, Kimmel and Matthew Mahler found a "striking similarity" between the young male, mostly white, teens who became mass murderers: They were all routinely harassed or "gay-baited" for "inadequate gender performance" of masculinity. They conclude, "These boys are not psychopathological deviants but rather overconformists to a particular normative construction of masculinity, a construction that defines violence as a legitimate response to a perceived humiliation."[101]

Violence is not only a means of policing the desires and practices of gender and sexual identities, but it also constitutes the dominant subject positions and thus the social structure. As Rich writes, the "failure to examine heterosexuality as an institution is like failing to admit that the economic system called capitalism or the caste system of racism is maintained by a variety of forces, including both violence and false consciousness."[102] That is, like capitalism and racism, heterosexuality is a social system and like all such systems it is maintained through violence and cultural hegemony. It is not an external tool but a defining social practice, a form of rule that configures identities. This is a very important point to keep in mind when theorizing any or all of these systems: The production of difference is not just the groundwork for forms of privilege, such as access to wealth and opportunity, cultural expression, and so forth. It also creates the opportunity to exercise violence beyond the law, to exercise "sovereignty," which is constitutive of dominant group identities. The above examples of mass shootings are spectacular forms of violence, but they are clearly *criminal*; they are not examples of the extra-juridical forms of violence that systematically reproduce identities. As forms of rule, masculinity and heterosexuality depend on more systematic articulations of violence and control either beyond the law or generally beyond accountability, because the law is not enforced. They would not be able to reproduce themselves if criminalized violence was their own means. Instead, the law must function to criminalize forms of resistance to their rule.

Systematic forms of violence can be exercised with state sponsorship (e.g., by police and military forces using systematic rape as an instrument of war or harassing and murdering LGBT people), as well as through the criminal code, resulting in state punishment, incarceration, and murder as a response to "deviance" and disobedience. The Stonewall riots, which are often considered to mark the beginning of the gay liberation movement—shifting from assimilation to resistance—began after the police raided and beat gay patrons at the Stonewall Inn in Greenwich Village in New York City in 1969.[103]

The most common forms of violence and aggression are pervasive hate speech and sexual harassment; rape and domestic violence, most often in the family and in intimate relations; and indiscriminate assaults on LGBT people.[104] A fundamental component of radical philosophical projects is therefore antiviolence work. The first Rape Crisis Centers in the United States in the 1970s were acts of political resistance by second-wave feminists, and organizations like the National Coalition of Anti-Violence Programs, founded in 1995, organize against violence in LGBT and HIV-affected communities.[105] In addition to creating and promoting services that assist the victims of violence, radical philosophical projects include politicizing and combating the sources of violence, destigmatizing the victims of violence, and capacitating communities to address violence and produce safe spaces without mobilizing the state and its coercive powers.[106]

Given that violence engenders multiple structures of domination and thus identity construction, intersectionalist theory and coalition organizing help prevent groups from responding to one system of violence in a way that might unintentionally strengthen other systems or render some groups more vulnerable, because of their residency status, race, or class. Incorporating a multiplicity of concerns and situated knowledge from various communities affected by a particular system of violence (and there are always multiple communities affected) can also potentially produce projects that address multiple systems of violence simultaneously. What is certain is that state institutions, and the law in particular, are always operative in constructing communities vulnerable to the most common forms of violence and aggression, which are necessary to reproduce social structures of domination.

Law, Patriarchy, and Labor

The Fourteenth Amendment (1868) to the US Constitution effectively overturned *Dred Scott v. Sandford* (1857), which had ruled that blacks could not be citizens (see Chapter 4). It was the first time that citizenship was gendered in the Constitution, protecting the right to vote of "male citizens."[107] In 1869, Myra Bradwell, a publisher, accomplished legal scholar, and activist, applied for a license to practice law in Illinois and was twice rejected by the Illinois Seventh Circuit. Bradwell appealed to the US Supreme Court, arguing that her right to practice law was covered under the Privileges or Immunities Clause of the Fourteenth Amendment. This clause was in the first section of the Amendment (together with the Citizenship Clause, Due Process Clause, and Equal Protection Clause) and was not qualified as "male," which presented an opening. The section reads, "All persons born or naturalized in the United States, and subject to the jurisdiction thereof, are citizens of the United States and of the State wherein they reside. No State shall make or enforce any law which shall abridge the privileges or immunities of citizens of the United States; nor shall any State deprive any person of life, liberty, or property, without due process of law; nor deny to any person within its jurisdiction the equal protection of the laws."

The justices ruled 8 to 1 against Bradwell, using a previous interpretation of the Amendment (*Slaughter-House Cases* of 1873), which distinguished federal and state privileges and immunities, viewing a law license as a state privilege and thus not protected by the Fourteenth Amendment. As in *Dred Scott*, the justices also invoked natural differences in their decision, this time between men and women, to support their rejection of Bradwell's efforts to practice law in *Bradwell v. State of Illinois* (1873). Justice Bradley writes in his opinion,

> On the contrary, the civil law, as well as nature herself, has always recognized a wide difference in the respective spheres and destinies of man and woman. Man is, or should be, woman's protector and defender. The natural and proper timidity and delicacy which belongs to the female sex evidently unfits it for many of the occupations of civil life. The Constitution of the family organization, which is founded in the divine ordinance as well as in the nature of things, indicates the domestic sphere as that which properly belongs to the domain and functions of womanhood. The harmony, not to say identity, of interest and views which belong, or should belong, to the family institution is repugnant to the idea of a woman adopting a distinct and independent career from that of her husband.[108]

The justice distinguishes civil from natural forms of organization, and both are said to follow the nature of reason and divine law. Women are viewed as helpless, and their proper place is the home in which they remain dependent upon the man financially, legally, and physically for protection. This dependency is clearly articulated by William Blackstone in his influential *Commentaries on the Laws of England* (1765–1769): "the husband and wife are one person in the law; that is, the very being or legal existence of the woman is suspended during the marriage, or at least incorporated and consolidated into that of the husband: under whose wing, protection, and cover she performs every thing."[109] The existence of the woman is subsumed by the man's, for she is situated beyond the law, yet appends to his legal standing. "The paramount destiny and mission of women are to fulfill the noble and benign offices of wife and mother. . . . And the rules of civil society must be adapted to the general constitution of things, and cannot be based upon exceptional cases," claims Justice Bradley.[110] The exceptional cases he refers to are unmarried women.

The *Bradwell* decision offers us insights into a web of intersecting oppressions and privileges, modes of power, spaces of rule, and hegemonic understandings. The topics I discuss in the following, all of which overlap, include the relation of domination in the "function" of wife; the construction of a nature/civil society distinction; the function and production of mother/sexuality; and the role of unwaged labor—which is what the case was ostensibly about, namely, whether Myra Bradwell could enter the waged labor force of the legal profession.[111] The first two points are mutually informing insofar as the function of "wife" is legally stipulated in relation to a husband, yet this relation is itself considered to have a natural basis in both *desire* and *necessity,* and thus exists beyond civil society. Justice Bradley argues that women are naturally weak and in need of a man's natural strength to protect her, making their pre-political biological traits complementary in a way that creates a functioning unit. This naturalized gender complex is echoed in a sexual complementarity insofar as the purpose of sex is assumed to be procreation—and in white supremacy, part of the protection the white man is assumed to provide includes protection from, for example, black desire. The fourteen-year-old Emmett Till was lynched in Mississippi in 1955 for talking to or whistling at a married white woman. An all-male and all-white jury acquitted his murderers.

In the *Bradwell* decision, and in the history of liberal theory generally, autonomy is doubled: The male is autonomous in civil society (public and political) and the family is autonomous insofar as it forms *natural* unity (private and familial), which becomes "one person in the law," as Blackstone put it. The civil sphere is marked as the space of freedom, rights, and universality, whereas the private sphere is marked as the space of necessity, duties, and particularity. "In this regard," writes Wendy Brown, "liberalism both produces and positions gendered subjects whose production and positioning it disavows through naturalization (an ideological moment) and produces abstract, genderless, colorless *sovereign subjects* (a more discursive moment)."[112] In Chapter 4, I discuss at length the practical relations of colonialism and slavery contributing to the discursive construction of these sovereign subjects as white.

Consistent with the philosophical and scientific traditions discussed in the previous chapters, the above dichotomies are variations on the theme of a mind-body dualism. Liberty, sovereignty, and reason are gendered as masculine and are achieved by transcending the particularity and dependencies of the body and emotional life, which are gendered as feminine.[113] Where one draws the line between the political and the natural is itself a political act, and what constitutes a natural condition or natural set of relations is thus politically determined. It is true that most women can get pregnant and men cannot, but how this difference is interpreted and informs social norms and institutions is political and always contested.[114] The same is true of the normalization of sex as procreative, the stigmatization of sex for pleasure, and the pathologizing of sex that threatens racial purity (and in particular white supremacy). Despite shifting borders and changing configurations, we can say that masculinity, as a form of rule, is impossible without the labor and body of the feminine subject, for their relation is reciprocally mediating and constitutive. To the extent that this gendered relation of rule is enforced in practice and normalized in psychiatric, medical, and juridical discourses, forms of sexual behavior that do not contribute to its reproduction are turned into pathologies—at first through stigmatizing sexual acts and ultimately by constructing a pathological sexual identity. Indeed, this was the origin of sexuality or sexual identity: the sexual deviant and uncontrollable black sexuality.

When the interpretive horizon is public life and wage labor, the gender relations and sexual identities of the home are situated beyond the margins of liberalism, and thereby more or less beyond history and justice as well.[115] In this scenario, the rational, rights-bearing subject is the foundation for the concepts of freedom and justice, which are constituted *by definition* through their opposition to the realm and relations of natural necessity that elude right. Only the man, and for the longest time only the white man, is recognized, while the rights-mediated social relations of civil society are the only relations that can be measured by liberalism's metric of justice, leaving the rest to nature. "The politics of domination and exploitation," writes Brown, "are converted ideologically as well as institutionally into what is given and natural."[116] Like an Egyptian sphinx, the masculine head sits atop and is thus sustained by the animal body of the feminine. Hegel interpreted the sphinx as the premodern aesthetic expression of a human rational spirit emerging from animal life—a representation of unfinished progress in the development of personhood—that remains "confused and associated with what is other than itself."[117] It is perhaps better viewed as the symbol of the patriarchal family of liberal politics and the capitalist mode of production—in Hegel's time and still very much in our own—which relegates to the realm of nature and prehistory that which in fact makes the sovereign masculine subject possible.[118] The confusion thus lies elsewhere—namely, in an atomistic understanding of freedom and the disavowal of the body.[119]

This particular notion and practice of freedom generate a space of extra-legal or noncriminal violence—the state of nature, plantation, colony, camp, prison, occupied territory, borderland, and home. These are spaces of violence against women's bodies, the ultimate embodiment of nature and pre-political life—particularly the bodies of women of color—that are more or less beyond the law.[120] The rape of black women during slavery (and after), of indigenous women during colonization (and after), and of Latina workers in the fields and factories of white men are methods of discipline and domination within these spaces.[121] Marital or spousal rape was only criminalized in the 1970s as a result of feminist organizing and resistance, and it wasn't until the 1990s that all fifty states had such a law. As Brown observes, "Everything under the auspices of the 'pre-political' is excluded from politics precisely because its [i.e., politics'] structure and organization is bound up with violence and inequality inherent in institutionalized subordination."[122] To politicize the body, particularly bodies of color, is to denaturalize this violence.

The family and economy came to be separate kinds of social relations in the development of capitalism and its theoretical expression in liberalism. The word *economy* is derived from the Greek term *oikos,* which means "household," and *economy* therefore referred to household management. The economy of the *oikos* or family was distinguished from the life of the city or *polis.* With the rise of capitalism, the site of economic production moved out of the household, creating a third distinct form of social relations that early liberalism called "civil society," distinct from both family and state. We now speak of it simply as the economy (i.e., the spaces of production and distribution discussed in Chapter 2). "The core of a gendered division of labor in modern societies," writes Young, "is the division between 'private' and 'public' work. An aspect of the basic structure of these societies is that the work of caring—for persons, their bodily needs, their emotional well being, and the maintenance of their dwellings—takes place primarily in unpaid labor in private homes."[123] In capitalism, the modern family transforms into a *"private service,"* writes Engels, and the "wife became the first domestic servant, pushed out of participation in social production"—with the exception of proletarian women, he notes.[124] In most cases, "the man has to be the earner, the bread-winner of the family, at least among the propertied classes, and this gives him a dominating position which requires no special legal privileges."[125] Until rather recently, the vast majority of wage-laborers in this "public" sphere had been male and the majority of those engaged in unwaged labor had been female, although many poor women have always worked for a wage (as Engels notes); this is disproportionately true of women of color. This economic reality has, together with cultural traditions and responses to white supremacy, contributed to family structures and community relations among people of color that are not reflected in traditional liberal theory or feminist critiques of it. The case of slave labor in capitalist production also presents a different dynamic, since the gendered division of labor was not as distinct: "the black woman was not systematically molded into an inferior being insofar as the internal workings of the slave community—the relations of the slaves among themselves—were concerned," writes Angela Davis.[126]

In *The German Ideology*, Marx and Engels argued that historical understanding almost always missed the "real basis of history"—namely, the mode of production.[127] This error arises from the naturalization of the mode of production, whereby "the antithesis of nature and history is created."[128] They set out to shed light on the political and historical sources of class domination, which had been pushed beyond the bounds of liberal theory and political economy, and argued that economic relations are "the true source and theater of all history."[129] Yet, in revealing one form of naturalization, they downplayed or concealed others (e.g., the "primitive accumulation" of women's unwaged labor in reproducing labor power), as well as the role of the family structure in producing gender and sexual identities.[130] While Engels did not view women as a class in his influential work, *The Origin of Family, Private Property, and State* (1884), he asserted that women's integration into social production, as well as making men and women "completely equal before the law," would spell the end of the family and thus of male domination.[131] However, as with his prediction about the withering away of the state under socialism (Chapter 2), Engels's notion that gender oppression would come to an end for economic reasons has proven unconvincing, given various socialist experiments and the experience of women in capitalist social production today. As with his prediction about the state, the central shortcoming of Engels's analysis was his reduction of all forms of oppression to class oppression. For the women who have worked their way into the sphere of social production, they are still paid less, and to the extent that domestic labor has been socialized (i.e., become an area of wage labor), it is mostly done by women of color for low wages—and often integrated into an international division of labor involving transnational migrant workers ("global care chains").[132] While "economic struggle is indispensable," writes Davis, "it is by no means the sole terrain of significant anti-capitalist activity."[133]

I began my discussion of gender and sexuality with Judith Butler's argument about sex as a gendered category—namely, that sex was masked as natural through an inversion situating it in a prediscursive realm. The *result* of practices, she points out, becomes the supposed cause, a fabricated origin (sex) that appears as the determining factor in gender performance. I subsequently introduced Foucault's notion of bio-power, which he describes as "numerous and diverse techniques for achieving the subjugations of bodies and the control of populations."[134] It is the power to enable and manage life at the level of the population, and it operates through various social institutions such as the family. All such institutions combine bio-power with various disciplinary practices that order and structure actions, with the goal of turning them into law-like relations with intelligible subjects and predictable outcomes (e.g., births, deaths, illnesses, etc.). Here, the two discussions converge, for the process of retroactive naturalization that Butler describes is mobilized through the family for the production of subjects, sexualities, and gender performances conducive to biological imperatives determined beyond the family—namely, by the imperatives of capital. "The adjustment of the accumulation of men to that of capital," writes Foucault, "the joining of the growth of human groups to the expansion of productive forces and the differential allocation of profit, were made possible in part by the exercise of bio-power in its many forms and modes of application."[135]

The description of woman's destiny and mission, as well as the "functions of womanhood," which Justice Bradley provides, is telling in this regard. The woman is being habituated to and discursively constructed as a wife and a mother; she maintains existing labor power and produces new labor power through manual, sexual, and affective labor. Foucault views this as a "deployment of sexuality," insofar as sexual activity is managed and normalized in a way that, as Butler argued, *produces* sexuality, or a particular form of sexual identity. The categories of heterosexual and homosexual are rather recent, and it was the latter that was defined first.[136] More importantly, Foucault traces the formation of sexual identity itself as the medical sciences moved from acts to agents: "Homosexuality appeared as one of the forms of sexuality when it was transposed from the practice of sodomy onto a kind of interior androgyny, a hermaphrodism of the soul. The sodomite had been a temporary aberration; the homosexual was now a species."[137]

Gender and sexual identities have been produced through interlocking practices and discourses of domination—patriarchy, capitalism, and white supremacy—and critical resistance to their contemporary configurations must remain attentive to the ways one form of liberation can result in assimilation to, and normalization of, other relations of domination. Ending the violence operating in the naturalized spaces of rule that support these relations is essential, which also means challenging the state that juridically constructs these spaces and the theories and values that normalize them. Foucault writes of the possibility of a future with a "different economy of bodies and pleasures," one of our own (collective) making, not tethered to contemporary deployments of sexuality.[138]

Speaking of female sexual desire, Hennessy writes, "The issue for feminists and transformative social movements generally should not so much be whether or not to endorse and celebrate female sexual desire in all of its possible forms, but how to understand the production of desire and subjectivity as a dialectical historical possibility and how to intervene in the ways that it works—often unevenly—in concert with capitalist advancement to open liberatory possibilities for some women but often at the expense of others."[139] What is certain is that future possibilities will only emerge through collective resistance and experimentation that changes the material conditions and practical relations so central to our subject formation. bell hooks defines feminism as "a struggle to end sexist oppression," rather than a fight for equality, for with whom would one want to be equal within existing structures of domination with their individualist notions of freedom?[140] In the next chapter, I turn to what is too often the implicit and problematic answer to this question—namely, the white sovereign subject whose masculinity and heterosexuality were discussed above.

CHAPTER 4
ANTIRACISM AND THE WHITENESS PROBLEM

> The idea of white supremacy rests simply on the fact that white men are the creators of civilization ... and are therefore civilization's guardians and defenders. Thus it was impossible for Americans to accept the black man as one of themselves, for to do so was to jeopardize their status as white men. But not so to accept him was to deny his human reality, his human weight and complexity, and the strain of denying the overwhelmingly undeniable forced Americans into rationalizations so fantastic that they approached the pathological.
>
> *—James Baldwin,* Notes of a Native Son[1]

> They talk to me about civilization, I talk about proletarianization and mystification.
>
> *—Aimé Césaire,* Discourse on Colonialism[2]

There is a powerful photograph from the US civil rights struggle depicting mostly black men marching single file on a sidewalk and carrying nothing more than sandwich-board signs stating "I AM A MAN." They are walking toward the photographer, and to their right is a neat row of helmeted white soldiers. The soldiers have their rifles held high and their left arms outstretched to grasp the barrels, bayonets jutting toward the marchers. They are blocking a roadway behind them, and as the protesters walk past, their long shadows lean toward the soldiers, running nearly parallel to the rifles. To the left of the marchers, in the middle of the street, is an evenly spaced row of military tanks heading in the same direction.

The date was March 29, 1968, in Memphis, Tennessee, and the National Guard had blocked off Beale Street. The marchers were sanitation workers on strike to demand recognition of their union, safer working conditions, and a pay raise. A few supporters accompanied them. Boundaries had been drawn and forces had been marshaled to defend them, but it was not the threat of violence by marchers that mobilized these instruments of war. One boundary defended that day was racial, the line between white supremacy and black subjugation, and any other racial group that might challenge their place for that matter. The "problem of the Twentieth Century," wrote W. E. B. Du Bois in 1903, "is the problem of the color-line."[3] Here it was, militarized, with white power policing it to protect its privilege. Part of that privilege is to never have to say, "I am a man," for in a white supremacist society, whites are synonymous with human beings and thus, by birthright, entitled to some degree of respect and social recognition. For blacks to publicly proclaim themselves worthy of similar respect and recognition was a direct threat to the foundation of white power. It challenged the natural identification of whiteness with human dignity and thus rendered particular what was taken by them to be universal. Accentuating this point is the presence of a lone white man among the marchers. In the photograph, he is walking in solidarity with them, yet, significantly, he doesn't carry a sign. As a white man, he doesn't need to demand his worthiness of recognition; he doesn't even need to state it as a fact. The social world he inhabits recognizes him as he recognizes himself in its norms, representations, institutions, history, and power.[4] White power "secures its dominance by seeming not to be anything at all," writes Richard Dyer.[5]

A second boundary policed that day was class, but in this struggle—like the Mexican and Filipino immigrant farmworker struggles occurring at the same time in California—it was a class divide that had become almost indistinguishable from the color-line. Dr. Martin Luther King Jr. spoke several times in Memphis to support the strikes, oscillating between the class struggle and the race struggle in his speeches. Indeed, class had been a theme of the March on Washington in August of 1963, where Dr. King delivered his "I Have a Dream" speech. The full title of the demonstration was the "March on Washington for Jobs and Justice," and it was organized by a coalition of civil rights and working-class organizations.[6] Dr. King was supposed to launch the Poor People's Campaign in May of 1968 in Washington, DC, as part of the second phase of the civil rights movement—namely, the multiracial class struggle. The last speech Dr. King gave was to the striking sanitation workers in Memphis the day before a white gunman assassinated him.

Unseen, but certainly framing the photograph as well, was the gender-line. Indeed, patriarchy was so well defended within both the race and class dimensions of this conflict that only men were visible, and visibility is part of gender privilege. Most of the public figures in this fight were men, from the mayor of Memphis, the National Guardsmen, and press, to the sanitation workers, union supporters, and civil rights leaders. The strike was a fight for dignity, but it was a masculine dignity. "I AM A MAN"—a response to the emasculating paternalism of whites referring to black men as "boy."[7] Out of frame, you could almost hear black women laboring as domestic workers in the kitchens and laundry rooms of white families all across the city, asking, "And Ain't I a Woman?"

Although black women were organizing and struggling as well, the gendered division of labor situating women's work in the domestic sphere (of reproductive labor) made their struggles longer and harder. The "family wage," which was afforded to white male workers to keep their wives at home for unpaid domestic work and child-rearing, was not paid to black men—thus forcing black women to do both paid and unpaid domestic labor. On Mother's Day, May 12, 1968, Coretta Scott King led the inaugural march of the Poor People's Campaign in DC, which included thousands of women. In that same year, Dorothy Bolden, a black domestic worker (and neighbor of the Kings) in Atlanta, Georgia, organized the National Domestic Workers Union and was elected its first president. Bolden was the granddaughter of a slave and had been a domestic worker for whites her entire adult life. She was fired from one of her jobs in the 1940s when she was leaving for the day and was told to stay and clean more dishes. Bolden refused and left, but her white employer called the police, who arrested her on her way home. She was jailed and given a psychiatric evaluation because her disobedience to whites was interpreted as a mental illness. Only after her uncle paid for two independent evaluations was she released five days later. "They told me I was crazy because I had talked back to a white woman, and called in some psychiatrists to prove it," Bolden said. "A white woman's word was gospel, and two psychiatrists actually thought I was crazy. . . . This was the way you got locked up. . . . This was the system."[8]

Race is a relation of power and a form of rule that relies on objectification and a system of classification. In order to reproduce race as a social relation of domination, the boundaries of racial identity must be continuously policed, and entire scientific discourses about race have been produced to legitimate its boundaries and authorize a group to enforce them. To justify a form of rule, the science of race, like the science of sex difference, created the notion of a physical racial essence.[9] Thus, each race had a certain biological substance, which determined one's social behavior, intelligence, abilities, and morality. This is a form of biological determinism intended to shield racial classification from social critique and resistance. In the case of Dorothy Bolden, her resistance to white rule was not taken to be evidence of a social pathology—namely, white supremacy—but rather of a psychological pathology located in the mind of a disobedient individual. As the biological discourses fade, contemporary political, scientific, and policy discourses about race are more often filtered through allegedly race-neutral categories, such as those of immigration, taxes, morality, religion, citizenship, sovereignty, security, and criminality.

The history of race as a social structure in the United States was shaped largely by the importation of African slaves for use by European colonists, beginning in the mid-seventeenth century, and the genocidal practices of settler colonialism that nearly wiped out indigenous peoples. From the beginning, North American race relations were class relations as well. It was primarily the dialectical relation of African slave labor to European slave owners and of European "civilization" to indigenous "savagery" that set the parameters of racial classification and constructed a white supremacist notion of whiteness.[10] Europeans of different ethnicities in this colonial context became *white*; surviving members of the Sioux, Comanche, Cherokee, Iroquois, and other nations became *Indian*; and slaves of different ethnicities became *black*, establishing a hierarchical spectrum into which subsequent immigrant groups entered (or, in the case of many residents of Mexico, where a migrating border placed them).

Ethnicity, as an identity generally associated with a country of origin, cultural traditions, religious practices, and language, is not synonymous with race, although race relations influence the characteristics and practices of cultural group identities.[11] As Harlon Dalton writes, "We embody our ethnicity without regard for the presence or absence of other ethnic groups. Of course, ethnic groups influence one another in myriad ways, and more than occasionally come into conflict. But they do not need each other to exist."[12] One way to conceal the interdependency of race as a social structure is to speak mostly, or only, of ethnic or cultural differences that entail neither hierarchy nor conflict. *Multiculturalism* and *ethnic diversity* have a pleasant and egalitarian ring to them, and even talk of discrimination does not entail an oppressive structure. "As a white person," writes Peggy McIntosh, "I realized that I had been taught about racism as something which puts others at a disadvantage, but had been taught not to see one of its corollary aspects, white privilege, which puts me at an advantage."[13] The hierarchical nature of race as a social structure does not mean there are only two races (just as there are more than two genders, sexualities, and classes), but rather that each race is constituted by its relative position within a hierarchy, in this case determined by white supremacy.[14] As Chimamanda Ngozi Adichie writes in her novel *Americanah,* "American racial minorities—blacks, Hispanics, Asians and Jews—all get shit from white folks, different kinds of shit but shit still."[15] Some might object that this is too simplistic, that discursive constructions and institutional mediations make such distinctions passé, but this is rarely said by those involved in critical resistance to white supremacy. For although "whiteness" (like "masculinity" and "heterosexuality") is discursively constituted, institutionally embedded, and therefore not synonymous with the direct rule of a particular group—and who can claim (or reject) whiteness as a sociopolitical identity changes over time—whiteness personifies itself in antagonistic group form when its privileges are challenged. In the face of resistance, the subtle mediations of contemporary life then mutate into the blunt instruments of racial conflict, and the ideological function of the policeman's hail is replaced by the swinging of his baton or worse.[16]

In the following, I begin with the hermeneutics of race, outlining some of the history of contested meanings and struggles over the authority to interpret texts, human nature, and social relations in the context of European colonialism, from which the first scientific and philosophical discourses about racial classification and hierarchy emerge. While their function in justifying European colonialism and North American slavery is not difficult to discern, the co-emergence of a racial hierarchy with Enlightenment notions of political freedom, moral autonomy, and individual reason had subtler and more insidious effects: it made whiteness synonymous with a peculiar and historically unprecedented *sovereign subject,* a fetish arising from the material conditions of colonial violence, primitive accumulation, and the despotic relations of chattel slavery. After reconstructing some of this colonial history, I turn to the role white identity plays in a dialectical relation of popular sovereignty and racial dictatorship—a *dialectic of Enlightenment.* My argument is that we should view the "association of modernity and slavery as a fundamental conceptual issue," to quote Paul Gilroy.[17] That is, there is a recognizable and necessary relation between extra-legal violence and domination and the notion of *freedom as sovereignty,* which undermines social praxis. I conclude with a discussion of the epistemic and pathological consequences of whiteness as sovereignty. Unlike previous chapters, my approach here is more historical than phenomenological.

Colonialism, Mastery, and the Hermeneutics of Race

In the British colonies, only the Bible was cited more often in political and legal texts than Charles de Montesquieu.[18] His work *The Spirit of the Laws* (1748) greatly influenced the development of the US Constitution and North American political thought more generally. He was particularly influential in his critique of despotism, the separation of powers, and defense of individual liberty, which means he had an opinion about slavery in the colonies as well. "If I had to defend the right we had of making Negroes slaves, here is what I would say," and he goes on to list several short arguments.[19] The first is economic: "The peoples of Europe, having exterminated those of America, had to make slaves of those of Africa in order to use them to clear so much land. Sugar would be too expensive if the plant producing it were not cultivated by slaves." His logic calls to mind the line from the *Communist Manifesto* about capitalism drowning everything in the "icy water of egotistical calculation." He makes a similar argument with regard to hot climates and mines: People don't want to work for you under such conditions, he says, because it's too difficult on the body. One must conclude that enslaving others is the only way to ensure that the work gets done—it is "natural reason," he says. The argument most insightful for us, however, is a succinct and accurate expression of the dialectic operative in the hermeneutics of race: "It is impossible for us to assume that these people are men because if we assumed they were men one would begin to believe we ourselves were not Christians."[20] Either Africans are full human beings and Europeans are moral monsters, or Africans are more like objects than subjects and Europeans can retain their Christian self-identity. Implicit in Montesquieu's argument is the belief that it is antithetical to Christianity to treat others the way Europeans treated Africans (i.e., enslaving, dispossessing, raping, and murdering them). Since Europeans did behave this way toward Africans, it must be that Africans are not born equal, that they are not "men," because Europeans are certain they are Christian—a determination that only Europeans are authorized to make. This is not an exceptional interpretation. From the standpoint of the dominant position, interests and values in economic profit and political rule are taken to be universal, and no one is better suited to interpret their actions, for only they can be rational and impartial. Before the question is even posed, the questioner is situated as the owner, the master, the one for whom others toil.

It is tempting to think that Montesquieu's line of reasoning is either marginal to his own theory of law and governance or lacking any real influence on jurisprudence or the practice of law. White supremacist arguments in the European Enlightenment tradition are often treated in this way. It was only recently that Immanuel Kant's influential theory of white supremacy and racial classification, for example, has been given serious attention.[21] In his essay "Of the Different Races of Human Beings" (1775), Kant presents a theory of biological determinism relating skin color to intelligence and physical strength. He asserts that "one makes use of the red slaves (Americans) in Surinam only for labors in the house because they are too weak for field labor, for which one uses Negros,"[22] and in his lectures on anthropology, he claims that "Negros" are "stupid," but they can at least be educated enough to be good slaves.[23] Like Montesquieu, he claims that "Negros are disinclined for labor," so if freed they become mere "tramps."[24] The "race of whites," however, "contains all incentives and talents," and are the "only one who always progress toward perfection."[25] Kant's proclamations about freedom, public reason, and one's exiting immaturity and entering the age of Enlightenment turn out to apply only to whites.[26] The difference between whites and blacks is an "essential" one, he argues, "and it seems to be just as great with regard to the capacities of the mind as it is with respect to color."[27]

Typically, such explicit references to racial superiority are left out of the anthologies, not taught in the classroom, or treated as minor aberrations from what is otherwise considered a work of reason or "pure philosophy" as Kant would say. Enlightenment philosopher David Hume put the following comment in a footnote to his essay "Of National Characters," published the same year as Montesquieu's *Spirit of the Laws* in 1748:

> I am apt to suspect the negroes, and in general all the other species of men (for there are four or five different kinds) to be naturally inferior to the whites. There scarcely ever was a civilized nation of any other complexion than white, nor even any individual eminent either in action or speculation. . . . On the other hand, the most rude and barbarous of the whites . . . have still something eminent about them, in their valour, form of government, or some other particular. . . . Not to mention our colonies, there are Negroe slaves, dispersed all over Europe, of whom none ever discovered any symptoms of ingenuity. . . . In Jamaica, indeed, they talk of one negroe as a man of parts and learning, but

it is likely he is admired for slender accomplishments, like a parrot, who speaks a few words plainly.[28]

To minimize the importance of this sentiment because it is in a footnote implies that explicit references to white supremacy do not indicate an inherent logic linking them to other claims about freedom or rationality. Since Kant, for example, so clearly argued that each person has reason, that morality is rational, and that all persons could be free if they were courageous enough to exercise their reason, his racist theories seem profoundly out of place, even contradictory. They are merely the beliefs of a bygone era, the thinking goes, so we can skip over them and retain only the theories about freedom, rationality, and moral autonomy, which are universal. In the case of Montesquieu's comments about slavery, there is a tradition of interpreting them as satire, because he clearly states elsewhere that slavery is wrong: "But, as all men are born equal, one must say that slavery is against nature."[29] This, however, overlooks a crucial point: although most Enlightenment thinkers argued either explicitly against slavery or for a concept of freedom that was defined as antithetical to enslavement, they made exceptions and often even argued that slavery was necessary. Their claims about universal reason and freedom were almost always supplemented with doctrines of racial hierarchies according to which nonwhites lacked reason and thus personhood. We will find that this contradictory supplement is necessary rather than contingent.

After Montesquieu's explicit rejection of slavery in the above quotation, he continues: "although in certain countries [slavery] may be founded on a natural reason, and these countries must be distinguished from those in which even natural reasons reject it, as in the countries of Europe where it has so fortunately been abolished."[30] Creative geography and the category of subpersonhood allow one to reconcile seemingly universal claims about freedom and practices of white supremacy. As Charles W. Mills puts it, "Subpersons are humanoid entities who, because of racial phenotype/genealogy/culture, are not fully human and . . . it is possible to get away with doing things to subpersons that one could not do to persons, because they do not have the same rights as persons."[31] Giorgio Agamben uses the Roman concept of *homo sacer* to describe those who are beyond the law and without rights; *bare life* is the dialectical counterpart of sovereign power.[32] To understand the nature of this dialectical relation—between rational person and subperson—it is helpful to understand how the rational person views reason, freedom, and social relations.

Generally speaking, reason in the Enlightenment tradition is conceptualized as a capacity to abstract from particular circumstances, interests, and emotions to make judgments in logical form. There is, of course, a long tradition of viewing reason this way, as we saw in Aristotle's three laws of logic (Chapter 1), and Plato's allegory of the cave argued that those not yet trained in the rules of philosophical thought remained slaves to deceptive appearances. In the Introduction, I also gave a brief sketch of the inductive and deductive methods of scientific reason developed by René Descartes and Francis Bacon, which were intended to achieve not just objectivity, but also mastery over the body and nature. In all of these cases, reason is viewed as liberation from the immediacy of the body and its desires as well as from unreflective or habitual ways of acting and thinking. A reflective stance allows for giving reasons, or articulating justifications for one's thoughts and actions, in a way comprehensible to others who might not share your particular interests or circumstance. As Kant writes, "*Thinking for oneself* means seeking the supreme touchstone of truth in oneself (i.e. in one's own reason); and the maxim of always thinking for oneself is enlightenment. . . . To make use of one's own reason means no more than to ask oneself ... whether one could find it feasible to make the ground or the rule on which one assumes it into a universal principle for the use of reason."[33]

The distinctive turn in late Enlightenment thinking about reason was to *make it a property of the individual,* an independent faculty of the mind, rather than viewing the mind as the means by which an objective reason (*logos*) in the world is intuited.[34] This is a *subject-centered* notion that involves an inward turn and, with it, social atomization. Developing an account of reason was achievable through introspection (inaugurated by Descartes), and thus to give an account of reason, as John Locke set out to do in *An Essay Concerning Human Understanding* (1689), was to give an account of one's own rational self—in a word, self-understanding. This entails a new concept of the self as disengaged from the world and body—a "punctual" self as Charles Taylor calls it—and with it the modern concept of autonomy.[35] If reason emanates from the subject or is contained, so to speak, within a discrete human being, then to be rational is to be self-legislating. *Autonomy* is the freedom achieved through reflexively applying reason, a form of rational self-determination or self-mastery in which one exerts absolute control over one's own thoughts and will. Locke writes, "The *Freedom* then of Man and Liberty of acting according to his own Will, is *grounded on* his having *Reason,* which is able to instruct him in that Law he is to govern himself by."[36] This process is somewhat similar to that of self-negation (see Chapter 1), in that our capacity for negation was—when we encountered another—turned back upon ourselves and in the process actually produced a particular kind of subject. Here, however, it is a claim of absolute *independence* from the other, rather than the recognition of the other and thus the interdependent and inter-subjective conditions of human freedom. Rational and moral autonomy, then, does not rely on an authority, social relations, inclination, or power outside of one's faculty of reason—Kant would call such dependence *heteronomy*. In short, it does not need an *Other*. "This idea," writes Charles Taylor, "has been a powerful, it is not overstated to say revolutionary, force in modern civilization. It seems to offer a prospect of pure self-activity, where my action is determined not by the merely given, the facts of nature (including inner nature), but ultimately by my own agency as a formulator of rational law."[37] As an individual, one is the Absolute, the rational "I," who as sovereign gives the law to oneself and only by doing so can one be free. "The fact that the human being can have the 'I' in his representations," writes Kant, "raises him infinitely above all other living beings on earth. Because of this, he is a *person* . . . i.e., through rank and dignity an entirely different being from *things,* such as irrational animals, with which one can do as one likes."[38]

We find in Kant's statement a succinct articulation of the *practical* conse-quences of this *theory* of rational autonomy, of the subject versus mere objects: If we, rather than God or an objective *logos,* are the source of law or the origin of the rules of reason, then we as subjects must legislate and rule over the world of objects, including "irrational beings." Freedom is a form of rule and *rank* relative to others; autonomy produces not only self-rule, but also the *self as ruler* or sovereign, for the exercise of freedom is the exercise of rule. As Hannah Arendt notes, the equating of freedom with power over the will (rather than social praxis), will have "fatal consequences for political theory," because it makes us "almost automatically equate power with oppression or, at least, with the rule over others."[39] What is more, others represent a potential threat to autonomy rather than a condition of it; if one does not rule over them, there is a possibility for them to corrupt one's reason and thereby undermine one's own freedom. Reason becomes defensive and autonomy is continuously in need of fortification against the other.

In the Enlightenment, then, we generally find an individualist or subject-centered notion of reason and the definition of *person* as someone who is auton-omous insofar as they can compel their will (and the will of others) to follow the laws of reason that they legislate. This is one dimension of C. B. Macpherson's notion of *possessive individualism,* which we discussed in Chapter 2: we master our will the way we exercise dominion over things in the world in the form of property. Dominion comes from the Latin *dominium,* which can mean mastery, rule, domination, or ownership.[40] The connection between property and self-mastery is not new. As Thomas Aquinas (1225–1274) writes, "Now nothing is more desirable to man than the liberty of his proper will [*propiae voluntatis*]. For it is this that he is a man and master [*dominus*] of other things, by this that he can use and enjoy them, by this even that he masters his own actions. So just as the man who relinquishes riches, or persons conjoined to him, denies their being, so he who foregoes the authoritative judgement [*arbitrium*] of his proper will, by which he is master [*dominus*] of himself, denies his own being."[41]

Aquinas's notion of (desirable) rational self-*dominium* or self-mastery, which generates *dominium* over external objects and persons, was asserted in a very specific context: he was arguing against the Franciscan notion of voluntary poverty. The Franciscans, such as William of Ockham (1287–1347), had argued that the renunciation of all forms of *dominium* was necessary, because they constituted types of command and ownership inconsistent with apostolic poverty. As the Franciscans grew in number and in popularity among the poor, the church, as a very wealthy organization with an interest in defending its right to property, viewed their claims to poverty (as the absence of *dominium*) as a threat. Aquinas, a Dominican, was tasked with providing a rebuttal. His response was that since we are rational beings, and rationality is a form of *dominium* over (or ownership of) oneself, to renounce it is to deny one's own (rational) being—that is, despite their professed hopes, the Franciscans could never completely renounce ownership (*dominium*).

Given the inconsistency of their position, the church was therefore not acting contrary to the teachings of Jesus in acquiring so much property. This is the origin of possessive individualism and rationality as self-*dominium*; it originated in Christian theology as a defense of the church's right to amass private property. You can hear the echo of Aquinas in William Blackstone's famous comment on property (again, emphasizing the *desire* for rule) in his *Commentaries on the Laws of England* (1765–1769): "There is nothing which so generally strikes the imagination, and engages the affections of mankind, as the right of property; or that sole and despotic dominion which one man claims and exercises over the external things of the world, in total exclusion of the right of any other individual in the universe."[42]

My point in reconstructing this history, and the modern derivations that follow, is to demonstrate the *material origins* of what in Enlightenment philosophy (and much philosophy today) is taken to be universal and ahistorical. Contemporary notions of rationality, personhood, law, right, property, and autonomy emerged from a particular context of disputes concerning primitive accumulation and colonial jurisdiction.[43] Indeed, the tradition of modern natural law (and thus international law) was developed in the service of European colonialism and conquest.[44] Different forms of accumulation gave rise to different political and legal theories as well as notions of the subject and freedom. The French, for example, were primarily, and for the longest period, interested in the fur trade, which necessitated some form of cooperation with indigenous Americans (rather than settlement). The Spanish under Columbus's governorship instituted the *encomienda* system of slavery, in which land and indigenous Americans were "commended" to Spaniards (*encomenderos*) in its early period. After slavery was formally abolished, Spaniards still held a milder, feudalistic title to indigenous labor.[45] The English quickly pursued a policy of displacement, land appropriation, and extensive settlement, which demanded new justifications of property and sovereignty and with them a different conception of the person (and thus subperson/savage).[46]

Aquinas's defense of property as an expression of rationality was very influential, but he had not posited the individual as the source of rational law (Kant), nor did he argue that self-dominium produced a *natural* right to property. The latter we find in the work of Locke, who was tasked with justifying English colonialism and was, next to Montesquieu, perhaps the second most influential philosopher in the colonies. Locke had both a philosophical and economic interest in colonialism, being in the employ of the Earl of Shaftesbury, serving as secretary of the Lord Proprietors of Carolina, playing a role in drafting the *Fundamental Constitutions of Carolina,* and having personal investments in the Royal Africa Company and the Company of Merchant Adventurers.[47] Unlike the colonialist (neo-Thomist) philosophers of Spain and Portugal, such as Francisco de Vitoria (1492–1546), who could rely on the Pope's universal jurisdiction (i.e., papal donation) or Catholic "just war" theory to justify their colonial practices, Locke was Protestant and therefore sought other means.[48] The famous "state of nature" argument in his *Two Treatises of Government* (1689) was a description of the condition in which English colonists were in a state of exception, beyond the jurisdiction of England.[49] In this condition, Locke posited two *nonconsensual* ways to establish colonial rule, both private (property) and public (sovereignty), which relied on natural law but not on a human authority beyond the individual. It was a very Protestant solution. We find that the uprooted "punctual" self of which Charles Taylor speaks is the self of the uprooted English colonist whose "pure self-activity" served as the juridical anchor in colonization and primitive accumulation.

According to Locke, property is established by individual labor (European sedentary agricultural labor, to be specific), whereby we "mix" the *dominium* or property in our person with the earth.[50] Locke was unique among his peers in arguing that a property right could be generated beyond a state or prior to a social contract. The role of personhood is foundational for Locke, who believed it bestows a *dominium*-founding capacity to individual labor outside of civil society and thus beyond consent—because one is said to have "property" (*dominium*) in one's person. "Though the Earth, and all inferior Creatures be common to all Men, yet every Man has a *Property* in his own *Person*. ... Whatsoever then he removes out of the State that Nature hath provided, and left it in, he hath mixed his *Labour* with, and joyned to it something that is his own, and thereby makes it his Property ... [and] no Man but he can have a right to what that is once joyned to."[51]

Locke's labor theory of property addressed the challenge of establishing private *dominium* without consent, but it was only via private *punishment* (violence) that "one Man comes by a Power over another" without an impartial judicial authority. It was an argument taken from Hugo Grotius, a Dutch colonial theorist and one of the founders of international law.[52] In a state of nature, "all the Power and Jurisdiction is reciprocal," writes Locke, "unless the Lord ... should by any manifest Declaration of his Will set one above another, and confer on him ... an undoubted Right to Dominion and Sovereignty."[53] This right is conferred through private punishment as the enforcement of law, which Locke admits is a "very strange doctrine."[54] How, then, is one supposed to rule another when there exists "between a Swiss and an Indian, in the woods of America" little more than a state of nature?[55]

In his *Second Treatise,* Locke argues that punishment for violations of the laws of nature allows the offended to appropriate "to himself, the Goods or Services of the Offender," resulting "in the perfect condition of *Slavery ... between a lawful Conqueror, and a Captive.*"[56] In his *First Treatise,* Locke writes, "A Planter in the *West Indies,*" for example, can gather forces "against the *Indians,* to seek Reparation upon any Injury ... and all this without the *Absolute Dominion of a Monarch.*"[57] Thus, when indigenous people violate the prevailing political and moral norms of the European elite (i.e., natural law), they "trespass against the whole Species" and have "declared War against all Mankind, and therefore may be destroyed as a *Lyon* or a *Tyger,* one of those wild Savage Beasts."[58] Locke's brutality brings to mind Alexis de Tocqueville's comment about the extermination of indigenous peoples when he toured the United States in the early nineteenth century: "It is impossible to destroy men with more respect for the laws of humanity."[59]

It is important to note that Locke's arguments about establishing property and sovereignty in a "state of nature" are *nonconsensual,* because Locke is a social contract theorist and most known for his *consensual* theory of legitimate government.[60] This is not surprising, since political liberalism is notoriously silent about primitive accumulation and the violence involved in the establishment of political sovereignty (law) and private property (right). Locke's influence on North American political theory and the Declaration of Independence is therefore acknowledged, but his active involvement in and philosophical justifications for English colonialism are typically ignored.[61]

European colonization was essentially a process of the primitive accumulation of private and public *dominium*—"Colonization is, above all, economic and political exploitation," writes Albert Memmi—and existing property relations, modes of production, and inter-imperialist rivalries of the colonizing countries shaped their philosophical justifications.[62] These processes did not involve the mere transference of preexisting rights, but rather accumulation and usurpation were considered to be the (violent) generative processes of right itself—a phenomenon I discuss at greater length in the next section. The relations of domination involved in this brutal enterprise gave rise to a new conception of European personhood, whose own self-dominium was thought to produce legitimate rule over objects and people—and in the case of slavery, people as objects—antecedent to any state or political power. The material origins of this concept of personhood, in the case of English settler colonialism, required it take private form.[63] The English colonialists prioritized right over law, insofar as the latter was predicated on the former—the state (law) was created only to protect property (right). Thus, the rise of the proprietary and sovereign nature of the self-understanding of the colonialist subject cannot be understood in abstraction from the particular policies and practices of European expansionism.[64] Its individualist and proprietary beginnings in the British colonies help clarify how an absolutist concept of private *dominium* came to be thought of as completely detached from, and even at times wielded against, political sovereignty: the origin of American libertarianism.

In his influential pamphlet *A Summary View of the Rights of British America* (1774), Thomas Jefferson argued that he and fellow colonists were analogous to his "Saxon ancestors" who migrated to Britain and "held their lands, as they did their personal property, in absolute dominion, disencumbered with any superior"—that is, before the imposition of the "Norman yoke" in the eleventh century.[65] Jefferson was appealing to individually sovereign property-holders in a Lockean state of nature, which, when wronged, were said to have the right of punishment, resistance, and private war. Elsewhere, Jefferson wrote of a historical rupture reminiscent of Montesquieu's assertion that natural law is different in Europe: "I strongly suspect that our geographical peculiarities may call for a different code of natural law to govern relations with other nations from that which the conditions of Europe have given rise to here."[66] Jefferson's statements reflected an emerging European American social imaginary of concurrent universalism and exceptionalism; the notion of a "Manifest Destiny" was rooted in absolutist *dominium* or mastery, which was synonymous with white (and male) supremacy. Freedom in both its Lockean and Kantian forms was not just "freedom from" but "freedom to"—the freedom to rule over property and other human beings, not within, but *beyond political society*. "In Western politics," writes Agamben, "bare life has the peculiar privilege of being that whose exclusions found the city of men."[67]

The logical entailment of freedom as sovereignty (i.e., rule) is traditionally conceptualized as "duty." As Locke writes in his *Essays on the Law of Nature*, "Each person is required to procure for himself and to retain in his possession the greatest possible number of useful things."[68] And nothing distresses Kant more than lazy whites not exercising the rational sovereignty he believed was granted them by virtue of their race. In the Declaration of Independence, Jefferson wrote of the colonists' freedom from monarchical rule and feudal property relations, yet speaks of "the merciless Indian Savages" and fails to mention the freedom to own African slaves or Euro-American women as wives. *Independence* in this concept of the person is the freedom of the master, the lord, which dialectically entails objects and persons over whom one can exercise such freedom—the *Other*. Kant writes, "[Native] Americans and Negros cannot govern themselves. Thus [they] serve only as slaves."[69]

Kant unwittingly captured the contradictory nature of *autonomy as rule over the other* in his famous comment about "unsocial sociability." He naturalizes this form of subjectivity, writing that the "unsocial characteristic of wanting to direct everything in accordance with his own ideas" is "obviously rooted in human nature." It is not, but the Kantian subject entails it. He writes that it is our resistance to others trying to direct us that "awakens all man's powers and induces him to overcome his tendency to laziness. Through the desire for honour, power or property, it drives him to seek status among his fellows whom he cannot *bear* yet cannot *bear to leave*."[70] His formulation articulates the dialectic of social domination (status) as it operates in masculinity, heterosexuality, white supremacy, and capital, which are the social relations that, according to this notion of the subject, produce honor, power, and property. As for laziness, it has racialized forms. When applied to whites, it is the cowardice that inhibits one from taking command. When applied to nonwhites, it is another name for pursuing pleasure, an aversion to subordination, a refusal to be mobilized in the subject formation of the master, or a condition of structural exclusion (from labor, political participation, etc.).[71] Kant writes that "the Negro" is "strong, fleshy, supple, but who, given the abundance of his mother land, is lazy, soft and trifling"—which according to his logic is a good reason to steal the abundance or steal the person away from his homeland in chains.[72] He speaks of "the happy inhabitants of Tahiti," for example, who live in "tranquil indolence," and questions if they should "exist at all, and whether it would not have been just as good to have this island populated with happy sheep and cattle as with human beings who are happy merely enjoying themselves?"[73] As with the lord in Hegel's dialectic of lordship and bondage, the ruler is dependent on the other for his own self-defeating understanding of independence ("he *cannot bear leave*"). He looks down on them, denigrates them, objectifies them, and necessarily judges them to be inferior, yet always threatening to undermine his rule ("he cannot *bear* them"). "For rule by a master cannot be preserved if the slave is destroyed," writes Aristotle.[74] To be "free" he must dominate—nature, women, people of color, and the laboring classes—and to dominate is to produce whiteness and masculinity. Most have heard the patriarchal saying that expresses this logic: "Women: can't live with them, can't live without them." Kant manages to comment on (and implicitly support) a similar sentiment expressed by a "Negro carpenter," while simultaneously demonstrating the pathology of his own white subjectivity. After the "Negro" was "reproached for haughty treatment of his wives, [he] replied: You whites are the real fools, for first you concede so much to your wives, and then you complain when they drive you crazy. There might be something here worth considering," writes Kant, "except for the fact that this scoundrel was completely black from head to foot, a distinct proof that what he said was stupid."[75]

Lazy, emotional, overly sexual, lacking in universal thought—all considered to be too closely associated with the body, nature, and pleasure—are rhetorical weapons in the discursive construction of subordinate groups rendered suitable for rule.[76] "Cultivated human beings," writes Hegel, "are the ones who know how to place the stamp of universality on everything that they do, say, and think; they surrender their particularity and act in accord with universal principles."[77] This is presumably the status of white, heterosexual men in European cultures, whereas "the Africans have not yet attained this recognition of the universal. . . . Thus, man as we find him in Africa has not progressed beyond his immediate existence."[78]

We find the logic of this white subjectivity operative in the US Supreme Court decision in *Dred Scott v. Sandford* (1857)—an instantiation of the argument by Montesquieu with which I began. Dred Scott was born a slave in Virginia but moved to a free state and sued for his freedom. Although the Court's decision found that they did not have the jurisdiction to decide the case and that Scott did not have the right to sue, they commented on the following question: "Can a negro, whose ancestors were imported into this country, and sold as slaves, become a member of the political community formed and brought into existence by the Constitution of the United States, and as such become entitled to all rights, and privileges, and immunities, guaranteed by that instrument to the citizen?"[79] The US Supreme Court is authorized to be the final interpreter of the Constitution and laws that potentially come into conflict with it—and in this case they were interpreting the meaning of race and citizenship. Dred Scott had argued that being in a free state meant that he should be recognized under the Constitution's "We, the people" and the Declaration of Independence's "self-evident" claim "that all men are created equal," and thus qualify as a free man and citizen.[80]

The Supreme Court did not agree, arguing that the framers of the Constitution were "great men—high in literary acquirements, high in their sense of honor, and incapable of asserting principles inconsistent with those on which they were acting."[81] What is more, the justices asserted that these white men transcended the finite world of hermeneutical horizons: "They perfectly understood the meaning of the language they used and how it would be understood by others . . . and no one misunderstood them."[82] The justices then stated their version of the white supremacist's moral dilemma (similar to Montesquieu's formulation of it a century earlier):

> It is too clear for dispute, that the enslaved African race were not intended to be included, and formed no part of the people who framed and adopted this

declaration; for if the language, as understood in that day, would embrace them, the conduct of the distinguished men who framed the Declaration of Independence would have been utterly and flagrantly inconsistent with the principles they asserted; and instead of the sympathy of mankind, to which they so confidently appealed, they would have deserved and received universal rebuke and reprobation.[83]

If the moral integrity of white men cannot be questioned, their use of "men" or "We, the people" cannot possibly include black people, since these white men owned black slaves. Independence was only possible for the white race (or white, property-owning men). If the Court were to concede that white people, like the justices themselves, could act immorally or even inconsistently, it would be possible that Dred Scott was right to hold up a sign, so to speak, and say, "I AM A MAN," and should be recognized as such. This was, however, an interpretation that only white men could make: "The unhappy black race were separated from the white by indelible marks ... and were never thought of or spoken of except as property, and when the claims of the owner or the profit of the trader were supposed to need protection."[84]

How could the highest judicial authority in the land make such incredible claims? They asserted that educated white men were incapable of immoral actions, that there could exist no distinction between the moral principles they espouse and the actions they take. The implication is that educated white men don't need such principles; they are, simply said, *without principle*. To quote James Baldwin, "Blacks are often confronted in American life with such devastating examples of the white descent from dignity; devastating not only because of the enormity of white pretensions, but because this swift and graceless descent would seem to indicate that white people have no principles whatsoever."[85] When whites are the norm, what they do simply *is* moral, and thus their actions can be used as a standard by which to judge others. As the norm, however, they (including the white male Supreme Court justices) cannot be judged.[86] "Humanity is at its greatest perfection in the race of the whites," writes Kant.[87]

Whiteness as Property, Sovereignty, and Fetish

The form of white subjectivity emerging from practical relations of domination, slavery, dispossession, and servitude is a fetish, a supposedly autonomous power within, which disavows its social origins and attributes to itself instead a fantastical ability to produce property, knowledge, law, and right directly out of itself. Like the fetish of finance capital, it appears as pure self-valorization.[88] It is an attempt to be self-identical in a nonidentical world. The analogy to capital is important, for the rights and privileges produced by *white dominium* have become legal forms of property. As George Lipsitz writes, "This whiteness is, of course, a delusion, a scientific and cultural fiction that like all racial identities has no valid foundation in biology or anthropology. Whiteness is, however, a social fact, an identity created and continued with all-too-real consequences for the distribution of wealth, prestige, and opportunity."[89] The fetish character of whiteness—manifest in the disavowal of the social and material conditions necessary for the development of subjectivity, practices of freedom, and the social-normative order from which subjectivity can emerge and freedom be enabled—generates a dialectical antagonism and an epistemology of ignorance.

Private property is a form of rule over others, even when it does not involve a property right to a person (i.e., a slave), for property is an active *social* relation. To claim a right is to claim a power of exclusion, the exclusion of others from the use and benefit of something, material or immaterial, that is backed by coercive power. The "origin of every contract," writes Walter Benjamin, "also points toward violence."[90] Whiteness is an identity of rule, over oneself and others through their exclusion from political or proprietary relations—the ideological construction of a sovereign subject without historical precedent. Aquinas argued that rationality is self-dominium and is therefore unalienable, while Locke wrote, "By *Property* I must be understood ... to mean that Property which Men have in the Persons as well as Goods," and elsewhere he summed one's property as one's "Life, Liberty and Estate."[91] This claim is the source of Jefferson's line in the Declaration of Independence about "unalienable Rights," which include "Life, Liberty and the pursuit of Happiness." For Locke, the most important active power of human beings is liberty: "the *Idea* of *Liberty,* is the *Idea* of a Power in any Agent to do or forbear any particular Action."[92] Exercised on the will (which itself is not free), liberty produces volitions that are free: "*Volition,* 'tis plain, is an Act of the Mind, knowingly exerting that Dominion it takes itself to have over any Part of the Man."[93] Liberty as the power of rule is concealed in positivist notions of property rights, for it makes it seem as if liberty—as a *property* in Locke's text or a *right* in the Declaration—is an object ruled, rather than the exercise of rule. In Locke's time, writers were transitioning from Latin to vernacular languages and *dominium* was often translated as "property," which has generated confusion (and Locke himself was not always consistent). In English, *property* does not reflect the sovereign dimension of *dominium,* thus obscuring the historical development of this pathological form of subjectivity.[94]

In an important and influential essay, "Whiteness as Property," Cheryl I. Harris reconstructs the historical development of a property interest in whiteness in US law.[95] "Becoming white," she writes, "meant gaining access to a whole set of public and private privileges that materially and permanently guaranteed basic subsistence needs and, therefore, survival. Becoming white increased the possibility of controlling critical aspects of one's life rather than being the object of another's domination."[96] The first benefit of whiteness is private *dominium* or ownership, which concerns property right, while the second is public *dominium* or self-determination, which concerns sovereignty. Despite an otherwise excellent analysis, Harris treats whiteness as an object possessed or a property right, the first of the above benefits. "Whiteness was an 'object' over which continued control was—and is—expected."[97] How she describes this private dimension, however, conceals the active component of the sovereign subject said to produce the rights and properties of rule. As Harris works through each of the classic characteristics of property to demonstrate that whiteness can be identified as a property interest in US history, she thus encounters a problem with alienability. The classic liberal understanding of property (as an object owned) is that it must be alienable or transferable. If whiteness is "incapable of being transferred or alienated either inside or outside the market," then it "would fail to meet a criterion of property," she writes.[98] Her solution is to find other exceptions to the definition, such as welfare entitlements, government licenses, or professional degrees. Given these exceptions, she concludes, "the inalienability of whiteness should not preclude the consideration of whiteness as property."[99] The tradition of *dominium* as an inalienable "property" in one's person—namely, as the power to rule (i.e., Locke's property as liberty and Jefferson's liberty as right)—is thereby overlooked and distorted.[100] This is clear when Harris turns to Locke's claim, quoted above, about people having property in their person. The positivist juridical framework Harris uses transforms Locke's claim into the "assertion that one's physical self was one's property."[101] This is not what Locke intended.[102] To "mix" our *dominium* with the earth is not to mix our physical body with the earth but to exercise power or rule over the earth through labor that negates its form to conform to our will. Harris's objectification of Locke's "property" transforms the law-making dimension of whiteness into an object of property as reputation: "The idea of self-ownership, then, was particularly fertile ground for the idea that reputation, as an aspect of identity earned through effort, was similarly property."[103] This concealment logically follows from liberal discourses about law and right, because such discourses are conceptually constructed to exclude the *extra-juridical violence* that establishes them. Power is only acknowledged *within* the juridical institution and text, thus occluding their dialectical mediation and dependency on violence and alterity. Therefore, Harris's account overlooks the active dimension of "property in one's person" in whiteness, and with it its fetish character, which is the basis for another historically unprecedented development—namely, popular sovereignty.[104]

Like capital and masculinity, white supremacy as sovereignty must be continuously reinvested in relations of domination, political and otherwise, to reproduce itself and its "inherent" right to rule and thus its antagonistic other. Recognizing whiteness as a form of rule affords us insight into its dialectical relationship with a class of subpersons or nonsovereign "others"—the US Constitution does not speak of race but of "free persons" and "other persons"; three-fifths of the latter (i.e., slaves) were acknowledged only insofar as they increased white political representation in slave states. Like the supposedly contradictory combination of universal reason and freedom with racial hierarchy and slavery in Enlightenment thought, the pairing of popular sovereignty and racial dictatorship in US history is often taken to be a historical mistake, an embarrassing confluence of universal truth and individual moral weakness. The traditional response to this "stain" on an otherwise noble American history is to express support for popular sovereignty and forgive those great but fallible white men who succumbed to racial prejudice. This once again conceals the dialectic of freedom and subordination at work here.

The fetish character of white subjectivity means everything that results from social or cooperative labor, mutual recognition, and intersubjectivity is projected onto an atomistic self. In Chapter 2, I discussed Marx's concept of commodity fetish, which concerns the projection of social relations onto commodities: "It is nothing but the definite social relation between men themselves which assumes here, for them, the fantastic form of a relation between things," writes Marx. "In order, therefore, to find an analogy we must take flight into the misty realm of religion. There the products of the human brain appear as autonomous figures endowed with a life of their own."[105] The autonomous figures Marx is referring to are gods, composed of projected human powers and thus representing a form of alienated human consciousness. To understand the fetish character of white subjectivity, it is best to return to the religious source of Marx's analysis, for white subjectivity attributes all of the social conditions of its freedom to its autonomous "punctual" self. This is not Marx's notion of the self as an "ensemble of social relations" whose form of consciousness is shaped by material conditions and social relations, but a godlike self that produces *ex nihilo* reason, law, morality, and property out of itself—as if it is a self-generative sovereign power.[106]

The assertion of sovereignty is made through establishing law (and right), which is violent and itself beyond the law. As Jacques Derrida writes, "The operation that consists of founding, inaugurating, justifying law (*droit*), making law, would consist of a *coup de force*, of a performative and therefore interpretive violence."[107] In his reading of the Declaration of Independence, Derrida asks, "How is a State made or founded, how does a State make or found itself. . . . And the autonomy of one which both gives itself, and signs its own law?"[108] In the signing of the Declaration, the "representatives" of the people create both "the people" and the authority of representation to sign it "in a sort of fabulous retroactivity."[109] As an act of violence beyond the law, the institution of law has a "mystical foundation," writes Derrida, which Benjamin describes as "mythical violence."[110] Authorization is produced retroactively through the violent act. In the context of US history, this violent foundation produced—through a growing patchwork of philosophy, theology, colonial law, and above all relations of domination—a white identity that understood itself to be the individuated, nonhistorical, and self-contained source or *author* of all law and right (i.e., an act of interpretive violence at the root of white subject formation). Whereas Derrida is speaking of the establishment of sovereignty at the level of the state, English colonists had been exercising absolute dominion for over a century through slavery, forcefully establishing the law of the sovereign—the "despotic dominion" of which Blackstone spoke—at the level of the individual white master.

In the previous chapter, I described how practical relations of domination become conventional, concretizing or embedding themselves in social norms, values, aesthetics, positive law, and built environments. The repetition of such social relations produces intelligible and relatively stable identities as well as associated behavioral expectations, thus creating social patterns and relations of domination that appear natural and law-like. There is, however, always resistance threatening to destabilize these practical relations, and thus the dominant group exercises what Benjamin called lawmaking and law-preserving violence to establish domination and continually reinstitute it. "The famous sovereignty of political bodies has always been an illusion, which, moreover, can be maintained only by the instruments of violence, that is, with essentially nonpolitical means," notes Arendt.[111]

In the context of English colonialism and slavery, the violent imposition of law in a racial dictatorship constituted "the people." Sovereignty thus rested with them, because as whites they had *rank,* as Kant called it, as rulers over others. This racialized form of sovereignty was coupled with an even older relation of domination in patriarchy, which forcefully established the male as sovereign in the family—the *dominus* or *paterfamilias.*[112] Indeed, as with the white colonists, the public and private dimensions of rule were commingled in the original Roman idea of *dominium,* which functioned as the anchor of Roman jurisprudence, while simultaneously *falling outside it.*[113] Arendt notes a similar structure in the ancient Greek polis, in which only men "who were already rulers (i.e. household heads who ruled over slaves and family)" could engage in political freedom, for they "were rulers among rulers, moving among peers."[114] This is the social scaffolding of masculine and white autonomy, whose social dependencies and violent nature continually fall outside its individualist self-understanding and legal institutions. "The paradox of sovereignty," writes Agamben, "consists in the fact that the sovereign is, at the same time, outside and inside the juridical order."[115]

The establishment of the Republic was the least violent stage in a long, vicious, and extra-judicial accumulation of sovereignty by white subjects in the colonies. For this reason, the Euro-Americans who founded the Republic did not see it as the establishment of a sovereign to rule over "the people," but rather as the rule of whites over "other persons"—thus solidifying the interdependent relation of white freedom and racial dictatorship. If you were not a master or *dominus,* you did not participate in the sovereignty of the *demos,* but because this mastery was exercised beyond the law, in a naturalized and lawless space of violence, the self-understanding of sovereignty was mystified—the origin of the fetish at work in Benjamin Franklin's description: "In free governments, the rulers are the servants and the people their superiors and sovereigns."[116] Popular sovereignty dialectically necessitates a class of subpersons, though their status escapes juridical comprehension within political liberalism. The American Republic was founded as a white supremacist state to facilitate the rule of white male slave owners and capitalists generally, yet the extra-judicial nature of their rule enabled a purely juridical and thus formal conception of justice and freedom to conceal it.[117]

Former slave and abolitionist Frederick Douglass confronted this state of affairs in a speech he gave in 1854 against the Kansas-Nebraska Bill (1854), which established the two states and the use of "popular sovereignty" to determine whether they would allow slavery.[118] Douglass asserts "that the only seeming concession to the idea of popular sovereignty in this bill is authority to enslave men."[119] He then draws a distinction between popular sovereignty as race-neutral—as it is uncritically understood in political liberalism today as well as how Douglass (genuinely or strategically) interpreted it then—and the way it was actually practiced by supposedly white *sovereign subjects*: "What is meant by Popular Sovereignty? It is the right of the people to establish a government for themselves, as against all others. Such was its meaning in the days of the revolution. It is the independent right of a people to make their own laws, without dictation or interference from any quarter. A sovereign subject is a contradiction in terms, and is an absurdity. When sovereignty becomes subject, it ceases to be sovereignty."[120]

Douglass's race-neutral interpretation of popular sovereignty and all-inclusive notion of "the people" contradicted existing social relations and was decisively undermined by the *Dred Scott* decision two years later. The Republic would remain a form of rule for whites only, with few exceptions, for another century, while white supremacy, patriarchy, and popular sovereignty continue to be wedded to this day. However, Douglass's critique of the *sovereign subject* as contradictory was on target. If the subject is conceived of as sovereign, then its freedom can only result from subjugation. Its independence is purchased through the production of an antagonistic form of alterity—the unstable and ultimately self-defeating condition of Hegel's dialectic of lordship and bondage. As Arendt writes, "Politically, the identification of freedom with sovereignty is perhaps the most pernicious and dangerous consequence of the philosophical equation of freedom and free will. For it leads either to a denial of human freedom—namely, if it is realized that whatever men may be, they are never sovereign—or to the insight that the freedom of one man, or a group, or a body politic can be purchased only at the price of the freedom, i.e., the sovereignty, of all others."[121] This holds true for the social structure of whiteness, masculinity, heterosexuality, and capital. The objectification and *othering* of its own social origins and dependencies render social relations seemingly burdensome to it—a white man's burden. Society becomes a world of "unsocial sociability," of others to be controlled, dominated, or destroyed, domestically and internationally through imperialism and colonialism.[122] This is not, however, a Hobbesian *bellum omnium contra omnes,* or war of all against all. Vulnerable populations must be produced, discursively and juridically, as beyond the law, or at least rendered precarious or indeterminate enough in their legal status for coercion and exploitation of them to be extra-juridical. If this extra-juridical condition is not clearly established, the violence of the sovereign becomes mere criminality and the racialization function is undermined.[123]

Consider, for example, *People v. Hall* (1854), in which the California Supreme Court ruled that, according to California's Act Concerning Civil Cases, Chinese residents could not testify against whites. The Act stipulated that "no black or mulatto person, or Indian, shall be allowed to give evidence in favor of, or against a white man," and thus the question was if Chinese could be categorized as black, mulatto, or Indian.[124] Chief Justice Hugh Murray concluded that Chinese residents could be considered *either* black *or* Indian. By the term "negro," he wrote, the justices "understand it to mean the opposite of 'white,' and that it should be taken as contradistinguished from all white persons."[125] It was a rather startling statement of logical, rather than biological, alterity. However, immigrants from China were also, amazingly, determined to be "Indian," because Columbus thought he was in Asia when he landed in the Americas (the Bahamas) and called the inhabitants Indians.[126] Setting aside this rather incoherent justification for exclusion, the real work to be done by the justices was to protect "the people" from an "actual and present danger."[127] They wrote, "The same rule which would admit them to testify would admit them to all the equal rights of citizenship, and we might soon see them at the polls, in the jury box, upon the bench, and in our legislative halls."[128] This would have represented the loss of an opportunity for racialized violence to be effectively beyond the law, which is needed to reproduce whiteness as an identity of rule. The justices' description of the Chinese community supports this logic: "a distinct people, living in our community, recognizing no laws of this State, except through necessity."[129] Indeed, this was a test case: white sovereign or white criminal? George Hall was a "free white citizen," previously convicted of murdering a Chinese miner, Ling Sing. Three Chinese witnesses had testified in the original case and Hall was convicted. He challenged the legitimacy of the decision on the grounds that Chinese witnesses should not have been allowed to testify against a white man. The Supreme Court justices agreed that the "privilege of participating with us in administering the affairs of our Government" should not be granted, and George Hall's conviction and death sentence were overturned.[130] Lynchings followed, as did a "police tax" on Chinese residents (1862); the Chinese Exclusion Act (1882); the Supreme Court decisions *Takao Ozawa v. United States* (1922) and *United States v. Bhagat Singh Thind* (1923), which ruled that Japanese and

Indian residents were not white and thus ineligible for citizenship; and Japanese internment camps, beginning in 1942.[131]

The juridical racialization of Latinos (or "Hispanics") in the United States began with the Treaty of Guadalupe Hidalgo (1848), which formally granted Latinos the privileges of whiteness (i.e., citizenship and property rights) in the Mexican territories (California, Utah, Nevada, and parts of Colorado, Wyoming, Arizona, and New Mexico) taken in the Mexican-American War (1846–1848). De jure protection from slavery and Jim Crow segregation did not, however, prevent de facto segregation, violence, and the theft of lands. The 2010 US Census states that "Hispanic origins are not races," and a majority of "Hispanics or Latinos" are identified as white in the Census. Yet the contemporary precarious status and social struggles of undocumented immigrants, the unprecedented numbers of Latinos in immigrant detention centers, and their disproportionate rates of incarceration in US prisons and jails all speak to a process of extra-juridical nonwhite racialization—a topic I return to momentarily.[132]

A fetish is by definition a form of misunderstanding or ignorance, and thus, we could say, the epistemology of the fetishized subject is an "epistemology of ignorance." Charles W. Mills describes such an epistemology as "inverted" and responsible for a "pattern of localized and globalized dysfunctions (which are psychologically and socially functional)." This pattern also has the "ironic outcome that whites will in general be unable to understand the world they themselves have made."[133] Historically, such an epistemic framework produced wonders such as the "sciences" of phrenology and physiognomy as well as the fabrication of entire histories and peoples, including the history of Europe, the colonies, sovereign whites, subpersons, and savages.[134] One need only reflect on the Supreme Court decisions and comments by influential philosophers cited above to witness this ignorance at work.

In order to understand Mills's idea of epistemology as "inverted," it helps to recall Marx and Engels's discussion of ideology in the *German Ideology*. They described it as a "camera obscura," in which practical relations "appear upside-down."[135] This is neither a natural phenomenon nor an automatic function of consciousness, but rather a sociohistorical result of long-term and prevalent social relations of domination. "The ruling ideas are nothing more than the ideal expression of the dominant material relationships, the dominant material relationships grasped as ideas."[136] In Chapter 3, I used Iris Marion Young's concept of cultural imperialism and Gramsci's notion of hegemony to describe this phenomenon. Those who control the means of production, thereby also control the means of consciousness production through which the ideas reflecting the dominant group's interest are expressed as "eternal law."[137] Out of the social structure of race, marked by white supremacy, privilege comes to be represented as merit, force as right, domination as protection, history as nature, theft as earned reward, and white supremacy as rugged individualism—"liberal individualism serves as a cover for coordinated collective group interests," writes George Lipsitz.[138] This is perhaps the strongest tie that binds poor and working-class whites to white capitalists, for the unacknowledged privileges secured by white political rule support a trans-class form of white identification. As W. E. B. Du Bois states, "It must be remembered that the white group of laborers, while they received a low wage, were compensated in part by a sort of public and psychological wage. They were given public deference and titles of courtesy because they were white. . . . The police were drawn from their ranks, and the courts, dependent on their votes, treated them with such leniency as to encourage lawlessness."[139] While Du Bois's observation of the *psychological* benefits of white privilege is cited often today, the *public* benefits he identified receive far less attention, although they are essential to understanding how white supremacy operates. They speak to the privileges of white *sovereign* power often granted to even working-class whites—"lawlessness" is a defining mark of sovereign power and a constitutive component of racialization. "White men became a law unto themselves," Du Bois asserts.[140]

After the abolition of slavery, a series of laws—the Black Codes and Jim Crow laws—quickly halted the enfranchisement that occurred during Reconstruction (1865–1877). The Black Codes, which criminalized blacks for offenses such as vagrancy and being late to work, aimed to curtail the freedom of movement of former slaves and coerce them into low-wage work. The Jim Crow laws, which legalized racial segregation, were upheld by *Plessy v. Ferguson* (1896): "We consider the underlying fallacy of the plaintiff's argument to consist in the assumption that the enforced separation of the two races stamps the colored race with a badge of inferiority."[141] For the next sixty years, through segregation, intimidation, incarceration, and systematic violence and murder by white supremacists, white sovereignty was by and large sustained. However, white sovereignty was challenged again in the mid-twentieth century: *Brown v. Board of Education* (1954) ruled public school segregation unconstitutional, the Civil Rights Act of 1964 made segregation and discrimination in private businesses and public institutions illegal, and the Voting Rights Act of 1965 ended explicit discriminatory practices in voting. These were compromises made in response to massive and courageous social struggles, a moment of which was captured in the photograph from 1963 that I described at the beginning of this chapter.

The Thirteenth Amendment (1865) to the US Constitution formally ended slavery but included an important exception—there is always an exception with sovereign power—namely, it made slavery constitutional as punishment for a crime. This brings us back full circle to Locke's justification for slavery in the state of nature: the violation of law. Since the end of Reconstruction, the criminal justice system was used to repopulate Southern plantations with black prison labor through the mechanisms of debt and the convict-leasing system.[142] Yet since the widespread Black Codes and Jim Crow laws allowed manifold forms of discrimination, coercion, and exploitation, prisons were not the only mechanisms to appropriate surplus value, exclude people of color from political participation, or mark them as a legally precarious population. However, when the civil rights movement dismantled much of the system of legal discrimination in the 1960s, the white power structure was facing a condition of legal equality, and thus a dilemma. This dilemma was not unlike what Locke faced in his colonial state of nature in which there existed no "undoubted Right to Dominion and Sovereignty." Like Locke, whites pursued criminalization and punishment, producing an unprecedented carceral system; the criminal "justice" system now became the primary mechanism to disenfranchise people of color and thereby support white subject formation. In 1972 there were approximately 350,000 people incarcerated in the United States, while today there are about 2.2 million and almost 5 million more on probation or on parole, left with the "indelible mark" of a criminal record and thus almost certainly lifelong marginalization.[143] With 5 percent of the world's population, the United States accounts for 25 percent of the world's prisoners (40 percent non-Hispanic black and 20 percent Hispanic of all races), and there are now more black Americans in prisons than there were slaves before the Civil War. Through the "war on drugs," racial profiling, and racial disparities in sentencing, an exception to formal equality was found, enabling the reproduction of white supremacy in the wake of Jim Crow: "a lower caste of individuals who are permanently barred by law and custom from mainstream society. Although this new system of racialized social control purports to be colorblind," writes Michelle Alexander, "it creates and maintains racial hierarchy much as earlier systems of control did. Like Jim Crow (and slavery), mass incarceration operates as a tightly networked system of laws, policies, customs, and institutions that operate collectively to ensure the subordinate status of a group defined largely by race."[144] We find a similar logic at work with the over

11 million undocumented immigrants in the United States, the vast majority of whom are Latino and suspended in a precarious and vulnerable condition. In Jim Crow, mass incarceration, and undocumented communities, economic exploitation is intensified, because most legal protections are either unavailable or unreliable.[145] Since the attacks of September 11, 2001, Arab and Muslim Americans have become a suspect population in the "war on terror," virtually erasing the distinction between foreign and domestic threats. With the Iraq and Afghanistan wars came the *state of exception* of "indefinite detention" at Gitmo in Guantanamo Bay, Cuba, as well as the widespread torture, most famously at the Abu Ghraib prison in Iraq.

What all of these examples have in common—from slavery, Jim Crow, and mass incarceration, to undocumented status, racialized surveillance/suspicion, and Gitmo—is the production of a legally precarious substatus (most extreme in the case of slavery and Gitmo), a "no-man's land between public law and political fact" that enables the exercise of sovereign violence, exploitation, and thus the reproduction of racialized identities.[146] Although she does not note its function in racial formation and limits her analysis to functionaries of the state, Judith Butler's description of sovereign subjects at Gitmo expresses the logic of popular sovereignty:[147]

> Rules that are not binding by virtue of established law or modes of legitimation, but fully discretionary, even arbitrary, wielded by officials who interpret them unilaterally and decide the condition and form of their invocation. . . . In a sense, the self-annulment of law under the condition of a state of emergency revitalizes the anachronistic "sovereign" as the newly invigorated subjects of managerial power. Of course, they are not true sovereigns: their power is delegated, and they do not fully control the aims that animate their actions. Power precedes them, and constitutes them as "sovereigns," a fact that already gives lie to sovereignty. They are not fully self-grounding; they do not offer either representative or legitimating functions to the policy. Nevertheless, they are constituted . . . as those who will and do decide on who will be detained, and who will not, who may see life outside the prison again and who may not, and this constitutes an enormously consequential delegation and seizure of power.[148]

The perceived absence of the state is the *exceptional presence of the law* in carving out a space, a population, upon which sovereign subjects—or "petty sovereigns" as Butler calls them elsewhere—can exercise domination and "lawlessness." This is the legal (public) structuring of a field of (private) practical relations from which various expressions of white power and privilege are ultimately derived; *inclusion* is provided by the other's exclusion, *safety* is enabled by the other's precariousness, and *material benefit* is made possible through dispossession.[149] State sovereignty is reproduced to the extent it sustains these naturalized forms of rule and group identities that operate through the suspension of law and right—which is why liberal theory reaches its limit precisely where the mechanisms of rule undergirding liberalism and state sovereignty actually begin (hence the epistemology of ignorance).

The function of the state is, therefore, to make possible "natural" relations of rule through the legal demarcation of their existence beyond the law (e.g., in heterosexuality, patriarchy, white supremacy, private property). Indeed, the enforcement of these practical relations of lawlessness and exploitation is the material condition of their discursive naturalization, giving rise, for example, to the unequal geography of "natural law" that Montesquieu and Jefferson invoke.[150] By *lawlessness,* I refer to either the absence of law or its unenforced presence, as well as moral law. As Horkheimer and Adorno observe, "the subjugation of everything natural to the sovereign subject [*selbstherrliche Subjekt*] culminates in the domination [*Herrschaft*] of what is blindly objective and natural. This tendency levels all the antitheses of bourgeois thought, especially that between moral rigor and absolute amorality."[151] That is to say, the radical objectification and disidentification with the other in the pursuit of freedom is, by the same process, the constitution of an objectified sovereign subject—the fetish character of the Kantian *person*—whose actions are stripped of all principle. The legal and discursive production of vulnerable populations, of a condition of precarity *within* a legal order marked as natural, allows for the sovereign subject to enact its (unprincipled) rule and thereby reproduce white supremacy. The same logic holds true for the construction of masculinity, heterosexuality, and capital, which operate through various but overlapping forms of accumulation by dispossession. Seeking equality with the master subject, or striving for the freedom of the sovereign, will only reproduce relations of domination in different form, and thus the crucial tasks ahead are to denaturalize relations of rule and heed Audre Lorde's call to "dismantle the master's house."

NOTES

Introduction

1. Audre Lorde, "The Uses of Anger: Women Responding to Racism," in *Sister Outsider: Essays and Speeches* (New York: Random House, 1984), 129.

2. John Holloway, *Change the World without Taking Power: The Meaning of Revolution Today* (London: Pluto Press, 2005), 1.

3. In Plato's *Theatetus*, Socrates states, "For this is an experience which is characteristic of a philosopher, this wondering: this is where philosophy begins and nowhere else." Plato, *Theatetus,* in *Plato: Complete Works,* ed. John M. Cooper and D. S. Hutchinson (Indianapolis: Hackett, 1997), 155d. Aristotle writes, "It was their wonder, astonishment, that first led men to philosophize and still leads them." Aristotle, *Metaphysics,* in *The Complete Works of Aristotle: The Revised Oxford Translations,* ed. Jonathan Barnes, vol. 2 (Princeton, NJ: Princeton University Press, 1984), 982b12.

4. Lorde, "The Uses of Anger," 127.

5. Due to space limitations, I am also unable to adequately address radical environmental philosophy, which is surely deserving of its own chapter.

6. bell hooks, "Killing Rage: Militant Resistance," in *Killing Rage: Ending Racism* (New York: Holt, 1996), 16.

7. See Plato's *Theatetus,* 174a.

8. Ibid., 174b.

9. Plato, *Republic,* in *Complete Works,* book VII, 514a.

10. Ibid., 515c.

11. Ibid.

12. On the idea of praxis as a new beginning or "rooted in natality," see Hannah Arendt, *The Human Condition* (Chicago: University of Chicago Press, 1958).

13. For a good historical and philosophical discussion of the shift from *vita activa* (e.g., work, labor, and action) to *vita contemplativa* (or contemplation), see ibid., particularly chs. 1 and 2.

14. Iris Marion Young usefully differentiates five forms of oppression: exploitation, marginalization, powerlessness, cultural dominance, and violence. See Iris Marion Young, *Justice and the Politics of Difference* (Princeton, NJ: Princeton University Press, 1990), ch. 2.

15. See Étienne Balibar, *The Philosophy of Marx,* trans. Chris Turner (New York: Verso, 1995), 2–6.

16. Karl Marx, *The Marx-Engels Reader,* 2nd ed., ed. Robert C. Tucker (New York: W. W. Norton and Company, 1978), 145. The role of theorists in political struggles generates debate. In the Marxist tradition, Antonio Gramsci speaks of the "organic intellectual" who, unlike the disinterested "traditional intellectual," carried out the labor of theorizing for the working class, giving it "homogeneity and an awareness of its own function not only in the economic but also in the social and political fields." Antonio Gramsci, *Selections from the Prison Notebooks,* ed. Quintin Hoare and Geoffrey Nowell Smith (New York: International Publishers, 1971), 5. Foucault's notion of a "specific intellectual" is perhaps a more appropriate description of those who theorize in social struggles: "Intellectuals have become used to working, not in the modality of the 'universal,' the 'exemplary,' the 'just-and-true-for-all,' but within specific sectors, at the precise points where their own conditions of life or work situate them (housing, the hospital, the asylum, the laboratory, the university, family, and sexual relations). That has undoubtedly given them a much more immediate and concrete awareness of struggles. And they have met there with problems that are specific, 'nonuniversal,' and often different from those of the proletariat or the masses. And yet I believe intellectuals have actually been drawn closer to the proletariat and the masses, for two reasons. Firstly, because it has been a question of real, material, everyday struggles, and secondly because they have often been confronted, albeit in different form, by the same adversary as the proletariat, namely, the multinational corporations, the judicial and police apparatuses, the property speculators, etc." Michel Foucault, "Truth and Power," in *The Foucault Reader,* ed. Paul Rabinow (New York: Pantheon Books, 1984), 68. Julia Kristeva also rejects Gramsci's notion of an organic intellectual, identifying three alternative kinds of "dissident intellectuals," the last of which she favors. There is the paranoid rebel who attacks political power, but in doing so cannot break free from the master-slave dialectic; the psychoanalyst who mostly combats religion; and the writer who is "playful" and subverts the law. Kristeva argues, unfortunately, that "true dissidence today is perhaps simply what it has always been: *thought.*" Julia Kristeva, "A New Type of Intellectual: The Dissident," in *The Kristeva Reader,* ed. Toril Moi (Oxford: Blackwell, 1986), 292–300.

17. Jean-Paul Sartre, *Search for a Method,* trans. Hazel E. Barnes (New York: Vintage, 1968), 5–6.

18. Axel Honneth makes a similar point about Left-Hegelian critical theory in his "Social Dynamics of Disrespect: On the Location of Critical Theory Today," in *Disrespect: The Normative Foundations of Critical Theory* (Malden, MA: Polity Press, 2007), 64–65.

19. Michel Foucault, *"Society Must Be Defended": Lectures at the College de France, 1975–1976*, trans. David Macey (New York: Picador, 2003), 10.

20. "As an historically oppressed group, U.S. Black women have produced social thought designed to oppose oppression. Not only does the form assumed by this thought diverge from standard academic theory—it can take the form of poetry, music, essays, and the like—but the *purpose* of Black women's collective thought is distinctively different." Patricia Hill Collins, *Black Feminist Thought: Knowledge, Consciousness, and the Politics of Empowerment* (New York: Routledge, 2002), 9.

21. Lorde, "The Master's Tools Will Never Dismantle the Master's House," in Lorde, *Sister Outsider*, 111.

22. Nancy Fraser, "What's Critical about Critical Theory: The Case of Habermas and Gender," in *Unruly Practices: Power, Discourse, and Gender in Contemporary Social Theory* (Minneapolis: University of Minnesota, 1989), 113.

23. Michel Foucault, *Discipline and Punish: The Birth of the Prison*, trans. Alan Sheridan (New York: Vintage, 1979), 27.

24. See Aristotle, *Nicomachean Ethics,* books 7–8, in *The Complete Works.* See also A. W. H. Atkins, "Theoria versus Praxis in the *Nicomachean Ethics* and the *Republic,*" *Classical Philology* 73, no. 4 (Oct. 1978): 300.

25. Aristotle, *Metaphysics*, in Aristotle, *The Complete Works,* 1074b20. In book IX of the *Nicomachean Ethics*, Aristotle does speak of *theoria* in the context of contemplation on a friend's life, rather than just one's own (1169b33–1170a1).

26. Ibid., 1072b24.

27. "Every philosophy is practical, even the one which at first appears to be the most contemplative. Its method is a social and political weapon." Sartre, *Search for a Method,* 5.

28. Jürgen Habermas, *Knowledge and Human Interests,* trans. Jeremy J. Shapiro (Boston: Beacon Press, 1971), 306.

29. Although at one point Aristotle speaks of probability rather than universality. See *Metaphysics,* book VI, 1027a20.

30. Aristotle, *Nicomachean Ethics,* 1142a24–25.

31. See Jürgen Habermas, *Theory and Practice,* trans. John Viertel (Boston: Beacon Press, 1973), ch. 1.

32. See Arendt, *The Human Condition,* ch. 6.

33. For Kant, what is knowable as universal and necessary are only those objects of experience that our understanding produces. See Georg Lukács, *History and Class Consciousness: Studies in Marxist Dialectics,* trans. Rodney Livingstone (Cambridge, MA: MIT Press, 1972), ch. 4.

34. Habermas, *Theory and Practice*, 61.

35. Thomas Hobbes, *Leviathan*, ed. Richard Tuck (New York: Cambridge University Press, 1991), 9.

36. The move from *civitas* to *societas* or from polity to society is important, argues Hannah Arendt, for the latter included the sphere of economic production that the former had excluded. This gave rise to a conflation of the political and the social—thanks in large part to Thomas Aquinas—allowing the introduction of a hierarchical form of rule in the economic sphere, namely, the household or *oikos* in Greece, into the political sphere, which had been defined by equal and free participants. See Arendt, *The Human Condition*. For a critique of Arendt's notion of the social and its relation to public justice, see Seyla Benhabib, "Models of Public Space: Hannah Arendt, the Liberal Tradition and Jurgen Habermas," in *Situating the Self: Gender, Community and Postmodernism in Contemporary Ethics* (New York: Routledge, 1992), 89–120.

37. See Thomas Hobbes, *On the Citizen*, ed. and trans. Richard Tuck and Michael Silverthorne (New York: Cambridge University Press, 1998), 10.

38. See David Gauthier, "The Social Contract as Ideology," *Philosophy and Public Affairs* 6, no. 2 (1977): 130–164.

39. Donald Rutherford, "Innovation and Orthodoxy in Early Modern Philosophy," in *The Cambridge Companion to Early Modern Philosophy*, ed. Donald Rutherford (New York: Cambridge University Press, 2006), 26.

40. See Francis Bacon, *The New Organon*, ed. Lisa Jardine and Michael Silverthorne (New York: Cambridge University Press, 2000).

41. Ibid., book II, 221.

42. Max Horkheimer and Theodor Adorno, *Dialectic of Enlightenment: Philosophical Fragments*, ed. Gunzelin Schmid Noerr and trans. Edmund Jephcott (Stanford, CA: Stanford University Press, 2002), 1.

43. To those who advocated a plurality of methods, Descartes responded, "Distinguishing the sciences by the differences in their objects, they think that each science should be studied separately, without regard to any of the others. But here they are surely mistaken." René Descartes, *Rules for the Direction of the Mind*, in *The Philosophical Writings of Descartes*, trans. John Cottingham, Robert Stoothoff, and Dugald Murdoch, vol. 1 (New York: Cambridge University Press, 1985), 9.

44. Ibid.

45. Immanuel Kant, *Metaphysics of Morals*, ed. and trans. Mary Gregor (New York: Cambridge University Press, 1996 [1797]), 62.

46. "The perceived fact," writes Horkheimer, "is therefore co-determined by human ideas and concepts, even before its conscious theoretical elaboration by the knowing individual." Horkheimer, "Traditional and Critical Theory," in *Critical Theory: Selected Essays*, trans. Matthew J. O'Connell (New York: Continuum, 1975), 222.

47. Horkheimer and Adorno, *Dialectic of Enlightenment*, 4.

48. Hobbes, *Leviathan*, 88.

49. Ibid., 90.

50. See Horkheimer and Adorno, *Dialectic of Enlightenment*, ch. 1.

51. Judith Butler, *The Psychic Life of Power: Theories in Subjection* (Stanford, CA: Stanford University Press, 1997), 8.

52. Friedrich Engels, "Socialism: Utopian and Scientific," in *The Marx-Engels Reader*, 695. As Paulo Freire writes, "every act of conquest implies a conqueror and someone or something which is conquered. The conqueror imposes his objectives on the vanquished, and makes of them his possession. He imposes his own contours on the vanquished, who internalize this shape and become ambiguous beings 'housing' another. From the first, the act of conquest, which reduces persons to the status of things, is necrophilic." Paulo Freire, *Pedagogy of the Oppressed*, trans. Myra Bergman Ramos (New York: Continuum, 1997), 119.

53. Immanuel Wallerstein et al., *Open the Social Sciences: Report of the Gulbenkian Commission on the Restructuring of the Social Sciences* (Stanford, CA: Stanford University Press, 1996), 50.

54. Ibid., 31.

55. Auguste Comte, *The Positive Philosophy of Auguste Comte*, trans. Harriet Martineau, vol. 1 (New York: Cambridge University Press, 1990), 5.

56. See Habermas, *Knowledge and Human Interests*, ch. 4.

57. Bertrand Russell, *History of Western Philosophy* (London: Routledge, 1996), 743. As A. J. Ayer writes, "it is necessary for the philosopher to become a scientist, in this sense, if he is to make any substantial contribution towards the growth of human knowledge." A. J. Ayer, *Language, Truth and Logic* (New York: Dover, 1946), 153. See also Wallerstein et al., *Open the Social Sciences*, 11.

58. Chris Daly argues that a philosophical method should have the following five qualities: (1) the logical form of a universally quantified biconditional; (2) be necessarily true; (3) be informative; (4) be knowable a priori; and (5) be testable by the methods of hypothetical cases. Chris Daly, *An Introduction to Philosophical Method* (Buffalo, NY: Broadview Press, 2010), 45–48.

59. See Richard J. Bernstein, *The Restructuring of Social and Political Theory* (Philadelphia: University of Pennsylvania Press, 1976), and Alasdair MacIntyre, *After Virtue: A Study in Moral Theory*, 3rd ed. (Notre Dame, IN: University of Notre Dame Press, 2007), particularly ch. 7.

60. Scott Soames, *Philosophical Analysis in the Twentieth Century: The Dawn of Analysis* (Princeton, NJ: Princeton University Press, 2003), xiv.

61. MacIntyre argues that the very nature of "fact" changed in "the transition from the Aristotelian to the mechanist view." In the Aristotelian understanding of human praxis, action must be "characterized with reference to the hierarchy of goods which provide the ends of human action." These are the motivating interests or values of our

praxis and thus the facts about human praxis include the motivating values. In the mechanistic understanding, no such values can be invoked: "there are no facts about what is valuable. 'Fact' becomes value-free, 'is' becomes a stranger to 'ought.'" MacIntyre, *After Virtue*, 84.

62. Max Weber, *Economy and Society: An Outline of Interpretive Sociology*, ed. Guenther Roth and Claus Wittich, vol. 1 (Berkeley: University of California Press, 1978), 15.

63. Alfred Schütz, *Collected Papers*, ed. Maurice Natanson, vol. 1 (The Hague: Martinus Nijhoff, 1962), 245.

64. See Paul Rabinow and William M. Sullivan, "The Interpretive Turn," in *Interpretive Social Science: A Second Look*, ed. Paul Rabinow and William M. Sullivan (Berkeley: University of California Press, 1987), 1–30.

65. "The scholar and his science," writes Horkheimer, "are incorporated into the apparatus of society; his achievements are a factor in the conservation and continuous renewal of the existing state of affairs, no matter what fine names he gives to what he does." Horkheimer, "Traditional and Critical Theory," 196.

66. "Each society has its regime of truth," writes Foucault, "its 'general politics' of truth; that is, the types of discourse which it accepts and makes function as true." Michel Foucault, *Power/Knowledge: Selected Interviews and Other Writings, 1972–77*, ed. Colin Gordon (New York: Vintage, 1980), 131.

67. Judith Butler, *Gender Trouble: Feminism and the Subversion of Identity* (New York: Routledge, 1990), 31.

68. Audre Lorde, "Age, Race, Class, and Sex: Women Redefining Women," in *Sister Outsider*, 123.

69. On the enabling and educative role of the Other, see Linda Martín Alcoff, *Visible Identities: Race, Gender and the Self* (New York: Oxford University Press, 2005), 122ff.

70. Dialectically understood, we could say that the diverse elements within an oppositional group are unified through the mediating other (i.e., the target of opposition) but stand in an unmediated and thus inherently unstable and potentially antagonistic relation to each other.

71. Alcoff, *Visible Identities*, 121.

72. Pierre Bourdieu, *In Other Words: Essays Towards a Reflexive Sociology*, trans. Matthew Adamson (Stanford, CA: Stanford University Press, 1990), 12–13. See also Pierre Bourdieu, *The Logic of Practice*, trans. Richard Nice (Stanford, CA: Stanford University Press, 1990); and Anthony Giddens, *The Constitution of Society: Outline of the Theory of Structuration* (Oxford, UK: Polity, 1985).

73. Bourdieu, *In Other Words*, 63.

74. Young, *Justice and the Politics of Difference*, 41.

75. Frederick Douglass, "The Significance of Emancipation in the West Indies" (speech), Canandaigua, New York, August 3, 1857, in *The Frederick Douglass Papers*,

Series One: Speeches, Debates, and Interviews, ed. John W. Blassingame, vol. 3 (New Haven, CT: Yale University Press, 1986), 204.

Chapter 1

1. Patricia Hill Collins, *Black Feminist Thought: Knowledge, Consciousness, and the Politics of Empowerment,* 2nd ed. (New York: Routledge, 2002), 15.

2. Herbert Marcuse, "On Concrete Philosophy," in *Heideggerian Marxism,* ed. Richard Wolin and John Abromeit (Lincoln: University of Nebraska, 2005), 36.

3. William James, *The Principles of Psychology,* vol. 1 (Cambridge: Harvard University Press, 1981), 109; Karl Marx, "Sixth Thesis on Feuerbach," in *Marx-Engels Reader,* ed. Robert C. Tucker (New York: W. W. Norton and Company, 1978), 145.

4. Immanuel Kant, *Anthropology from a Pragmatic Point of View,* ed. and trans. Robert B. Louden (New York: Cambridge University Press, 2006), §12, 40.

5. Aristotle famously argued that habit is necessary for moral virtue (*Nicomachean Ethics,* 1103a32–33), and Hegel made it central to ethical life. We also find bodily and intellectual habits important in phenomenological perception (Merleau-Ponty); performative practices of identity (Judith Butler); American pragmatist understandings of thought, belief, and character (Dewey, Peirce, and James); and performance of class and status in the sociology of Pierre Bourdieu.

6. John Dewey, *Human Nature and Conduct: An Introduction to Social Psychology* (New York: Henry Holt and Co., 1922), 177.

7. Bertolt Brecht, "On Chinese Acting," in *Brecht Sourcebook,* ed. Carol Martin and Henry Bial (New York: Routledge, 2000), 13.

8. See Bertolt Brecht, "A Short Organum for Theater," in *Brecht on Theatre: The Development of an Aesthetic,* trans. and ed. John Willett (London: Methuen, 1964).

9. I am using Brecht's epic theater as an analogy, rather than suggesting that theater should always incorporate a reflexive dimension or estrangement effect. On the recent revival of the critique of spectatorship and a critique of the traditional categories used in its analysis, see Jacques Rancière, *The Emancipated Spectator,* trans. Gregory Elliott (New York: Verso, 2009). For an insightful discussion of participatory art generally, see also Claire Bishop, *Artificial Hells: Participatory Art and the Politics of Spectatorship* (New York: Verso, 2012).

10. Theodor W. Adorno, *Against Epistemology: A Metacritique; Studies in Husserl and the Phenomenological Antinomies,* trans. W. Domingo (Cambridge, MA: MIT Press, 1982), 74.

11. Karl Marx, "Letter to Arnold Ruge," September 1843, in *The Marx-Engels Reader,* 13.

12. Aristotle, *Nicomachean Ethics, The Complete Works of Aristotle,* book 1.3 (Princeton, NJ: Princeton University Press, 1984), 1095a13–15.

13. Hans-Georg Gadamer, *Truth and Method,* 2nd rev. ed., trans. Joel Weinsheimer and Donald G. Marshall (New York: Continuum, 2006), 556.

14. See Ludwig Wittgenstein, *Philosophical Investigations,* trans. G. E. M. Anscombe, P. M. S. Hacker, and Joachim Schulte, 4th ed. (Oxford: Blackwell Publishing, 2009), §§65–66.

15. Georg Lukács, *History and Class Consciousness: Studies in Marxist Dialectics,* trans. Rodney Livingstone (Cambridge, MA: MIT Press, 1972), 5.

16. The definition of knowledge (*epistēmē*) as justified true belief is found in Plato's *Theaetetus,* where he speaks of knowledge as "true belief with an account [*meta logou alêthê doxan*]" (201c8).

17. The word *metaphysics* comes from the Latin *metaphysica,* itself derived from the ancient Greek phrase *Ta meta ta phusika,* which roughly translates as "the works after the physical works." The phrase was originally intended by a subsequent editor to describe works by Aristotle that followed his writings on what we now call physics (*phusika*). At the time, it was not intended to mean beyond or transcendent of the physical.

18. As Emilio, a seventeen-year-old activist in Argentina, told the author Marina Sitrin, "So, today we're constructing something different. And, in the process, a whole new language and new forms of expression come into being. *Horizontalidad,* direct democracy, sharing and effecting one another's movements, contamination, articulation, organizing in networks—these expressions are not often heard from the traditional left." Marina Sitrin, ed., *Horizontalism: Voices of Popular Power in Argentina* (Oakland, CA: AK Press, 2006), vi.

19. See Butler, *Excitable Speech: A Politics of the Performative* (New York: Routledge, 1997), 140. See also Stuart Hall, "Ethnicity: Identity and Difference," *Radical America* 23, no. 4 (1989): 9–20.

20. The Catholic Church had traditionally considered itself the only authorized source of scriptural interpretation, which was challenged by Martin Luther (1483–1546), among others. This challenge was systematized in Matthias Flacius Illyricus's *Clavis Scripturae sacrae* [Key to the Holy Scripture] (1567). See Kurt Mueller-Vollmer, ed., *The Hermeneutics Reader* (New York: Continuum, 1988), 2.

21. For a helpful discussion of different forms of meaning beyond the merely linguistic, see Charles Taylor, "Interpretation and the Sciences of Man," *Review of Metaphysics* 25, no. 1 (Sept. 1971): 3–51.

22. A transitional work in this narrative is *The First New Science* (1725) by Giambattista Vico (1668–1744). In this humanist text, Vico argues against the universalistic method of Descartes and modern science generally, with its clear and distinct ideas, emphasizing instead the value and truth of common sense (*sensus communis*) that emerges in particular communities and is in need of interpretation. Giambattista Vico,

The First New Science, ed. and trans. Leon Pompa (New York: Cambridge University Press, 2002).

23. "Up to now it has been assumed that all our cognition must conform to the objects; but all attempts to find out something about them *a priori* through concepts that would extend our cognition have, on this presupposition, come to nothing. Hence, let us once try whether we do not get farther with the problems of metaphysics by assuming that the objects must conform to our cognition." Immanuel Kant, *Critique of Pure Reason,* ed. and trans. Paul Guyer and Allen Wood (bxvi), 110. Kant called this reversal his Copernican Revolution.

24. Wilhelm Dilthey, *Gesammelte Schriften,* I, xviii; quoted in Gadamer, *Truth and Method,* 246.

25. Friedrich Ast, *Hermeneutics,* in *The Hermeneutic Tradition: From Ast to Ricoeur,* ed. Gayle L. Ormiston and Alan D. Schrift (New York: SUNY Press, 1990), §82, 48.

26. Ibid., §75, 43.

27. Dilthey, *Gesammelte Schriften,* 5:144; quoted in Jean Grondin, *Introduction to Philosophical Hermeneutics,* trans. Joel Weinsheimer (New Haven, CT: Yale University Press, 1994), 86.

28. "Understanding and interpretation is the method used throughout the human sciences. It unites all their functions and contains all their truths. At each instance understanding opens up a world." Wilhelm Dilthey, "The Understanding of Other Persons and Their Life-Expressions," in *The Hermeneutics Reader,* ed. Kurt Mueller-Vollmer, 152. The term *Geisteswissenschaften* was popularized in German as a translation of John Stuart Mill's term *moral sciences* in his *System of Logic* (1843). John Stuart Mill, *A System of Logic, Ratiocinative and Inductive,* 8th ed. (New York: Harper and Brothers, 1882).

29. Quoted in Josef Bleicher, *Contemporary Hermeneutics: Hermeneutics as Method, Philosophy and Critique* (New York: Routledge, 1980), 23.

30. He calls this an *existentiale.* It is, he writes, "neither a definite species of cognition, distinguished, let us say, from explaining and conceiving, nor any cognition at all in the sense of grasping something thematically." Martin Heidegger, *Being and Time,* trans. John Macquarrie and Edward Robinson (New York: Harper and Row, 1962), 385.

31. Ibid., 375.

32. Gadamer, *Truth and Method,* 276–277.

33. Ibid., 302.

34. Ibid., 291.

35. "Like conversation, interpretation is a circle closed by the dialectic of question and answer. It is a genuine historical life comportment achieved through the medium of language, and we can call it a conversation with respect to the interpretation of texts as well." Ibid., 389.

36. See Richard Bernstein, *Beyond Objectivism and Relativism* (Philadelphia: University of Pennsylvania Press, 1983); Robin Pappas and William Cowling, "Toward a

Critical Hermeneutics," in *Feminist Interpretations of Hans-Georg Gadamer*, ed. Lorraine Code (University Park: Pennsylvania State University Press, 2003), 203–227; Nancy J. Holland and Patricia Huntington, eds., *Feminist Interpretations of Heidegger* (University Park: Pennsylvania State University Press, 2001); and Sandra Bartky, *Femininity and Domination: Studies in the Phenomenology of Oppression* (New York: Routledge, 1990).

37. Jürgen Habermas, "A Review of Gadamer's *Truth and Method*," in Ormiston and Schrift, *The Hermeneutic Tradition*, 239.

38. Habermas distinguishes three kinds of knowledge interests that determine our various orientations in the world: "Orientation toward technical control, toward mutual understanding in the conduct of life, and toward emancipation from seemingly 'natural' constraint establish the specific viewpoints from which we can apprehend reality as such in any way." Jürgen Habermas, *Knowledge and Human Interests*, trans. Jeremy J. Shapiro (Boston: Beacon Press, 1971), 312. These knowledge interests are technical, practical, and emancipatory. "The approach of the empirical-analytic sciences incorporates a technical cognitive interest; that of the historical-hermeneutic sciences incorporates a practical one; and the approach of critically oriented sciences incorporates the emancipatory cognitive interest that, as we saw, was at the root of traditional theories." Ibid., 308. The technical interest is most relevant to the empirical sciences that so often translate into technologically mediated manipulation and control of the objective environment. The practical interest is most relevant to the dialogical domain of hermeneutics, for it relates to dialogue participants working toward mutual understanding and agreement concerning shared goals in a community. Lastly, the emancipatory interest is at the center of critical social theory, which aspires for freedom from forces of domination that inhibit our capacity to exercise self-reflective reason and in turn self-understanding. Axel Honneth incorporates much of this critique but locates a more fundamental interest in social recognition, which Habermas is said to already presuppose in his theory of communicative action. Marx similarly located an "interest" in the free development of oneself in one's labor, which is always social, because labor as a process of externalization is necessary to the development of human freedom.

39. "With every speech act, by virtue of the validity claims it raises, the speaker enters into an interpersonal relationship of mutual obligation with the hearer: The speaker is obliged to support her claims with reasons." Maeve Cooke, *Language and Reason: A Study in Habermas's Pragmatics* (Cambridge, MA: MIT Press, 1994), 12–13.

40. See Jürgen Habermas, *Communication and the Evolution of Society*, trans. Thomas McCarthy (Boston: Beacon, 1979), and Jürgen Habermas, *On the Pragmatics of Communication*, trans. Barbara Fultner (Cambridge, MA: MIT Press, 1998).

41. See Linda Martín Alcoff, *Visible Identities: Race, Gender, and the Self* (New York: Oxford University Press, 2005), 88.

42. See ibid., ch. 4.

43. Ibid., 96. See also Alcoff, "Gadamer's Feminist Epistemology," in *Feminist*

Interpretations of Hans-Georg Gadamer, ed. Lorraine Code (University Park: Pennsylvania State University Press, 2003), 231–258.

44. See Nancy C. M. Hartsock, "The Feminist Standpoint: Developing the Ground for a Specifically Feminist Historical Materialism," in *Discovering Reality: Feminist Perspectives on Epistemology, Metaphysics, Methodology, and Philosophy of Science,* ed. Sandra Harding and Merrill B. Hintikka (Norwell, MA: Kluwer, 1983).

45. Donna J. Haraway, "Situated Knowledges: The Science Question in Feminism and the Privilege of Partial Perspective," in *Simians, Cyborgs, and Women: The Reinvention of Nature* (New York: Routledge, 1991), 187. "Feminists don't need a doctrine of objectivity that promises transcendence, a story that loses track of its mediations just where someone might be held responsible for something, and unlimited instrumental power." Ibid.

46. See Patricia Hill Collins, *Fighting Words: Black Women and the Search for Justice* (Minneapolis: University of Minnesota Press, 1998).

47. See Donna Haraway, *Simians, Cyborgs, and Women: The Reinvention of Nature* (New York: Routledge, 1991); Donna Haraway, *Primate Visions: Gender, Race, and Nature in the World of Modern Science* (New York: Routledge, 1989); Emily Martin, "The Egg and the Sperm: How Science Constructed a Romance Based on Stereotypical Male-Female Roles," *Signs: Journal of Women in Culture and Society* 16, no. 3 (1991): 485–501; Stephen Jay Gould, *The Mismeasure of Man* (New York: W. W. Norton and Company, 1996).

48. Collins, *Black Feminist Thought,* 257. "Subordinates ... know much more about the dominants than vice versa. They have to. They become highly attuned to the dominants, able to predict their reactions of pleasure and displeasure," writes Jean Baker Miller. Subordinates also, she adds, "often know more about the dominants than they know about themselves." Jean Baker Miller, *Toward a New Psychology of Women* (Boston: Beacon Press, 1986), 10.

49. Sandra Harding, "Introduction: Standpoint Theory as a Site of Political, Philosophic, and Scientific Debate," in *The Feminist Standpoint Theory Reader: Intellectual and Political Controversies,* ed. Sandra Harding, 1–16 (New York: Routledge, 2004), 3.

50. For a Marxist perspective on working-class standpoint, see Lukács, *History and Class Consciousness,* 149ff.

51. Hartsock, "The Feminist Standpoint," 285.

52. Edmund Husserl, *Logical Investigations, Two Volumes,* trans. J. M. Findlay (New York: Routledge, 2001).

53. "For Kant and for Husserl the *I* is a formal structure of consciousness. We have tried to show that an *I* is never formal, that it is always, even when conceived abstractly, an infinite contraction of the material *me.*" Jean-Paul Sartre, *The Transcendence of the Ego: An Existentialist Theory of Consciousness,* trans. Forrest Williams and Robert Kirkpatrick (New York: Hill and Wang, 1991), 54.

54. Edmund Husserl, "Pure Phenomenology, Its Method and Its Field of

Investigation" in *The Phenomenology Reader*, ed. Dermot Moran and Timothy Mooney (New York: Routledge, 2002), 124.

55. Edmund Husserl, "The Critique of Historicism," in *The Essential Husserl: Basic Writings in Transcendental Phenomenology*, ed. Donn Welton (Bloomington: Indiana University Press, 1999), 23.

56. Edmund Husserl, *The Crisis of the European Sciences and Transcendental Philosophy: An Introduction to Phenomenological Philosophy*, trans. David Carr (Evanston, IL: Northwestern University Press, 1970), 152.

57. Ibid., 355.

58. Ibid., 152.

59. "The word means 'going beyond,' based on its Latin root, *transcendere*, to climb over or go beyond, from *trans* and *scando*. Consciousness, even in the natural attitude, is transcendental because it reaches beyond itself to the identities and things that are given to it. The ego can be called transcendental insofar as it is involved, in cognition, in reaching out to things." Robert Sokolowski, *Introduction to Phenomenology* (New York: Cambridge University Press, 2004), 58.

60. Husserl, *The Crisis of the European Sciences*, 60.

61. Ibid., 59.

62. Husserl, *Experience and Judgment*, trans. James S. Churchill and Karl Ameriks (Evanston, IL: Northwestern University Press, 1973 [1938]), §10, 41.

63. Ibid., 42.

64. Husserl, *The Crisis of the European Sciences*, 109.

65. Ibid., 106.

66. Iris Marion Young, "Throwing Like a Girl: A Phenomenology of Feminine Body Comportment, Motility, and Spatiality," in *On Female Body Experience: "Throwing Like a Girl" and Other Essays* (New York: Oxford University Press, 2005), 44.

67. Kevin Paterson and Bill Hughs, "Disability Studies and Phenomenology: The Carnal Politics of Everyday Life," *Disability and Society* 14, no. 5 (1999): 603. See also Rosemarie Garland-Thomson, "Misfits: A Feminist Materialist Disability Concept," *Hypatia* 26, no. 3 (Summer 2011): 591–609.

68. Frantz Fanon, *Black Skin, White Masks*, trans. Charles Lam Markmann (London: Pluto Press, 2008), 83. According to Merleau-Ponty, our bodily schema "gives us at every moment a global, practical, and implicit notion of the relation between our body and things, of our hold on them." Maurice Merleau-Ponty, *The Primacy of Perception: And Other Essays on Phenomenological Psychology*, ed. James M. Edie and trans. William Cobb (Evanston, IL: Northwestern University Press, 1964), 5.

69. Fanon, *Black Skin, White Masks*, 82.

70. Judith Butler, "Performative Acts and Gender Constitution: An Essay in Phenomenology and Feminist Theory," *Theatre Journal* 40, no. 4 (1988): 519 [519–531]. See

also Judith Butler, *Gender Trouble* (New York: Routledge, 1990); and Sara Ahmed, *Queer Phenomenology: Orientations, Objects, Others* (Durham, NC: Duke University Press, 2006).

71. Hegel calls Plato's *Parmenides* "surely the greatest artistic achievement of the ancient dialectic." G. W. F. Hegel, *Phenomenology of Spirit*, trans. A. V. Miller (New York: Oxford University Press, 1977), §71.

72. Ibid., §18.

73. Hegel, *Science of Logic*, trans. George di Giovanni (New York: Cambridge University Press, 2010), 33.

74. Ibid.

75. This is the sphere of what Hegel calls "objective spirit." For Hegel, his phenomenological and historical account of the development of human consciousness is merely a coming-of-age story of philosophy. Philosophy only truly begins with the positive reconciliation of subjectivity and objectivity in absolute spirit, which is the narrative of his *Phenomenology of Spirit* and to which his phenomenological method is limited. All of his other works are examples of *philosophy* (or post-phenomenology).

76. Theodor Adorno, *Negative Dialectics*, trans. E. B. Ashton (New York: Routledge and Kegan Paul, 1973), 5.

77. The second law, the law of non-contradiction, is according to one of Aristotle's versions: "It is impossible for anything at the same time to be and not to be." Aristotle, *Metaphysics*, in *The Complete Works of Aristotle: The Revised Oxford Translations*, vol. 2, ed. Jonathan Barnes (Princeton, NJ: Princeton University Press, 1984), 1105b37–38. With the third law, the law of the excluded middle, according to Aristotle, "there cannot be an intermediate between contradictories, but of one subject we must either affirm or deny any one predicate." Ibid., 1011b23–24.

78. See the Preface to Hegel, *Phenomenology of Spirit*.

79. This sense of nonidentity is what Judith Butler means when she writes, "the body is not a self-identical or merely factical materiality." Judith Butler, "Performative Acts," 521.

80. Hegel, *Phenomenology of Spirit*, §20.

81. Ibid., §184.

82. Ibid., §175.

83. Ibid., §177.

84. G. W. F. Hegel, *Encyclopaedia of the Philosophical Sciences in Basic Outline, Part I, Logic*, ed. and trans. Klaus Brinkmann and Daniel O. Dahlstrom (New York: Cambridge University Press, 2010), §119.

85. Hegel, *Phenomenology of Spirit*, §171.

86. See ibid., "Lordship and Bondage," §§178–196.

87. Said another way, the desire to be free is what it is to be human, and Hegel describes human self-consciousness as a desiring form of consciousness. Ibid., §§174–175.

88. For social theory informed by this account, see Judith Butler, *The Psychic Life of Power: Theories in Subjection* (Stanford, CA: Stanford University Press, 1997); Cynthia Willet, *Maternal Ethics and Other Slave Moralities* (New York: Routledge, 1998); Axel Honneth, *The Struggle for Recognition: The Moral Grammar of Social Conflicts,* trans. Joel Anderson (Cambridge, MA: MIT, 1996); and Charles Taylor, "The Politics of Recognition," in *Multiculturalism: Examining the Politics of Recognition,* ed. Amy Gutmann (Princeton, NJ: Princeton University Press, 1992), 25–73. See Kelly Oliver, *Witnessing: Beyond Recognition* (Minneapolis: University of Minnesota Press, 2001) for an alternative model of subject formation.

89. Hegel, *Phenomenology of Spirit,* §§194–195.

90. See Judith Butler's excellent discussion of this "turning" in her Introduction to *The Psychic Life of Power,* 1–30.

91. Elsewhere in the *Phenomenology of Spirit,* Hegel describes an "I" that "finds that it is outside of itself and belongs to another, finds its personality as such dependent on the contingent personality of another, on the accident of the moment, on a caprice, or some other utterly unimportant circumstance." Hegel, *Phenomenology of Spirit,* §517. Alcoff has referred to this fundamental predicament as a "double gesture of acknowledgment/anxiety about our dependence on the Other." Alcoff, *Visible Identities,* 63.

92. See Susan Buck-Morss, *Hegel, Haiti and Universal History* (Pittsburgh: University of Pittsburgh Press, 2009).

93. See Jean-Paul Sartre, *Anti-Semite and Jew: An Exploration of the Etiology of Hate,* trans. George J. Becker (New York: Schocken, 1995); Simone de Beauvoir, *The Second Sex,* trans. Constance Borde and Sheila Malovany-Chevallier (New York: Vintage, 2011); Butler, *Gender Trouble*; Frantz Fanon, *Wretched of the Earth,* trans. Richard Philcox (New York: Grove, 2005); Aimé Césaire, *Discourse on Colonialism,* trans. Joan Pinkham (New York: Monthly Review Press, 2000). Axel Honneth has also reconstructed Hegel's theory of recognition as a paradigm for critical social theory generally. See Honneth, *The Struggle for Recognition,* and Honneth, *Freedom's Right: The Social Foundations of Democratic Life,* trans. Joseph Ganahl (New York: Columbia University Press, 2014).

94. See G. W. F. Hegel, *Elements of a Philosophy of Right,* trans. H. B. Nisbet (New York: Cambridge University Press, 1991).

95. Indeed, it was the critique of Hegel's system as a totalizing meta-narrative that forces multiplicity into an oppressive binary logic, which gave birth to postmodern theory. See Jean-François Lyotard, *The Postmodern Condition: A Report on Knowledge,* trans. Geoff Bennington and Brian Massumi (Minneapolis: University of Minnesota Press, 1984), xxiv. Derrida developed his notion of *différance* (as both difference and deferral) as a way to "operate a kind of infinitesimal and radical displacement" of Hegelian discourse. Jacques Derrida, *Margins of Philosophy,* trans. Alan Bass (Chicago: University of Chicago Press, 1982), 14. Against Hegel's totalizing tendency and metaphysics of presence, Derrida advocates "play" within the field of language. Jacques Derrida, "Structure, Sign, and

Play in the Discourse of the Human Sciences," in *Writing and Difference,* trans. Alan Bass (Chicago: University of Chicago Press, 1978), 289. According to Gilles Deleuze, we should replace identity, negation, and contradiction with difference and repetition, the latter of which is a better conceptualization of movement, he argues, than Hegel's notion of dialectical opposition or mediation. Gilles Deleuze, *Difference and Repetition,* trans. Paul Patton (New York: Columbia University Press, 1994), xix.

96. Adorno, *Negative Dialectics,* 5.

97. Nancy Fraser and Axel Honneth, *Redistribution or Recognition? A Political-Philosophical Exchange,* trans. Joel Golb, James Ingram, and Christiane Wilke (New York: Verso, 2004), 202.

98. Ibid., 244.

99. Karl Marx, "Letter to Arnold Ruge," September 1843, in *The Marx-Engels Reader,* 13.

100. Lukács, *History and Class Consciousness,* 3.

101. Engels Letter to Joseph Bloch, in *The Marx-Engels Reader,* 760.

102. Karl Marx, "Theses on Feuerbach," in *The Marx-Engels Reader,* 145.

103. The pedagogy of the oppressed "must be forged with, not for, the oppressed (whether individuals or peoples) in the incessant struggle to regain their humanity. This pedagogy makes oppression and its causes objects of reflection by the oppressed, and from that reflection will come their necessary engagement in the struggle for their liberation. And in the struggle this pedagogy will be made and remade." Paulo Freire, *Pedagogy of the Oppressed,* trans. Myra Bergman Ramos (New York: Continuum, 1997), 30.

104. Marx, *Manifesto of the Communist Party,* in *The Marx-Engels Reader,* 473.

105. Ibid.

106. Lukács, *History and Class Consciousness,* 2.

107. Ibid., 224–225.

108. See, for example, Rosemary Hennessy and Chrys Ingraham, eds., *Materialist Feminism: A Reader in Class, Difference, and Women's Lives* (New York: Routledge, 1997); Cedric J. Robinson, *Black Marxism: The Making of the Black Radical Tradition* (London: Zed Press, 1983); David R. Roediger, *The Wages of Whiteness: Race and the Making of the American Working Class* (New York: Verso, 2007); Fanon, *Wretched of the Earth*; Vivek Chibber, *Postcolonial Theory and the Specter of Capital* (New York: Verso, 2013); Donald Morton, ed., *The Material Queer: A LesBiGay Cultural Studies Reader* (Boulder, CO: Westview Press, 1996); Haraway, *Simians, Cyborgs, and Women*; and Rosemary Hennessy, *Profit and Pleasure: Sexual Identities in Late Capitalism* (New York: Routledge, 2000).

109. Chandra Talpade Mohanty, *Feminism without Borders: Decolonizing Theory, Practicing Solidarity* (Durham, NC: Duke University Press, 2003), 229.

110. Karl Marx, *Capital,* vol. 3, trans. David Fernbach (New York: Penguin, 1991), 957. Marx continues: "Those conditions, like these social relations, are on the one hand

the presuppositions of the capitalist production process, on the other its results and creations." Ibid.

111. Henri Lefebvre, *Dialectical Materialism*, trans. John Sturrock (London: Jonathan Cape, 1968), 153–154.

112. "If the accumulation of capital has been an essential feature of our society, the accumulation of knowledge has not been any less so. Now the exercise, production, and accumulation of this knowledge cannot be dissociated from the mechanisms of power; complex relations exist which must be analyzed." Michel Foucault, *Remarks on Marx: Conversation with Duccio Trombadori*, trans. R. James Goldstein and James Cascaito (New York: Semiotext(e), 1991), 165.

113. See Marx, "On the Jewish Question."

114. Marx and Engels, *Communist Manifesto*, in *The Marx-Engels Reader*, 475.

115. "Postwar Fordism has to be seen, therefore, less as a mere system of mass production and more as a total way of life. Mass production meant standardization of product as well as mass consumption; and that meant a whole new aesthetic and a commodification of culture." David Harvey, *The Condition of Postmodernity: An Enquiry into the Origins of Cultural Change* (Cambridge, MA: Blackwell, 1990), 135.

116. Antonio Gramsci, "Americanism and Fordism," in *Selections from the Prison Notebooks*, trans. Quintin Hoare and Geoffrey Nowell Smith (New York: International Publishers, 1971), 302. F. W. Taylor's *The Principles of Scientific Management* (New York: Harper and Brothers, 1911), used time and motion studies to measure every part of the production process and make it more efficient, a method that came to be known as Taylorism. Following Taylorist principles of management, it expressed "with brutal cynicism the purpose of American society—developing in the worker to the highest degree automatic and mechanical attitudes, breaking up the old psycho-physical nexus of qualified professional work, which demands a certain active participation of intelligence, fantasy and initiative on the part of the worker, and reducing productive operations exclusively to the mechanical, physical aspect." Ibid.

117. See Chad Kautzer, "The Urban Roots of the Crisis: An Interview with David Harvey on Class, Crisis, and the City," *Radical Philosophy Review* 11, no. 2 (2009): 53–60.

118. See Harvey, *The Condition of Postmodernity*.

119. "I define *postmodern* as incredulity toward meta-narratives," wrote Lyotard. Lyotard, *The Postmodern Condition*, xxiv. Although Lyotard popularized the term *postmodernism* in philosophy, its origins are earlier, probably with Federico de Onís in the 1930s. See Perry Anderson, *The Origins of Postmodernity* (New York: Verso, 1998). See also Gilles Deleuze and Félix Guattari, *Anti-Oedipus: Capitalism and Schizophrenia, Anti-Oedipus: Capitalism and Schizophrenia,* trans. Robert Hurley, Mark Seem, and Helen R. Lane (Minneapolis: University of Minnesota Press, 1983 [1972]); and Habermas's influential critique of the conservatism of postmodern philosophy in Jürgen Habermas,

The Philosophical Discourse of Modernity: Twelve Lectures, trans. Frederick G. Lawrence (Cambridge, MA: MIT Press, 1987).

120. Fredric Jameson, *Postmodernism or, the Cultural Logic of Late Capitalism* (New York: Verso, 1991), xii.

121. Harvey, *The Condition of Postmodernity,* 121.

122. On the relation of debt and guilt, see Walter Benjamin, "Fragment 74: Capitalism as Religion," in *Religion as Critique: The Frankfurt School's Critique of Religion,* ed. Eduardo Mendieta (New York: Routledge, 2005), 259–262.

123. Maurizio Lazzarato, *The Making of the Indebted Man: An Essay on the Neoliberal Condition,* trans. Joshua David Jordan (New York: Semiotext(e), 2012), 30. See also Maurizio Lazzarato, *Signs and Machines: Capitalism and the Production of Subjectivity,* trans. Joshua David Jordan (New York: Semiotext(e), 2014); David Graeber, *Debt: The First 5,000 Years* (Brooklyn, NY: Melville House, 2011); Andrew Ross, *Creditocracy and the Case for Debt Refusal* (New York: OR Books, 2013); Jubilee Debt Campaign Report, *Life and Debt: Global Studies of Debt and Resistance* (October 2013), http://jubileedebt.org.uk/reports-briefings/report/life-debt-global-studies-debt-resistance.

124. *The Debt Resisters' Operations Manual* (Brooklyn: Common Notions, 2014), compiled by Strike Debt, an outgrowth of Occupy Wall Street.

Chapter 2

1. Rosa Luxemburg, *The Accumulation of Capital,* trans. Agnes Schwartzschild (New York: Routledge, 2003 [1913]), 432–433.

2. Karl Marx, "Theses on Feuerbach," in Marx and Engels, *The Marx-Engels Reader* 2nd ed., ed. Robert C. Tucker (New York: W. W. Norton and Company, 1978), 145; *Marx/Engels Collected Works,* vol. 5 (New York: International Publishers, 1976), 6. For references to shorter works by Marx and Engels, I use the popular anthology edited by Robert C. Tucker, *The Marx-Engels Reader* (*MER*), followed by the *Marx/Engels Collected Works* (*MECW*). For citations of Marx's *Grundrisse* and *Capital,* I use the Penguin editions, which are complete and accessible.

3. Jenny Chan, "A Suicide Survivor: The Life of a Chinese Worker," *New Technology, Work and Employment* 28 (2013): 86. For more first-person accounts from young workers in electronics assembly, see Jenny Chan, Esther de Haan, Sara Nordbrand, and Annika Torstensson, *Silenced to Deliver: Mobile Phone Manufacturing in China and the Philippines* (Stockholm: SOMO and SwedWatch, 2008).

4. Kam Wing Chan, "China, Internal Migration," in *The Encyclopedia of Global Migration,* ed. Immanuel Ness and Peter Bellwood (New York: Blackwell Publishing, 2011), 88. Over the last twenty years of urbanization in China, writes David Harvey, "more than a hundred cities have passed the one-million population mark in this period,

and previously small villages, such as Shenzhen, have become huge metropolises of 6 to 10 million people." David Harvey, "The Right to the City," *New Left Review* 53 (2008): 29.

5. It was also a month's pay that managers threatened to withhold if workers didn't return to the Rana Plaza building in Bangladesh's capital when cracks in the structure were discovered on April 24, 2013. After workers reluctantly returned to the garment factories illegally operating there, the building collapsed, killing over 1,100 and wounding more than 2,500, most of whom were women. It was the deadliest building collapse in history.

6. Chan, "China, Internal Migration," 92. After public outcry, Foxconn retracted the pledge.

7. On deindustrialization, see Barry Bluestone and Bennett Harrison's classic study, *Deindustrialization of America: Plant Closings, Community Abandonment and the Dismantling of Basic Industry* (New York: Basic Books, 1983).

8. Michael Hardt and Antonio Negri, *Multitude: War and Democracy in the Age of Empire* (New York: Penguin, 2004), 106.

9. Arlie Russell Hochschild, *The Managed Heart: Commercialization of Human Feeling* (Berkeley: University of California Press, 1983), 4.

10. C. Wright Mills, *White Collar: The American Middle Classes* (New York: Oxford University Press, 2002), 182.

11. Ibid., 183.

12. Marketing and the products themselves are also the means by which gender, sexuality, race, and class are represented, performed, and reproduced. See Chapter 3.

13. Mills, *White Collar,* 188. "The personality market, the most decisive effect and symptom of the great salesroom, underlies the all-pervasive distrust and self-alienation so characteristic of metropolitan people." Ibid., 187–188.

14. Edward Palmer Thompson, *The Poverty of Theory and Other Essays,* in *The Essential E. P. Thompson,* ed. Dorothy Thompson (New York: The New Press, 2001), 468.

15. Karl Marx, *Capital: A Critique of Political Economy,* vol. 1, trans. Ben Fowkes (New York: Penguin, 1976), 167.

16. Ibid., 92.

17. Ellen Meiksins Wood, *Democracy against Capitalism: Renewing Historical Materialism* (New York: Cambridge University Press, 1995), 19.

18. Karl Marx, "Estranged Labour," in *Economic and Philosophic Manuscripts of 1844,* in Marx and Engels, *MER,* 70–81; *MECW,* vol. 3 (New York: International Publishers, 1975), 270–282.

19. Marx, "Critique of the Hegelian Dialectic and Philosophy as a Whole," in Marx and Engels, *MER,* 112; *MECW,* vol. 3, 332.

20. Ibid., 112; *MECW,* vol. 3, 332–333.

21. Marx rightly called Hegel's *Phenomenology* the "true point of origin and the secret

of the Hegelian philosophy," for it is the pre-history of Hegel's philosophical concepts grasped phenomenologically. Marx, "Critique of the Hegelian Dialectic and Philosophy as a Whole," Marx and Engels, *MER*, 109; *MECW*, vol. 3, 329.

22. Hegel, *Phenomenology of Spirit*, §37. Hegel speaks of the subject as "living substance" and "pure, *simple negativity*" (i.e., "the movement of positing itself, or is the mediation of its self-othering with itself"). Ibid., §18. As both subject and substance, we divide ourselves, creating a "doubling which sets up opposition, and then again the negation of this indifferent diversity and of its antithesis." Ibid., §18. "Now, although this negative appears at first as a disparity between the 'I' and its object,' writes Hegel, "it is just as much the disparity of the substance with itself." Ibid., §37. For Hegel, this substance is "spiritual" or "conceptual," whereas for Marx it is human activity or praxis. This is perhaps the most important difference between their respective projects. For an excellent discussion of this topic, see Richard J. Bernstein, "Praxis: Marx and the Hegelian Background," in *Praxis and Action: Contemporary Philosophies of Human Activity* (Philadelphia: University of Pennsylvania Press, 1971), 11–83.

23. "Let us now look at the residue of the products of labour. There is nothing left of them in each case but the same phantom-like objectivity; they are merely congealed qualities of homogenous human labour, i.e. of human labour-power expended without regard to the form of its expenditure. . . . As crystals of this social substance, which is common to them all, they are values—commodity values." Marx, *Capital*, vol. 1, 128.

24. Marx, "Critique of the Hegelian Dialectic and Philosophy as a Whole," Marx and Engels, *MER*, 116; *MECW*, vol. 3, 337.

25. As Georg Lukács writes, "There is not yet any interiority, for there is not yet any exterior, any 'otherness' for the soul." Georg Lukács, *The Theory of the Novel: A Historico-Philosophical Essay on the Forms of Great Epic Literature*, trans. Anna Bostock (Cambridge, MA: MIT Press, 1971 [1920]), 30. See also Judith Butler, *The Psychic Life of Power: Theories in Subjection* (Stanford, CA: Stanford University Press, 1997).

26. Marx, "Estranged Labour," Marx and Engels, *MER*, 76; *MECW*, vol. 3, 276.

27. Marx, "Theses on Feuerbach," Marx and Engels, *MER*, 143; *MECW*, vol. 5 (New York: International Publishers, 1976), 3.

28. Marx, "Estranged Labour," Marx and Engels, *MER*, 73–74; *MECW* vol. 3, 272.

29. Ibid., 78; *MECW*, vol. 3, 278. Conversely, if there is alienation, it "can only become manifest through the real practical relationship to other men. The medium through which estrangement takes place is itself *practical*." Ibid.

30. Ibid., 70; *MECW*, vol. 3, 270–271.

31. Ibid., 71; *MECW*, vol. 3, 271.

32. In *Capital*, Marx writes that the "categories of bourgeois economy" are "forms of thought expressing with social validity the conditions and relations of a definite, historically determined mode of production," viz., the production of commodities. The whole mystery of commodities, all the magic and necromancy that surrounds the products

of labor as long as they take the form of commodities, vanishes therefore, so soon as we come to other forms of production." Marx, *Capital,* vol. 1, 169.

33. Maurice Merleau-Ponty, *Phenomenology of Perception,* trans. Donald A. Landes (New York: Routledge, 2012), 431.

34. Marx, "Estranged Labour," Marx and Engels, *MER,* 73–74; *MECW,* vol. 3, 272.

35. Ibid., 76–77; *MECW,* vol. 3, 277.

36. See Marx's description of the bodily effects of factory work in *Capital,* vol. 1, 481–482.

37. "The emphasis comes to be placed not on the state of being *objectified,* but on the state of being *alienated,* dispossessed, sold; on the condition that the monstrous objective power which social labour itself erected opposite itself as one of its moments belongs not to the worker, but to the personified conditions of production, i.e. to capital." Marx, *Grundrisse: Foundations of the Critique of Political Economy (Rough Draft),* trans. Martin Nicolaus (New York: Penguin Books, 1973), 831.

38. See Marx, "Estranged Labour," Marx and Engels, *MER,* 77–78; *MECW,* vol. 3, 278.

39. Marx, *Capital,* vol. 1, 163.

40. Georg Lukács, *History and Class Consciousness: Studies in Marxist Dialectics,* trans. Rodney Livingstone (Cambridge, MA: MIT Press, 1972), 14.

41. "The mysterious character of the commodity-form consists therefore simply in the fact that the commodity reflects the social characteristics of men's own labour as objective characteristics of the products of labour themselves, as the socio-natural properties of these things," writes Marx. Marx, *Capital,* vol. 1, 164–165.

42. John Holloway, *Change the World without Taking Power* (London: Pluto Press, 2005), 47.

43. Karl Marx, *Capital: A Critique of Political Economy,* vol. 3, trans. David Fernbach (New York: Penguin, 1991), 516.

44. Ibid.

45. Marx, *Capital,* vol. 1, 168.

46. Ibid., 125.

47. Ibid., 126.

48. Ibid.

49. See Michael Heinrich, *An Introduction to the Three Volumes of Karl Marx's Capital,* trans. Alexander Locascio (New York: Monthly Review Press, 2004), 44.

50. Marx, *Capital,* vol. 1, 130.

51. Ibid., 129.

52. Adam Smith, *An Inquiry into the Nature and Causes of the Wealth of Nations,* vol. 1, ed. R. H. Campbell and A. S. Skinner, vol. 2 of the *Glasgow Edition of the Works and Correspondence of Adam Smith* (Indianapolis: Liberty Fund, 1981), 4. Smith's famous example of the increased efficiency of production with a division of labor is the

pin factory, which in his example goes from making one pin per worker per day to 4,800 pins per worker per day. Ibid., ch. 1.

53. See Marx, *Capital*, vol. 1, 992–993.

54. Marx and Engels, *Manifesto of the Communist Party*, in Marx and Engels, *MER*, 476; *MECW*, vol. 6 (New York: International Publishers, 1976), 487.

55. Ibid., 480; *MECW*, vol. 6, 492.

56. Ibid.

57. For an analysis of "time-space compression," see David Harvey, *The Condition of Postmodernity: An Enquiry into the Origins of Cultural Change* (Cambridge, MA: Blackwell, 1990).

58. Marx, *Grundrisse*, 164.

59. For a technical analysis of this form of abstraction, or what is often called "real abstraction," see Alberto Tuscano, "The Open Secret of Real Abstraction," *Rethinking Marxism* 20, no. 2 (2008): 273–287; and Alfred Sohn-Rethel, *Intellectual and Manual Labour: A Critique of Epistemology* (London: Macmillan, 1978).

60. Marx, *Capital*, vol. 1, 1038.

61. "Capital is therefore not only personal; it is a social power." Marx and Engels, *Manifesto of the Communist Party*, in Marx and Engels, *MER*, 485; *MECW*, vol. 6, 499.

62. Ibid., 474; *MECW*, vol. 6, 485.

63. Michael Hardt and Antonio Negri name this class "the multitude" and characterize its antagonistic other as "empire" (rather than the imperialism of industrial capital), both of which are effects of the de-territorialization of production and the rise of "immaterial" labor. See Michael Hardt and Antonio Negri, *Empire* (Cambridge, MA: Harvard University Press, 2000), and Hardt and Negri, *Multitude*. Marx's chapter on "General Intellect" in the *Grundrisse* has been particularly influential in contemporary theory about "immaterial labor," knowledge, and cultural forms of production. See Marx, *Grundrisse*, 706ff.

64. Marx, *Capital*, vol. 1, 743.

65. See Marx and Engels, *Manifesto of the Communist Party*, in Marx and Engels, *MER*, 484–485; *MECW*, vol. 6, 498–499.

66. See Marx, *Capital*, vol. 1, 169.

67. Friedrich Engels, *The Origin of the Family, Private Property and the State* (New York: Penguin, 2010).

68. See Marx, *Capital*, vol. 1, 250.

69. Ibid., 251.

70. Ibid., 253. There exists another form of M-C-M' in the case of "merchant's capital." This exchange does not employ labor as the commodity, but rather takes advantage of place or access for profitable trade, for example, when someone buys bottles of water at the grocery store for $2 and then sells them outside a park on a hot day for $3.

71. Marx, *Capital*, vol. 1, 270.

72. "The process ... which creates the capital-relation can be nothing other than the process which divorces the worker from ownership of the conditions of his own labour," writes Marx. "It is a process which operates two transformations, whereby the social means of subsistence and production are turned into capital, and the immediate producers are turned into wage-labourers." Marx, *Capital*, vol. 1, 874.

73. See ibid.

74. See C. B. Macpherson, *The Political Theory of Possessive Individualism: Hobbes to Locke* (Oxford: Oxford University Press, 1962). I discuss this subject at greater length in Chapter 4.

75. See Marx, *Capital*, vol. 1, 272–273.

76. Michael Perelman, *The Invention of Capitalism: Classical Political Economy and the Secret History of Primitive Accumulation* (Durham, NC: Duke University Press, 2000), 14.

77. Karl Polanyi, *The Great Transformation: The Political and Economic Origins of Our Time* (New York: Beacon, 2001 [1944]), 37.

78. Marx, *Capital*, vol. 1, 885.

79. Luxemburg, *The Accumulation of Capital*, 432.

80. Marx, *Capital*, vol. 1, 874.

81. For a list of various forms of accumulation by dispossession, see David Harvey, *The New Imperialism* (Oxford: Oxford University Press, 2003), ch. 4.

82. See Giovanni Arrighi, *Adam Smith in Beijing: Lineages of the Twenty-First Century* (New York: Verso, 2007).

83. Vandana Shiva, *Biopiracy: The Plunder of Nature and Knowledge* (Cambridge, MA: South End Press, 1997), 45.

84. Naomi Klein, *The Shock Doctrine: The Rise of Disaster Capitalism* (New York: Picador, 2008), 7. The shock doctrine is often used in the event of natural disasters, such as Hurricane Katrina in New Orleans in 2005 and the 2004 tsunami in Sri Lanka, which were exploited to dispossess, dislocate, and privatize. After Katrina, the entire public school system in New Orleans was privatized.

85. Quoted in ibid., 339. See also Rajiv Chandrasekaran, *Imperial Life in the Emerald City: Inside Iraq's Green Zone* (New York: Knopf, 2006).

86. See Angela Davis, *Are Prisons Obsolete?* (New York: Seven Stories Press, 2003); and Michelle Alexander, *The New Jim Crow: Mass Incarceration in the Age of Colorblindness* (New York: New Press, 2010).

87. Marx and Engels, *Manifesto of the Communist Party*, in Marx and Engels, *MER*, 483; *MECW*, vol. 6, 496.

88. Rather than speak of individual rights or engage in moral condemnation, Marx shifted the focus to concepts of freedom and value. Readers of Marx often overlook this shift, because rights are so central to contemporary political and economic discourse. Indeed, many people today find it impossible to develop a political critique or formulate

claims within political struggles without invoking the concept of individual rights. Given that the notion of the inherent or inalienable rights of individuals—sometimes referred to as *natural* or *human rights*—has an identifiable history, beginning in medieval theological works and becoming ubiquitous in the constitutionalist traditions of the late eighteenth and nineteenth centuries, the supposed "impossibility" of thinking without them should set off alarm bells in radical philosophy. For excellent scholarly treatments of the history of rights, see Brian Tierney, *The Idea of Natural Rights: Studies on Natural Rights, Natural Law and Church Law 1150–1625* (Atlanta, GA: Scholars Press for Emory University, 1997); and Richard Tuck, *Natural Right Theories: Their Origin and Development* (New York: Cambridge University Press, 1979).

89. W. E. B. Du Bois, *Black Reconstruction in America, 1860–1880* (New York: Free Press, 1995 [1935]), 700. In Chapter 4, I discuss the "public wage" of white sovereignty.

90. bell hooks, *Where We Stand: Class Matters* (New York: Routledge, 2000), 5.

91. Marx's most famous and systematic critique of this form of individuality and its abstract rights is found in his early essay "On the Jewish Question" (1843). As a work of ideology critique, Marx's essay traces how these ideas of individual private rights (particularly to property) became naturalized, moving them out of the realm of history and human creation and into a realm of ahistorical necessity. This has in effect isolated from critique precisely the notions essential to reproducing capitalism and class rule.

92. The opportunity for corporate personhood to gain the Constitutional rights of natural persons is found in an innocent omission in the Fourteenth Amendment (1868) of the US Constitution, which referred to "persons" rather than "natural persons." The US Supreme Court ruling in *Santa Clara County v. Southern Pacific Railroad Company* (1886) was taken to be a precedent including corporate persons under the category "person" of the Fourteenth Amendment (although the decision didn't actually make that determination). It was the Supreme Court decision in *Buckley v. Valeo* (1976) that ruled that money spent in order to affect election outcomes is constitutionally protected speech, and *Citizens United v. Federal Election Commission* (2010) removed most of the spending limits on such money/speech.

93. Marx, *Critique of the Gotha Program*, Marx and Engels, *MER*, 531; *MECW*, vol. 24 (New York: International Publishers, 1989), 87. The phrase did not originate with Marx.

94. These are reflected in, for example, divisions of labor; currency; social norms and cultural traditions; state laws; individual rights; sexual desires and intimate relations; ethical values and notions of justice; religious beliefs; family structure; scientific discourses; common sense; art; entertainment, political rule, and representation; divisions of public and private life; and systems of incarceration, policing, banking, housing, health care, education, and child rearing.

95. There are also nationalist and religious forms of anti-capitalism that are explicitly repressive in myriad ways.

96. For a wonderful account of the question in the form of a children's book, see Bini Adamczak, *Kommunismus: kleine geschichte, wie endlich alles anders wird* (Munster: UNRAST-Verlag, 2004).

97. Marx and Engels would call the attempt to do so "utopian" as opposed to "scientific" (i.e., historical materialist), because it would be based on free speculation rather than material possibilities. The clearest statement of this idea is found in Engels, "Socialism: Utopian and Scientific," Marx and Engels, *MER*, 683–717; Engels, *Anti-Düring*, Part III, Socialism, and Appendix, *MECW*, vol. 25 (New York: International Publishers, 1987), 254–271, 630–644.

98. Marx and Engels, *German Ideology*, Marx and Engels, *MER*, 162; *MECW*, vol. 5, 49.

99. Marx, *The Civil War in France*, Marx and Engels, *MER*, 634–635; *MECW*, vol. 22 (New York: International Publishers, 1986), 334.

100. Ibid., 635–636; *MECW*, vol. 22, 335.

101. Ibid., 652; *MECW*, vol. 22, 355.

102. Marx and Engels, *Manifesto of the Communist Party*, in Marx and Engels, *MER*, 491; *MECW*, vol. 6, 506.

103. Engels, "Socialism," Marx and Engels, *MER*, 711; *MECW*, vol. 25, 266.

104. Marx, *Critique of the Gotha Program*, Marx and Engels, *MER*, 538; *MECW*, vol. 24, 95.

105. Vladimir Lenin was well aware of this argument and extensively developed it in his book *The State and Revolution*, ed. and trans. Robert Service (New York: Penguin, 1992 [1918]).

106. Engels, "Socialism," Marx and Engels, *MER*, 713; *MECW*, vol. 25, 268.

107. This was a decisive debate between the Marxists and Bakunists within the International Working Men's Association—the Marxists prevailed and Bakunin and his supporters were expelled from the organization.

108. See Emma Goldman, "There Is No Communism in Russia," in *Red Emma Speaks: An Emma Goldman Reader*, ed. Alix Kates Shulman (Amherst, NY: Humanity Books, 1996), 405–420.

109. Against Lenin's vanguard party (a "small minority") that ruled over the majority of workers, Luxemburg advocated social democratic "self-centralism," which relied on a "significant stratum of the proletariat that had already been schooled in political struggle and the opportunity to express their battle-readiness through the exercise of direct political influence." Rosa Luxemburg, "Organizational Questions of Russian Social Democracy," in *The Rosa Luxemburg Reader*, ed. Peter Hudis and Kevin B. Anderson (New York: Monthly Review, 2004), 253.

110. As Harry Cleaver states, "What gives meaning to the concept of 'autonomist

Marxism' as a particular tradition is the fact that we can identify, within the larger Marxist tradition, a variety of movements, politics and thinkers who have emphasized the autonomous power of workers—autonomous from capital, from their official organizations (e.g. the trade unions, the political parties) and, indeed, the power of particular groups of workers to act autonomously from other groups (e.g. women from men)." An Interview with Harry Cleaver, https://libcom.org/library/interview-cleaver.

111. See Silvia Federici, *Revolution at Point Zero: Housework, Reproduction, and Feminist Struggle* (Oakland, CA: PM Press, 2012); and Mariarosa Dalla Costa and Selma James, *The Power of Women and the Subversion of the Community*, 3rd ed. (Bristol, UK: Falling Wall Press, 1975).

112. Marx and Engels, *German Ideology*, Marx and Engels, *MER*, 161; *MECW*, vol. 5, 78.

113. Ibid., 157; *MECW*, vol. 5, 52.

114. "Founding itself upon love, humility, and faith, dialogue becomes a horizontal relationship of which mutual trust between the dialoguers is the logical consequence," writes Freire. Paulo Freire, *Pedagogy of the Oppressed*, trans. Myra Bergman Ramos (New York: Continuum, 1997), 72. He also advocates a "horizontal" or dialogical form of leadership. Ibid., 144–148.

115. See Marina Sitrin, ed., *Horizontalism: Voices of Popular Power in Argentina* (Oakland, CA: AK Press, 2006); and Subcomandante Marcos, *Ya Basta! Ten Years of the Zapatista Uprising*, ed. Žiga Vodovnik (Oakland, CA: AK Press, 2004). I discuss this at greater length in Chapter 4.

Chapter 3

1. Simone de Beauvoir, *The Second Sex*, trans. Constance Borde and Sheila Malovany-Chevallier (New York: Vintage, 2011), 283.

2. Gloria Anzaldúa, *Borderlands/La Frontera: The New Mestiza*, 3rd ed. (San Francisco: Aunt Lute Books, 2007), 26.

3. Poet and fellow suffragist, Frances D. Gage, published this transcription of Truth's speech more than a decade after it was delivered, and some of the details have been questioned, although Truth never challenged its accuracy. For a detailed analysis of the text, see Carleton Mabbe, *Sojourner Truth: Slave, Prophet, Legend* (New York: New York University Press, 1995), ch. 6. See also Sojourner Truth, *Narrative of Sojourner Truth* (New York: Penguin, 1998).

4. Paula Giddings, *When and Where I Enter: The Impact of Black Women on Race and Sex in America* (New York: William Morrow, 1984), 55.

5. Although the concept is not new—it has been variously referred to as a "simultaneity of oppressions," "interlocking oppressions," and "matrix of domination"—Kimberlé

Crenshaw coined the term *intersectionality*. See Kimberlé Crenshaw, "Demarginalizing the Intersection of Race and Sex: A Black Feminist Critique of Antidiscrimination Doctrine, Feminist Theory and Antiracist Politics," *University of Chicago Legal Forum* 139 (1989): 139–167. As bell hooks writes, "My life experience had shown me that the two issues were inseparable, that at the moment of my birth, two factors determined my destiny, my having been born black and my having been born a woman." bell hooks, *Ain't I a Woman: Black Women and Feminism* (Boston, MA: South End Press, 1981), 12.

    6. Audre Lorde, "There Is No Hierarchy of Oppressions," *Interracial Books for Children Bulletin* 14, Special Issue: Homophobia and Education: How to Deal with Name-Calling, (1983): 9.

    7. Even the abolitionist Frederick Douglass, who sat on the stage with Sojourner Truth that day in 1851, publicly argued that black men should be granted the right to vote before women of any race: "No class of men, without insulting their own nature, be content with any deprivation of their rights." Frederick Douglass, "What the Black Man Wants," delivered at the Annual Meeting of the Massachusetts Anti-Slavery Society in Boston, April 1865, *The Life and Writings of Frederick Douglass,* ed. Philip S. Foner, vol. 4 (New York: International Publishers, 1955); cited in hooks, *Ain't I a Woman,* 90.

    8. "They have us doing to those within our ranks what they have done and continue to do to us—*Othering* people—that is, isolating them, pushing them out of the herd, ostracizing them." Gloria Anzaldúa, "En Rapport, in Opposition," in *The Gloria Anzaldúa Reader,* ed. AnaLouis Keating (Durham: Duke University Press, 2009), 112.

    9. "The assumption of women as an already constituted, coherent group with identical interests and desires, regardless of class, ethnic, or racial location, or contradictions, implies a notion of gender or sexual difference or even patriarchy that can be applied universally and cross-culturally." Chandra Talpade Mohanty, *Feminism without Borders: Decolonizing Theory, Practicing Solidarity* (Durham, NC: Duke University Press, 2003), 21. "By and large within the women's movement today," wrote Audre Lorde in 1980, "white women focus upon their oppression as women and ignore differences of race, sexual preference, class, and age. There is a pretence to a homogeneity of experience covered by the word *sisterhood* that does not in fact exist." Audre Lorde, "Age, Race, Class, and Sex: Women Redefining Women," in *Sister Outsider,* 116.

    10. "In the absence of a viable Black feminism that investigates how intersecting oppressions of race, gender, and class foster these contradictions," writes Patricia Hill Collins, "the angle of vision created by being deemed devalued workers and failed mothers could easily be turned inward, leading to internalized oppression." Patricia Hill Collins, *Black Feminist Thought: Knowledge, Consciousness, and the Politics of Empowerment,* 2nd ed. (New York: Routledge, 2001), 11–12.

    11. See Linda J. Nicholson and Nancy Fraser, "Social Criticism without Philosophy:

An Encounter between Feminism and Postmodernism," in *Feminism/Postmodernism,* ed. Linda J. Nicholson (New York: Routledge, 1990), 19–38.

12. For an early and influential argument about why sexuality and gender should be treated differently, see Gayle Rubin, "Thinking Sex: Notes for a Radical Theory of the Politics of Sexuality," in *The Lesbian and Gay Studies Reader,* ed. Henry Abelove, Michèle Aina Barale, and David M. Halperin (New York: Routledge, 1994), 3–44.

13. Judith Butler, *Undoing Gender* (New York: Routledge, 2004), 54.

14. "The critical relation depends as well on a capacity, invariably collective, to articulate an alternative, minority version of sustaining norms or ideals that enable me to act." Ibid., 3.

15. "Every power to exert symbolic violence, i.e. every power which manages to impose meanings and to impose them as legitimate by concealing the power relations which are the basis of its force, adds its own specifically symbolic force to the power relations." Pierre Bourdieu and Jean-Claude Passeron, *Reproduction in Education, Society and Culture,* trans. Richard Nice (London: Sage, 1977), 4.

16. Linda Nicholson, "Gender," in *A Companion to Feminist Philosophy,* ed. Alison Jaggar and Iris Marion Young (Malden, MA: Blackwell, 1998), 293.

17. See Judith Butler, *Bodies That Matter: On the Discursive Limits of Sex* (New York: Routledge, 1993), ch. 8.

18. Adrienne Rich, "Compulsory Heterosexuality and Lesbian Existence," *Signs* 5, no. 4 (Summer 1980): 631–660. For a nice summary of queer activism, visibility, and representation, see Rosemary Hennessy, *Profit and Pleasure: Sexual Identities in Late Capitalism* (New York: Routledge, 2000), ch. 4.

19. Queer Nation Manifesto, "Queers Read This," distributed at the New York Gay Pride Day parade, 1990, accessed May 5, 2014, www.historyisaweapon.com/defcon1/queernation.html.

20. Eve Kosofsky Sedgwick, *The Epistemology of the Closet* (Berkeley: University of California Press, 1990), 29. This is not to say, of course, that there are not also radical philosophies characterized (or self-identified) as gay, lesbian, or transgender projects. On the emergence of a queer movement out of earlier liberation movements, see Annamarie Jagose, *Queer Theory: An Introduction* (New York: New York University Press, 1997). A conversation about the future of queer theory has also recently begun. See Michael Warner, "Queer and Then," *Chronicle of Higher Education* (January 1, 2012), accessed May 7, 2014, http://chronicle.com/article/QueerThen-/130161/; and in response Elahe Haschemi Yekani, Eveline Kilian, and Beatrice Michaelis, eds., *Queer Futures: Reconsidering Ethics, Activism, and the Political* (Burlington, VT: Ashgate, 2013).

21. Roderick Ferguson describes queer of color critique as presuming that "liberal ideology occludes the intersecting saliency of race, gender, sexuality, and class in forming social practices. Approaching ideologies of transparency as formations that have worked to conceal those intersections means that queer of color analysis has to debunk the idea

that race, class, gender, and sexuality are discrete formations, apparently insulated from one another. . . . As queer of color analysis claims an interest in social formations, it locates itself within the mode of critique known as historical materialism." Roderick A. Ferguson, *Aberrations in Black: Toward a Queer of Color Critique* (Minneapolis: University of Minnesota Press, 2003), 4.

22. Maurice Merleau-Ponty, *Phenomenology of Perception*, trans. Donald A. Landes (New York: Routledge, 2012), 431. The "life of the body, or the flesh, and the life of the psyche are always involved in a relationship of reciprocal expression ... bodily event always has a psychic meaning," he writes. Ibid., 186.

23. An early argument for the separate treatment of sex and gender is found in Gayle Rubin, "The Traffic in Women: Notes on the 'Political Economy' of Sex," in *Toward an Anthropology of Women*, ed. Rayna Reiter (New York: Monthly Review Press, 1975), 157–210. See also Monique Wittig, "One Is Not Born a Woman," in *The Lesbian and Gay Studies Reader*, ed. Henry Abelove, Michèle Aina Barale, and David M. Halperin (New York: Routledge, 1994), 103–109.

24. Butler, *Gender Trouble*, 6.

25. Katrina Karkazis, *Fixing Sex: Intersex, Medical Authority, and Lived Experience* (Durham, NC: Duke University Press, 2008); Elizabeth Reis, "Impossible Hermaphrodites: Intersex in America, 1620–1960," *Journal of American History* 92, no. 2 (Sept. 2005): 411–441; Alice Domurat Dreger, *Hermaphrodites and the Medical Invention of Sex* (Cambridge, MA: Harvard University Press, 1998); and Michel Foucault, *Herculine Barbin: Being the Recently Discovered Memoirs of a Nineteenth-Century French Hermaphrodite*, trans. Richard McDougall (New York: Pantheon, 1980).

26. As Linda Alcoff writes, "Sexism has more to work with [than race], one might say. The role one plays in the biological division of reproduction, the capacity to sustain an infant entirely on the production of one's own body, to give birth, to nurse, are much more significant attributes" than skin color, hair type, and so on. Alcoff, *Visible Identities*, 164.

27. For a nuanced discussion of various arguments about the metaphysics of gender sex difference, see ibid., ch. 6.

28. Butler, *Gender Trouble*, 7.

29. Lukács, *History and Class Consciousness*, 241.

30. Butler is arguing against so-called humanist positions that assume a core subject, a substance or substrate, which has attributes like gender and race. This "metaphysics of substance" is untenable if we accept the relational constitution of gender, race, and sexuality. "This relational or contextual point of view suggests that what the person 'is,' and, indeed, what gender 'is' is always relative to the constructed relations in which it is determined." Butler, *Gender Trouble*, 10.

31. "Gender reality is performative which means, quite simply, that it is real only to the extent that it is performed." Judith Butler, "Performative Acts and Gender Constitution:

An Essay in Phenomenology and Feminist Theory," *Theatre Journal* 40, no. 4 (1988): 527. Such performance is not the conscious choice of a subject, however: "Performativity cannot be understood outside of a process of iterability, a regularized and constrained repetition of norms. And this repetition is not performed by a subject; this repetition is what enables a subject and constitutes the temporal condition for the subject." Butler, *Bodies That Matter*, 95.

32. Beauvoir, *The Second Sex*, 283.

33. See Butler, "Performative Acts."

34. Young qualifies her analysis: "The account developed here claims only to describe the modalities of feminine bodily existence for women situated in contemporary advanced industrial, urban, and commercial society." Young, "Throwing Like a Girl," 30.

35. Ibid., 35.

36. Edward S. Casey, *Getting Back into Place: A Philosophical History* (Berkeley: University of California Press, 1997), 234.

37. This means, says Jean-Paul Sartre, "that transcendence is the constitutive structure of consciousness; that is that consciousness emerges supported by a being which is not itself." Jean-Paul Sartre, *Being and Nothingness*, trans. Hazel E. Barnes (New York: First Washington Square Press, 1992 [1943]), 23.

38. Young, "Throwing Like a Girl," 36.

39. Ibid., 37.

40. Merleau-Ponty, *Phenomenology of Perception*, 140.

41. Young, "Throwing Like a Girl," 39.

42. Butler, *Gender Trouble*, 17.

43. See David Bell and Gill Valentine, eds., *Mapping Desire* (New York: Routledge, 1995).

44. Anzaldúa, *Borderlands/La Frontera*, 25.

45. Collins, *Black Feminist Thought*, ch. 4.

46. Sara Ahmed, *Queer Phenomenology: Orientations, Objects, Others* (Durham, NC: Duke University Press, 2006), 92.

47. Alcoff, *Visible Identities*, 176.

48. Young, "Throwing Like a Girl," 43.

49. Beauvoir, *The Second Sex*, 284.

50. Patricia Mees, "The Ripple Effect of Title IX on Women's Health Issues: Treating an Increasingly Active Population," *Physician and Sports Medicine* 31, no. 4 (2003): 21. I leave aside the very important normative question about assimilation to these sports, which are ritualistic practices with their own raced, gendered, and sexed histories.

51. Ahmed, *Queer Phenomenology*, 56.

52. Ibid., 9.

53. Beauvoir, *The Second Sex*, 16. See also Robin Schott, "Whose Home Is It Anyway? A Feminist Response to Gadamer's Hermeneutics," in *Gadamer and Hermeneutics*, ed.

Hugh Silverman (New York: Routledge, 1991), 202–209; Martin Biddy and Chandra Talpade Mohanty, "Feminist Politics: What's Home Got to Do with It?" in *Feminist Studies/Critical Studies,* ed. Teresa de Laurentiis (Bloomington: Indiana University Press, 1986), 191–212; and Young's mildly critical response in Iris Marion Young, "House and Home: Feminist Variations on a Theme," in *Feminist Interpretations of Heidegger,* ed. Nancy J. Holland and Patricia Huntington (University Park: Pennsylvania State University Press, 2003), 252–288.

54. Merleau-Ponty, *Phenomenology of Perception,* 170.

55. Beauvoir, *The Second Sex,* 33.

56. Catharine MacKinnon, *Feminism Unmodified: Discourses on Life and Law* (Cambridge, MA: Harvard University Press, 1988), 51.

57. Iris Marion Young, *Justice and the Politics of Difference* (Princeton, NJ: Princeton University Press, 1990), 58–59.

58. "Women are essential and central to creating society; they are and always have been actors and agents in history. Women have 'made history,' yet they have been systematically excluded from the enterprise of creating symbolic systems, philosophies, science, and law. Women have not only been educationally deprived throughout historical time in every known society, they have been excluded from theory-formation." Gerda Lerner, *The Creation of Patriarchy,* in *Women and History,* vol. 1 (Oxford: Oxford University Press, 1987), 5.

59. Freire, *Pedagogy of the Oppressed,* 120.

60. Young, *Justice and the Politics of Difference,* 59–60.

61. W. E. B. Du Bois, *The Souls of Black Folk* (New York: Oxford University Press, 2007 [1903]), 8–9. See also Paul Gilroy, *The Black Atlantic: Modernity and Double-Consciousness* (New York: Verso, 1993).

62. Du Bois, *The Souls of Black Folk,* 9. "Because group standpoints are situated in, reflect, and help shape unjust power relations, standpoints are not static," writes Patricia Hill Collins. Collins, *Black Feminist Thought,* 25.

63. Mohanty, *Feminism without Borders,* 231.

64. Foucault, *Society Must Be Defended,* 51.

65. Beauvoir, *The Second Sex,* 7.

66. Butler, *The Psychic Life of Power: Theories in Subjection* (Stanford, CA: Stanford University Press, 1997), 28.

67. Susan Bordo, *Unbearable Weight: Feminism, Western Culture, and the Body* (Berkeley: University of California Press, 2003), 166. "Viewed historically, the discipline and normalization of the female body—perhaps the only gender oppression that exercises itself, although to different degrees and in different forms, across age, race, class, and sexual orientation—has to be acknowledged as an amazingly durable and flexible strategy of social control." Ibid., 166.

68. Young, "Throwing Like a Girl," 39.

69. MacKinnon, *Feminism Unmodified*, 50.

70. Beauvoir, *The Second Sex*, 349. See also Sandra Bartky, *Femininity and Domination: Studies in the Phenomenology of Oppression* (New York: Routledge, 1990), ch. 5.

71. Martha Nussbaum identifies seven forms of objectification: instrumentality, denial of autonomy, inertness, fungibility, violability, ownership, and denial of subjectivity. See Martha Nussbaum, "Objectification," *Philosophy and Public Affairs* 24, no. 4 (1995): 249–291. Rae Langton adds three more: reduction to body, reduction to appearance, and silencing. Rae Langton, *Sexual Solipsism: Philosophical Essays on Pornography and Objectification* (New York: Oxford University Press, 2009), ch. 10.

72. Frantz Fanon, *Black Skin, White Masks,* trans. Charles Lam Markmann (London: Pluto Press, 2008 [1952]), 90.

73. Lukács, *History and Class Consciousness*, 83.

74. Ibid., 131.

75. Bartky, *Femininity and Domination*, 36. "Sexualized objectification is what defines women as sexual and as women under male supremacy." MacKinnon, *Feminism Unmodified*, 50.

76. "Since, before he enters the process, his own labor has already been alienated [*entfremdet*] from him, appropriated by the capitalist, and incorporated with capital, it now, in the course of the process, constantly objectifies itself so that it becomes a product alien to him [*fremder Produkt*]." Karl Marx, *Capital*, vol. 1, trans. Ben Fowkes (New York: Penguin, 1976), 716.

77. Michel Foucault, *History of Sexuality*, vol. 1, trans. Robert Hurley (New York: Vintage, 1978), 139. See also Foucault, *Discipline and Punish*.

78. Bartky, *Femininity and Domination*, 35.

79. Foucault, *History of Sexuality*, 139.

80. Ibid., 140.

81. John Stuart Mill, *On Liberty and the Subjection of Women*, ed. Alan Ryan (New York: Penguin, 2007), 180.

82. Ibid., 222.

83. Ibid., 174, 222.

84. Ibid., 220.

85. Indeed, Mill was one of its most important architects of mid-nineteenth-century British colonialism. His father, who ran the East India Company, got him his first job there. His comment about colonialism within his critique of English masculinity is telling: "Despotism is a legitimate mode of government in dealing with barbarians." Ibid., 16.

86. Mill also discusses the use of violence, but he attributes it mostly to working-class culture.

87. Ibid., 148.

88. Ibid., 148.

89. Ibid., 155.

90. Antonio Gramsci, *Selections from the Prison Notebooks,* ed. Quintin Hoare and Geoffrey Nowell Smith (New York: International Publishers, 1971), 12.

91. "Law is not pacification, for beneath the law, war continues to rage in all the mechanisms of power, even in the most regular. War is the motor behind institutions and order. In the smallest of its cogs, peace is waging a secret war. To put it another way, we have to interpret the war that is going on beneath peace; peace is itself a coded war. We are therefore at war with one another; a battlefront runs through the whole of society, continuously and permanently, and it is this battlefront that puts us all on one side or the other." Michel Foucault, *"Society Must Be Defended": Lectures at the College de France, 1975–1976,* trans. David Macey (New York: Picador, 2003), 51.

92. Ibid., 148.

93. Foucault, *History of Sexuality,* 95.

94. See Michael Kimmel, "Masculinity as Homophobia: Fear, Shame, and Silence in the Construction of Gender Identity," in *Theorizing Masculinities,* Research on Men and Masculinities Series, ed. H. Brod and M. Kaufman (Thousand Oaks, CA: SAGE Publications, 1994), 132.

95. See Susan Brownmiller, *Against Our Will: Men, Women and Rape* (New York: Ballantine, 1993).

96. Kimmel, "Masculinity as Homophobia," 135.

97. As Gloria Anzaldúa writes, "Most societies try to get rid of their deviants. Most cultures have burned and beaten their homosexuals and others who deviate from the sexual common. The queer are the mirror reflecting the heterosexual tribe's fear: being different, being other and therefore lesser, therefore sub-human, in-human, non-human." Anzaldúa, *Borderlands/La Frontera,* 40.

98. Hennessy, *Profit and Pleasure,* 25.

99. Beauvoir, *The Second Sex,* 13.

100. "Transcript of the Disturbing Video 'Elliot Rodger's Retribution,'" *Los Angeles Times,* May 24, 2014, accessed June 3, 2014, www.latimes.com/local/lanow/la-me-ln -transcript-ucsb-shootings-video-20140524-story.html.

101. Michael Kimmel and Matthew Mahler, "Adolescent Masculinity, Homophobia, and Violence: Random School Shootings, 1982–2001," *American Behavioral Scientist* 46, no. 10 (June 2003): 1440.

102. Adrienne Rich, *Blood, Bread and Poetry: Selected Prose, 1979–1985* (New York: Norton, 1986), 51.

103. As Annamarie Jagose puts it, "Stonewall functions in a symbolic register as a convenient if somewhat spurious marker of an important cultural shift away from assimilationist policies and quietist tactics, a significant if mythological date for the origin of the gay liberation movement." Annamarie Jagose, *Queer Theory: An Introduction* (New York: New York University Press, 1996), 30.

104. See Joey L. Mogul, Andrea J. Ritchie, and Kay Whitlock, *Queer (In)Justice:*

The Criminalization of LGBT People in the United States (Boston: Beacon Books, 2011).

105. See Nancy A. Matthews, *Confronting Rape: The Feminist Anti-Rape Movement and the State* (New York: Routledge, 1994).

106. See Sarah Tyson, "Experiments in Responsibility: Pocket Parks, Radical Anti-Violence Work, and the Social Ontology of Safety," *Radical Philosophy Review* 17, no. 2 (2014): 421–434.

107. The exclusion of women from voting was reinforced in the Fifteenth Amendment (1870), which barred discrimination based "on account of race, color, or previous condition of servitude." These amendments created divisions within the white suffragist movement: Suffragists such as Susan B. Anthony, co-drafter of the Nineteenth Amendment, and Elizabeth Cady Stanton, co-author of the "Declaration of Sentiments" and co-drafter with Anthony of the Nineteenth Amendment, opposed adoption until universal suffrage was included. Other suffragists, such as Lucy Stone, who co-organized the Seneca Falls Women's Rights Convention in 1848, and Julia Ward Howe, author of "Battle Hymn of the Republic," supported it as a first step. The disagreement led Anthony and Stanton to break away from the American Equal Rights Association and co-found the National Woman Suffrage Association in 1869, while Stone and Howe left to found the American Woman Suffrage Association that same year. On the politics of race and racism in the Women's Suffrage Movement, see Angela Davis, *Women, Race, and Class* (New York: Vintage, 1983), chs. 2–4.

108. *Bradwell v. The State*, 83 US 16 Wall. 130 (1872), 141.

109. William Blackstone, *Commentaries on the Laws of England,* vol. 1 (Chicago: University of Chicago Press, 1979), 430.

110. Ibid.

111. I leave aside the less interesting claims about divine law, since the divine is always invoked by rulers to justify their rule and does not provide any insights into specific social or theoretical relations.

112. Wendy Brown, *States of Injury: Power and Freedom in Late Modernity* (Princeton, NJ: Princeton University Press, 1995), 142, emphasis added.

113. As Angela Davis describes this construction, "Men (i.e. males) have severed the umbilical cord between themselves and nature. They have deciphered its mysteries, subdued its forces, and have forged their self-definition in contradistinction to nature they have conquered. But women are projected as embodiments of nature's unrelenting powers. In their alienated portrait, women are still primarily undifferentiated beings— sexual, childbearing, natural." Angela Davis, "Women and Capitalism: Dialectics of Oppression and Liberation," in *The Angela Y. Davis Reader,* ed. Joy James (Malden, MA: Wiley-Blackwell, 1998), 148.

114. For example, in the case of medical insurance, reproductive services, such as contraception and abortion, are considered "unique to women," treated as less important

or less than universal (i.e., they are not male concerns). In the case of labor law, pregnancy and childbirth are still treated by the federal government as disabilities, thereby gendering ability as masculine. In the US Supreme Court decision *Burwell v. Hobby Lobby*, 573 US (2014), the majority ruled that corporations could refuse to provide health insurance that includes contraceptives for women. Although Title VII of the Civil Rights Act of 1964 prohibited discrimination on the basis of sex, the US Supreme Court decision *Geduldig v. Aiello*, 417 US 484 (1974), found that an employer could deny workers compensation to women who could not work due to pregnancy (although this was reversed by the Pregnancy Discrimination Act of 1978). The US Equal Employment Opportunity Commission considers pregnancy and childbirth to be disabilities and any impairments that result from them are covered under the Americans with Disabilities Act.

115. Aristotle made a similar move: "we cannot regard the elements which are necessary for the existence of the state ... as being parts of the state." Aristotle, *Politics*, 1328a.

116. Wendy Brown, *Manhood and Politics: A Feminist Reading in Political Theory* (Totowa, NJ: Rowman and Littlefield, 1988), 42.

117. G. W. F. Hegel, *Aesthetics: Lectures on Fine Art*, vol. 1, trans. T. M. Knox (New York: Oxford University Press, 1975), 361.

118. And in the long history of liberalism's partnership with racial dictatorship, we can see this natural body as including the bodies of slaves and black labor power—it was, after all, the African's animal nature, in body and thought, that Hegel argued needed to be left behind by the rational spirit. See Chapter 4.

119. "The liberal formulation of liberty is thus not merely opposed to but premised upon encumbrance; it is achieved by displacing the embodied, encumbered, and limited nature of existence onto women." Brown, *States of Injury*, 156.

120. "As people of color, our struggle against racial imperialism should have taught us that wherever there exists a master/slave relationship, an oppressed/oppressor relationship, violence, mutiny, and hatred will permeate all elements of life. There can be no freedom for black men as long as they advocate subjugation of black women. There can be no freedom for patriarchal men of all races as long as they advocate subjugation of women. Absolute power for patriarchs is not freeing." hooks, *Ain't I a Woman*, 117.

121. "One of racism's salient historical features has always been the assumption that white men—especially those who wield economic power—possess an incontestable right of access to Black women's bodies." Davis, *Women, Race, and Class*, 175.

122. Brown, *Manhood and Politics*, 43–44.

123. Iris Marion Young, *On Female Body Experience: "Throwing Like a Girl" and Other Essays* (New York: Oxford University Press, 2005), 22.

124. Friedrich Engels, *The Origin of Family, Private Property, and State*, in Marx and Engels, *The Marx-Engels Reader* (*MER*), ed. Robert C. Tucker (New York: W. W. Norton and Company, 1978), 744; *Marx/Engels Collected Works* (*MECW*), vol. 26 (New York: International Publishers, 1990), 181.

125. Ibid.

126. Davis, "Women and Capitalism," 171.

127. Marx and Engels, *German Ideology, MER*, 165.

128. Ibid.

129. Ibid., 163.

130. Silvia Federici argues that there are three areas where the process of primitive accumulation is operating: the gendered division of labor, which makes women's work primarily that of reproduction of labor-power; the construction of the social structure of gender that makes women subordinate to men; and the transformation of a woman's body into a mechanism for the reproduction of the workforce. See Silvia Federici, *Caliban and the Witch: Women, the Body and Primitive Accumulation* (Brooklyn, NY: Autonomedia, 2004), 12. See also Silvia Federici, *Revolution at Point Zero: Housework, Reproduction, and Feminist Struggle* (Oakland, CA: PM Press, 2012); and Maria Mies, *Patriarchy and Accumulation on a World Scale: Women in the International Division of Labor* (London: Zed Books, 2014).

131. Engels, *The Origin of Family, MER*, 744; *MECW*, vol. 26, 181.

132. See Arlie Russell Hochschild, "Global Care Chains and Emotional Surplus Value," in *On the Edge: Living with Global Capitalism*, ed. William Hutton and Anthony Giddens (London: Jonathan Cape, 2000), 130–146.

133. Davis, "Women and Capitalism," 185.

134. Foucault, *History of Sexuality*, 140.

135. Ibid., 141.

136. See David M. Halperin, *One Hundred Years of Homosexuality: And Other Essays on Greek Love* (New York: Routledge, 1990).

137. Foucault, *History of Sexuality*, 43.

138. Ibid., 159.

139. Hennessy, *Profit and Pleasure*, 198–199.

140. bell hooks, "Feminism: The Struggle to End Sexist Oppression," in *Feminist Theory: From Margin to Center* (Cambridge, MA: Southend Press, 2000), 51.

Chapter 4

1. James Baldwin, *Notes of a Native Son* (New York: Beacon Press, 1955), 172.

2. Aimé Césaire, *Discourse on Colonialism*, trans. Joan Pinkham (New York: Monthly Review Press, 2000), 44.

3. W. E. B. Du Bois, *The Souls of Black Folk* (New York: Oxford University Press, 2007 [1903]), 3.

4. This is not to say that other identities of white men were fully reflected.

5. Richard Dyer, "White," *Screen* 29, no. 4 (1998): 44.

6. Communist groups were banned from participating, although this didn't stop the FBI from labeling Dr. King a communist and spying on him. Most civil rights organizations were labeled as internal threats to American security, which was just a different way of saying they represented a threat to the way of life of American white supremacy. W. E. B. Du Bois, who had been living in Ghana, died on the eve of the march, and one of the organizers, Roy Wilkins, almost didn't announce it to the crowd, because Du Bois was a communist. Wilkins had a similar problem with Bayard Rustin, one of the march's lead organizers and a longtime leader in the movement, who was a communist and gay.

7. Bill Lucy and other "community leaders," presumably all men, decided upon "I AM A MAN" as a slogan earlier that month. See Steve Estes, *I Am a Man! Race, Manhood, and the Civil Rights Movement* (Chapel Hill: University of North Carolina Press, 2005).

8. Dorothy Bolden, "Dorothy Bolden Portrait," in *Nobody Speaks for Me! Self-Portraits of American Working-Class Women,* ed. Nancy Seifer (New York: Simon and Schuster, 1976), 142. See also Elizabeth Beck, "The National Domestic Workers Union and the War on Poverty," *Journal of Sociology and Social Welfare* 18, no. 4 (Dec. 2001): 195–211.

9. See Naomi Zack, "Race and Philosophic Meaning," in *Race and Racism,* ed. Bernard Boxill (New York: Oxford University Press, 2001), 43–57.

10. See Ronald L. Meek, *Social Science and the Ignoble Savage* (Cambridge: Cambridge University Press, 1976); Anthony Pagden, *The Fall of Natural Man: The American Indian and the Origins of Comparative Ethnology* (Cambridge: Cambridge University Press, 1986); and Robert A. Williams Jr., *The American Indian in Western Legal Thought: The Discourses of Conquest* (New York: Oxford University Press, 1990).

11. This is not to say that individuals do not often incorporate and intentionally defend racial identities.

12. Harlon Dalton, "Failing to See," in *White Privilege: Essential Readings on the Other Side of Racism,* ed. Paula S. Rothenberg (New York: Worth Publishers, 2005), 16.

13. Peggy McIntosh, "White Privilege: Unpacking the Invisible Knapsack," in *White Privilege,* ed. Rothenberg, 109–113.

14. Falguni Sheth has argued that hierarchical relations between two races are often stabilized via a third subject race. See Falguni A. Sheth, *Toward a Political Philosophy of Race* (New York: SUNY Press, 2009), 171.

15. Chimamanda Ngozi Adichie, *Americanah* (New York: Alfred A. Knopf, 2013), 207. On Jews and whiteness, see Karen Brodkin, *How Jews Became White Folks and What That Says about Race in America* (New Brunswick, NJ: Rutgers University Press, 1998).

16. Louis Althusser describes how *"ideology has the function (which defines it) of 'constituting' concrete individuals as subjects"* through a "hail" or *interpellation.* By

responding to the call or hail, we are constituted as subjects. His famous example was "the most commonplace everyday police (or other) hailing: 'Hey, you there!'" to which we respond as an addressee. Louis Althusser, "Ideology and Ideological State Apparatuses (Notes towards an Investigation)," in *Lenin and Philosophy and Other Essays,* trans. Ben Brewster (New York: Monthly Review Press, 1971), 171, 174.

17. Paul Gilroy, *The Black Atlantic: Modernity and Double-Consciousness* (New York: Verso, 1993), 53. This association is similar to what Giorgio Agamben identifies as the "hidden point of intersection between the juridico-institutional and the biopolitical models of power." Giorgio Agamben, *Homo Sacer: Sovereign Power and Bare Life,* trans. Daniel Heller-Roazen (Stanford, CA: Stanford University Press, 1998), 6.

18. Donald S. Lutz, "The Relative Influence of European Writers on Late Eighteenth-Century American Political Thought," *American Political Science Review* 78, no. 1 (1984): 189–197.

19. Charles de Montesquieu, *The Spirit of the Laws,* ed. and trans. Anne M. Cohler, Basia C. Miller, and Harold S. Stone (New York: Cambridge University Press, 1989), 250.

20. Ibid.

21. See Emmanuel Chukwudi Eze, "The Color of Reason: The Idea of 'Race' in Kant's Anthropology," in *Postcolonial African Philosophy: A Critical Reader,* ed. Emmanuel Chukwudi Eze (Cambridge, MA: Blackwell, 1997), 103–140; Robert Bernasconi, "Who Invented the Concept of Race? Kant's Role in the Enlightenment Construction of Race," in *Race,* ed. Robert Bernasconi (Oxford: Blackwell, 2001), 11–36; Robert Bernasconi, "Kant as an Unfamiliar Source of Racism," in *Philosophers on Race: Critical Essays,* ed. Julie Ward and Tommy Lee Lott (Malden, MA: Blackwell, 2002), 145–166; Charles W. Mills, "Kant's *Untermenschen,*" in *Race and Racism in Modern Philosophy,* ed. Andrew Valls (Ithaca, NY: Cornell University Press, 2005), 169–193; Todd Hedrick, "Race, Difference, and Anthropology in Kant's Cosmopolitanism," *Journal of the History of Philosophy* 46 (2008): 245–268; Pauline Kleingeld, *Kant and Cosmopolitanism: The Philosophical Ideal of World Citizenship* (Cambridge: Cambridge University Press, 2012), ch. 4; and Jon M. Mikkelsen, ed. and trans., *Kant and the Concept of Race: Late Eighteenth-Century Writings* (Albany, NY: SUNY Press, 2013).

22. Immanuel Kant, "Of the Different Races of Human Beings," in *Kant: Anthropology, History, and Education,* ed. Günter Zöller and Robert Louden (New York: Cambridge University Press, 2007), 92.

23. See Kleingeld, *Kant and Cosmopolitanism,* 96–97.

24. Immanuel Kant, "On the Use of Teleological Principles in Philosophy," in *Kant: Anthropology, History, and Education,* ed. Zöller and Louden, 209.

25. *Immanuel Kants physische Geographie, Kant's gesammelte Schriften,* vol. 9 (Berlin: Walter de Gruyter, 1923), 319, cited in Eduardo Mendieta, "Geography Is to History as Woman Is to Man: Kant on Sex, Race, and Geography," in *Reading Kant's Geography,* ed. Stuart Elden and Eduardo Mendieta (New York: SUNY, 2011), 359.

26. See Immanuel Kant, "An Answer to the Question: 'What Is Enlightenment?'" in *Kant: Political Writings,* ed. H. S. Reiss (New York: Cambridge University Press, 1991), 54–60.

27. Immanuel Kant, *Observations on the Feeling of the Beautiful and Sublime,* in *Kant: Anthropology, History, and Education,* ed. Zöller and Louden, 59.

28. David Hume, "Of National Characters," in *Hume: Political Essays,* ed. Knud Haakonssen (New York: Cambridge University Press, 1994), 86.

29. Montesquieu, *Spirit of the Laws,* 252.

30. Ibid.

31. Charles W. Mills, *The Racial Contract* (Ithaca: Cornell University Press, 1997), 56.

32. See Agamben, *Homo Sacer.*

33. Immanuel Kant, "What Does It Mean to Orient Oneself in Thinking?," in *Religion and Rational Theology,* ed. and trans. Allen Wood and George di Giovanni (Cambridge: Cambridge University Press, 1996), 18.

34. "Philosophers from Anaxagoras to Spinoza felt no intellectual embarrassment in speaking of Reason itself as a subject with its own power and *telos.* From this point of view, we are rational insofar as *we* manifest or participate in universal Reason or *Noûs*—a universal Reason closely associated with the concept of the Divine." Richard J. Bernstein, *Praxis and Action: Contemporary Philosophies of Human Activity* (Philadelphia: University of Pennsylvania Press, 1971), 15–16.

35. See Charles Taylor, *Sources of the Self: The Making of Modern Identity* (Cambridge, MA: Harvard University Press, 1989), ch. 9. The "punctual" self is "defined in abstraction from any constitutive concerns and hence from any identity. . . . Its only constitutive property is self-awareness." Ibid., 49.

36. John Locke, *Two Treatises of Government,* ed. Peter Laslett (Cambridge: Cambridge University Press, 1999), *Second Treatise,* §63.

37. Taylor, *Sources of the Self,* 364.

38. Immanuel Kant, *Anthropology from a Pragmatic Point of View,* in *Kant: Anthropology, History, and Education,* ed. Zöller and Louden, 239.

39. Hannah Arendt, "What Is Freedom?," in *Between Past and Future: Six Exercises in Political Thought* (New York: Viking Press, 1961), 162.

40. See Richard Tuck, *Natural Rights Theories: Their Origin and Development* (New York: Cambridge University Press, 1979); and Brian Tierney, *The Idea of Natural Rights: Studies on Natural Rights, Natural Law and Church Law 1150–1625* (Atlanta: Scholars Press for Emory University, 1997).

41. Cited in Annabel Brett, *Liberty, Right and Nature: Individual Rights in Later Scholastic Thought* (Cambridge: Cambridge University Press, 1997), 14.

42. William Blackstone, *Commentaries on the Laws of England,* vol. 2 (Chicago: University of Chicago Press, 1979), 2.

43. See Chad Kautzer, "Kant, Perpetual Peace, and the Colonial Origins of Modern Subjectivity," *Peace Studies Journal* 6, no. 2 (March 2013): 58–67. See also Edward Keene, *Beyond the Anarchical Society: Grotius, Colonialism and Order in World Politics* (Cambridge: Cambridge University Press, 2002).

44. See, for example, Ken MacMillan, *Sovereignty and Possession in the English New World: The Legal Foundations of Empire, 1576–1640* (Cambridge: Cambridge University Press, 2006).

45. See Lyle N. McAlister, *Spain and Portugal in the New World, 1492–1700* (Minneapolis: University of Minnesota Press, 1984); Lewis Hanke, *The Spanish Struggle for Social Justice in the Conquest of America* (Philadelphia: University of Pennsylvania Press, 1949); Anthony Pagden, *Lords of All the World: Ideologies of Empire in Spain, Britain and France c. 1500–c. 1800* (New Haven, CT: Yale University Press, 1995); and James Muldoon, *The Americas in the Spanish World Order: The Justification for Conquest in the Seventeenth Century* (Philadelphia: University of Pennsylvania Press, 1994).

46. Their exclusionary theory of property reflected England's burgeoning agrarian capitalism and increasing enclosure of the commons at home as well. See Neal Wood, *John Locke and Agrarian Capitalism* (Berkeley: University of California Press, 1984).

47. On Locke's involvement with English colonialism, see Barbara Arneil, *John Locke and America: The Defence of English Colonialism* (New York: Clarendon Press, 1996); David Armitage, "John Locke, Carolina, and the *Two Treatises of Government*," *Political Theory* 32 (2004): 602–627; James Tully, *An Approach to Political Philosophy: Locke in Contexts* (Cambridge: Cambridge University Press, 1993); and James Tully, *A Discourse of Property: John Locke and His Adversaries* (Cambridge: Cambridge University Press, 1980).

48. The Spanish theologian Francisco de Vitoria, for example, begins his *On the American Indians* (1537–1538) by asking, "Whether these barbarians, before the arrival of the Spaniards, had true dominium, public or private?" He elaborates: "That is to say, whether they were true masters of their private chattels and possessions, and whether there existed among them any men who were true princes and masters of the others." Vitoria, *On the American Indians [De Indis]*, 1.1.4, in *Vitoria: Political Writings,* ed. Anthony Pagden and Jeremy Lawrance (Cambridge: Cambridge University Press, 1991), 239. Vitoria argued that the only way for the Spanish to establish *dominium* in the colonies was either (privately) through first occupation or, if the natural right of Spaniards to travel, trade, occupy land, or preach is resisted, then, under the law of nations (*ius gentium*), a just war can be fought and victory entailed dispossession and enslavement, establishing both public *and* private *dominium*. His arguments did not settle the matter. After tales of genocide returned to the homeland, King Charles V, the Holy Roman Emperor, formally suspended all overseas conquests in April of 1550 until they were proven just. In Valladolid (1550–1551), in the most important debate concerning natural *dominium* since the Franciscan poverty controversy, Juan Ginés de Sepúlveda and Bartolomé de Las Casas debated whether indigenous

Americans had *dominium* and thus personhood or were natural slaves. In the exchange, Sepúlveda coupled a reading of Aristotle's doctrine of natural slavery with an Augustinian notion of *dominium,* which is lost in sin. Las Casas argued, "Not all barbarians are irrational or natural slaves or unfit for government. Some barbarians, in accordance with justice and nature, have kingdoms, royal dignities, jurisdiction, and good laws, and there is among them lawful government." Las Casas, *In Defense of the Indians,* ed. and trans. Stafford Poole (DeKalb: Northern Illinois University Press, 1974), 42.

49. "Men living together according to reason, without a common Superior on Earth, with Authority to judge between them, is *properly the State of Nature.*" Locke, *Second Treatise,* §19.

50. See Janet Coleman, "*Dominium* in Thirteenth and Fourteenth-Century Political Thought and Its Seventeenth-Century Heirs: John of Paris and Locke." *Political Studies* 33 (1985): 73–100.

51. Locke, *Second Treatise,* §27. There are actually four cases of the state of nature in Locke's work: (1) relations between independent states; (2) our initial condition at birth and until we consent to citizenship by oath or tacitly do so by remaining in the state; (3) relations between a ruler (absolute monarch) and the people when there is no impartial judge to mediate political rule; and (4) when there is no state or two or more people relate to each other without sharing common sovereign. The last is the one operative in Locke's discussion of property and private punishment and is often illustrated with examples from "America" and the "Indians."

52. In the *Second Treatise,* Locke claims that natural law is "writ in the Hearts of all Mankind." The phrase is adapted from Paul in Romans 2:14–15; Locke, *Second Treatise,* §11. See also Hugo Grotius, *De Iure Praedae Commentarius,* I, trans. Gladys L. Williams and Walter H. Zeydal (Oxford: Oxford University Press, 1950), 91–92.

53. Locke, *Second Treatise,* §4. Quentin Skinner has suggested that Locke's doctrine of private punishment is taken from Jacques Almain, but J. H. Burns has a strong argument against this association. See Quentin Skinner, *The Foundations of Modern Political Thought,* vol. 2 (Cambridge: Cambridge University Press, 1978), 119; and J. H. Burns, "Jus Gladii and Jurisdictio: Jacques Almain and John Locke," *Historical Journal* 26, no. 2 (June 1983): 369–374.

54. Locke, *Second Treatise,* §9.

55. Ibid., §14. "Those who have the supreme power of making laws in England, France or Holland, are to an Indian, but like the rest of the world, men without authority." Ibid., §9.

56. Ibid., §11, §24. "In transgressing the law of nature, the offender declares himself to live by another rule than that of reason and common equity," he writes. Ibid., §8.

57. Locke, *First Treatise,* §130. See also §131.

58. Ibid., §8, §11. For agrarian capitalists, the land indigenous Americans made use of in their community was "*waste,*" because it wasn't creating commodities (i.e.,

marketable exchange-values). See Locke, *Second Treatise*, §45. Locke turned Genesis 1:29 into a duty to create exchange values, rather than merely to use the resources provided by nature.

59. Alexis de Tocqueville, *Democracy in America*, vol. 1 (New York: Vintage, 1990), 355.

60. "That the *beginning* of *Politik Society* depends upon the consent of the Individuals, to joyn into and make one Society; who, when they are thus incorporated, might set up what form of Government they thought fit." Locke, *Second Treatise*, §106.

61. Locke also influenced international law through Emerich de Vattel, who wrote that every nation "is obliged by the law of nature to cultivate the land that has fallen to its share," and for those who do not make their land productive, "Those nations ... who inhabit fertile countries, but disdain to cultivate their lands, and choose rather to live by plunder, are wanting to themselves, are injurious to all their neighbors, and deserve to be extirpated as savage and pernicious beasts." Emerich de Vattel, *The Law of Nations; or, Principles of the Law of Nature Applied to the Conduct and Affairs of Nations and Sovereigns*, trans. Joseph Chitty (London: Stevens and Sons, 1834), book I, ch. VII, §81, 35.

62. Albert Memmi, *The Colonizer and the Colonized* (Boston: Beacon Press, 1965), 149.

63. By Kant's time, the pressure to justify settler colonialism had passed and in this national context was less pressing in any case.

64. For a defense of the thesis that the "sovereignty doctrine acquired its character through the colonial encounter," see Antony Anghie, *Imperialism, Sovereignty and the Making of International Law* (Cambridge: Cambridge University Press, 2005), ch. 1. For a parallel point about conceptual abstraction following from private property, see Max Horkheimer and Theodor Adorno, *Dialectic of Enlightenment: Philosophical Fragments*, ed. Gunzelin Schmid Noerr and trans. Edmund Jephcott (Stanford, CA: Stanford University Press, 2002), 9–10.

65. Thomas Jefferson, *A Summary View of the Rights of British America*, in *The Works of Thomas Jefferson, 1771–1779*, vol. 2, federal ed., ed. Paul Leicester Ford (New York and London: G. P. Putnam's Sons, 1904–1905), 84–85, 673–675. "America was not conquered by William the Norman, nor its lands surrendered to him, or any of his successors. Possessions there are undoubtedly of the allodial nature." Ibid., 85.

66. Thomas Jefferson, "Letter to Samuel Latham Mitchill, June 13, 1800," in *The Papers of Thomas Jefferson*, vol. 32, ed. Barbara B. Oberg (Princeton, NJ: Princeton University Press, 2005), 19.

67. Agamben, *Homo Sacer*, 7.

68. John Locke, *Essays on the Law of Nature: The Latin Text with a Translation, Introduction and Notes, Together with Transcripts of Locke's Shorthand in His Journal for 1676*, ed. W. von Leyden (Oxford: Oxford University Press, 1988), VIII, 211–213.

69. Immanuel Kant, *Reflexionen aus den Nachlass,* in *Kants gesammelte Schriften,* vol. 15 (Berlin: Walter de Gruyter, 1923), 878, cited in Kleingeld, *Kant and Cosmopolitanism,* 97.

70. Kant, "Idea for a Universal History with a Cosmopolitan Purpose," in *Kant: Political Writings,* ed. Reiss, 44.

71. As Marx writes mockingly of capitalist mythology, "Long, long ago there were two sorts of people; one, the diligent, intelligent and above all frugal elite; the other, lazy rascals, spending their substance, and more, in riotous living." Karl Marx, *Capital,* vol. 1, 873. "Such insipid childishness," he writes, "is every day preached to us in defense of property." Ibid., 873–874.

72. Kant, "Of the Different Races of Human Beings," 93.

73. Immanuel Kant, "Review of Herder's Ideas on the Philosophy of the History of Mankind," in *Kant: Political Writings,* 219. See Kant's comments about competition (for "boys") combating laziness in Kant, *Anthropology from a Pragmatic Point of View,* 375–376.

74. Aristotle, *Politics,* 1278b37.

75. Immanuel Kant, *Observations on the Feeling of the Beautiful and Sublime,* 61.

76. Hume is something of an exception here insofar as he famously argued, "Reason is, and ought only to be the slave of the passions, and can never pretend to any other office than to serve and obey them." David Hume, *A Treatise on Human Nature,* ed. L. A. Selby-Bigge (Oxford: Oxford University Press, 1978), II, 3.3, 415. That said, there is a passion for exercising power over the will of others: "For the same reason, that riches cause pleasure and pride, and poverty excites uneasiness and humility, power must produce the former emotions, and slavery the latter. Power or an authority over others makes us capable of satisfying all our desires; as slavery, by subjecting us to the will of others, exposes us to a thousand wants, and mortifications." Ibid., II, 1.10, 315.

77. Hegel, *Lectures on the Philosophy of World History,* vol. 1, ed. and trans. Robert F. Brown and Peter C. Hodgson (Oxford: Oxford University Press, 2011), 158.

78. Hegel, "Introduction," in *Lectures on the Philosophy of World History,* trans. H. B. Nisbet (Cambridge: Cambridge University Press, 1975), 177. "The negro is an example of animal man in all his savagery and lawlessness, and if we wish to understand him at all, we must put aside all our European attitudes." Ibid. The "eating of human flesh is quite compatible with the African principle; to the sensuous negro, human flesh is purely an object of the senses, like all other flesh." Ibid., 183.

79. *Scott v. Sandford,* 60 US 393 (1856), 404.

80. The Constitution recognized slaves as property, but Dred Scott was no longer in a slave state and, therefore, he argued that his "I" was a part of the "We," the "We" of citizens that constitute the "I" of the polity—namely, the "I which is a We, and the We which is an I," as Hegel described mutual recognition (see Chapter 1).

81. *Scott v. Sandford,* 60 US 393 (1856), 410.

82. Ibid.

83. Ibid.

84. Ibid.

85. James Baldwin, *The Devil Finds Work* (New York: Knopf, 2011), 61.

86. As Baldwin writes, "Therefore, a vast amount of the energy that goes into what we call the Negro problem is produced by the white man's profound desire not to be judged by those who are not white, not to be seen as he is, and at the same time a vast amount of the white anguish is rooted in the white man's equally profound need to be seen as he is, to be released from the tyranny of his mirror." Baldwin, *The Fire Next Time* (New York: Vintage, 1963), 95.

87. *Immanuel Kants physische Geographie, Kant's gesammelte Schriften*, vol. 9 (Berlin: Walter de Gruyter, 1923), 316, cited in Kleingeld, *Kant and Cosmopolitanism*, 93.

88. Hegel's dialectical, historical, and social understanding of the self is an exception, despite the white supremacist and patriarchal conclusions he draws from it.

89. George Lipsitz, *The Possessive Investment in Whiteness* (Philadelphia: Temple University Press, 2006), vii.

90. Walter Benjamin, "Critique of Violence," in *Reflections: Essays, Aphorisms, Autobiographical Writings*, ed. Peter Demetz (New York: Schocken, 1986), 288.

91. Locke, *Second Treatise*, §173, §87.

92. John Locke, *An Essay Concerning Human Understanding*, ed. Peter H. Nidditch (Oxford: Oxford University Press, 1975), book II, ch. 21, §8, 237.

93. Ibid., §15.

94. On the pathology of whiteness, or what I call "self-defensive subjectivity," see Chad Kautzer, "Self-Defensive Subjectivity: The Diagnosis of a Social Pathology," *Philosophy and Social Criticism* 40, no. 8 (2014): 743–756.

95. Cheryl I. Harris, "Whiteness as Property," *Harvard Law Review* 106, no. 8 (June 1993): 1710–1791.

96. Ibid., 1713.

97. Ibid., 1730.

98. Ibid., 1732.

99. Ibid., 1732–1734.

100. Harris moves closer to an active sense of *dominium* when she writes, "As whiteness is simultaneously an aspect of identity and a property interest, it is something that can both be experienced and deployed as a resource. Whiteness can move from being a passive characteristic as an aspect of identity to an active entity that—like other types of property—is used to fulfill the will and to exercise power." Ibid., 1734. However, just as she is about to reflexively relate the resource deployed to the power deploying it, she makes the "active" entity "like other types of property" used as instruments or means, and *dominium* as liberty is left unanalyzed.

101. Ibid., 1735.

102. By "Life," Locke meant something like our entire being (which would include our body) as the "workmanship" of God and thus God's property. We have a property right to what results from our labor and any government instituted has a duty to preserve it, says Locke. See Locke, *Second Treatise*, §6.

103. Harris, "Whiteness as Property," 1735.

104. Harris gestures toward this fetish character when she writes, "The law constructed 'whiteness' as an objective fact, although in reality it is an ideological proposition imposed through subordination. This move is the central feature of 'reification.'" Ibid., 1730. She then cites Lukács on reification and appears to be claiming that the fetish or reification is whiteness as objective property, which is only an "ideological proposition," whereas I'm referring to the fetish character of the *autonomous subject* of whiteness.

105. Marx, *Capital,* vol. 1, 165.

106. In 1932, Adolf Hitler drew a connection between German anti-Semitic white supremacy and what he called the *Herrenrecht* or the "brutal right to dominate" that emerged in European colonialism, "not on the basis of any legal claim, but from the absolute, inborn feeling of superiority of the white race." It represented, Hitler wrote, an indispensable "marriage between the concept of domination in political will and the concept of domination (*Herrensinn*) in economic activity." He speaks of Cortés and Pizarro conquering and colonizing, "not on the basis of any legal claim, but from the absolute, inborn feeling of superiority of the white race. The settlement of the North American continent was similarly a consequence not of any higher claim in a democratic or international sense, but rather of a consciousness of what is right which had its sole roots in the conviction of the superiority and thus the right of the white race. . . . Regardless of what external disguise this right assumed in a given case—in reality, it was the exercise of an extraordinarily brutal right to dominate (*Herrenrecht*). From this view there evolved the basis for the economic takeover of the rest of the world." Adolf Hitler, Düsseldorf Speech, Jan. 27, 1932, in *The Years 1932 to 1934,* vol. 1 of *Hitler: Speeches and Proclamations, 1932–1945,* ed. Max Domarus, trans. Mary Fran Gilbert (Wauconda, IL: Bolchazy-Carducci Publishers, 1990), 96; cited in part in Mills, *The Racial Contract,* 106.

107. Jacques Derrida, "Force of Law," *Cardozo Law Review* 11 (1990): 941, 943.

108. Jacques Derrida, "Declarations of Independence," *New Political Science* 7, no. 1 (1986): 13.

109. Ibid., 10.

110. Ibid. See also Benjamin, "Critique of Violence."

111. Arendt, "What Is Freedom?," 164.

112. For Foucault, the *patria potestas* of the *paterfamilias* is the *locus classicus* of sovereign power (i.e., the power to take life). See Michel Foucault, *History of Sexuality,* vol. 1, trans. Robert Hurley (New York: Vintage, 1978), 135.

113. Although the patriarchal family served as a foundation from which and through

which all other relations and rights (*iura*) were conceptualized, there did not yet exist a conception of subjective rights as a "property of one's person."

114. Arendt, "What Is Freedom?," 166.

115. Agamben, *Homo Sacer*, 15.

116. Benjamin Franklin, *The Political Thought of Benjamin Franklin*, ed. Ralph Ketchum (Indianapolis, IN: Hackett Publishing, 2003), 398.

117. "The slaveholders fell back on a kind of dual power: that which they collectively exercised as a class, even against their own impulses, through their effective control of state power; and that which they reserved to themselves as individuals who commanded other human beings in bondage." Eugene D. Genovese, *Roll, Jordan, Roll: The World the Slaves Made* (New York: Vintage, 1976), 46. Genovese's work is an excellent analysis of the operations of cultural hegemony in the dialectics of race and class relations in US slavery.

118. For Lincoln's discussion of popular sovereignty in this context, see Abraham Lincoln, *Collected Works of Abraham Lincoln*, vol. 2, ed. Roy P. Basler, Marion Dolores Pratt, and Lloyd A. Dunlap (New Brunswick, NJ: Rutgers University Press, 1953), 240.

119. Frederick Douglass, "The Kansas-Nebraska Bill Speech," October 30, 1854, in *Frederick Douglass: Selected Speeches and Writings,* ed. Philip S. Foner (Chicago: Chicago Review Press, 2000), 309.

120. Ibid., 308.

121. Arendt, "What Is Freedom?," 164. For an excellent historical and philosophical critique of sovereignty, see Daniel Loick, *Kritik der Souveränität* (Frankfurt: Campus Verlag, 2012).

122. "Human beings purchase the increase in their power with estrangement from that over which it is exerted. Enlightenment stands in the same relationship to things as the dictator to human beings." Horkheimer and Adorno, *Dialectic of Enlightenment*, 6.

123. A contemporary example of this distinction is the very recent criminalization of marital rape.

124. *People v. Hall,* 4 Cal. 399; 1854 Cal. LEXIS 137, 400.

125. Ibid., 404.

126. Ibid., 403.

127. Ibid., 405.

128. Ibid.

129. Ibid.

130. Ibid., 406.

131. While the internment camps for Japanese residents were up and running, the Magnuson Act of 1943 repealed the Chinese Exclusion Act of 1882. It was passed when China officially joined the allied nations in WWII.

132. For a subtle discussion of the politics and historical conditions shaping and reshaping Latino identities in the United States, see Alcoff, *Visible Identities,* chs. 10 and 11.

133. Mills, *The Racial Contract*, 18. Alasdair MacIntyre writes that the Enlightenment is "the period *par excellence* in which most intellectuals lack self-knowledge." Alasdair MacIntyre, *After Virtue: A Study in Moral Theory*, 3rd ed. (Notre Dame, IN: University of Notre Dame Press, 2007), 81. "Ruthless toward itself, the Enlightenment has eradicated the last remnant of its own self-awareness." Horkheimer and Adorno, *Dialectic of Enlightenment*, 2.

134. For a pathbreaking work on this subject, see Edward Said, *Orientalism* (New York: Penguin, 2003).

135. Marx and Engels, *German Ideology*, in *The Marx-Engels Reader* (*MER*), 2nd ed., ed. Robert C. Tucker (New York: W. W. Norton and Company, 1978), 154; *Marx/Engels Collected Works* (*MECW*), vol. 5 (New York: International Publishers, 1976), 36.

136. Ibid., *MER*, 172–173; *MECW*, vol. 5, 59.

137. Ibid., *MER*, 173; *MECW*, vol. 5, 59.

138. Lipsitz, *Possessive Investment in Whiteness*, 22.

139. W. E. B. Du Bois, *Black Reconstruction in America, 1860–1880* (New York: Free Press, 1995), 700–701. See also David R. Roediger, *The Wages of Whiteness: Race and the Making of the American Working Class* (New York: Verso, 2007).

140. Du Bois, *Black Reconstruction in America*, 700.

141. *Plessy v. Ferguson*, 163 US 537 (1896), 552.

142. As Du Bois notes, "Since 1876, Negroes have been arrested on the slightest provocation and given long sentences or fines which they were compelled to work out. The resulting peonage of criminals extended into every Southern state and led to the most revolting situations." Du Bois, *Black Reconstruction*, 698. See Angela Davis, "From the Prison of Slavery to the Slavery of Prison: Frederick Douglass and the Convict Lease System," in *The Angela Y. Davis Reader*, ed. Joy James (Malden, MA: Wiley-Blackwell, 1998), 74–95.

143. As of 2010, there were approximately 5.85 million people disenfranchised by felony convictions. Christopher Uggen, Sarah Shannon, and Jeff Manza, "State-Level Estimates of Felon Disenfranchisement in the United States, 2010," a Sentencing Project Report, accessed February 2, 2014, http://felonvoting.procon.org/sourcefiles/2010_State_Level_Estimates_of_Felon_Disenfranchisement.pdf.

144. Michelle Alexander, *The New Jim Crow: Mass Incarceration in the Age of Colorblindness* (New York: New Press, 2010), 13. See also Angela Davis, *Are Prisons Obsolete?* (New York: Seven Stories Press, 2003). In addition to federal and state prisons and jails, there is a vast network of over 250 immigrant detention facilities around the country, which in 2011 held over 400,000 people.

145. Police forces all over the country have been militarized, a process that began in the 1960s in the face of rebellions, such as Watts in 1965, and social movements fighting for more than integration. As Angela Davis reminds us, "SWAT [Special Weapons and Tactics] is now a common name, but its very first public appearance was the attack on

the Black Panther Party office." Chad Kautzer and Eduardo Mendieta, "Law and Resistance in the Prisons of Empire: An Interview with Angela Davis," *Peace Review* 16, no. 3 (2004): 340. That was in Los Angeles in 1969; its predecessor appeared a few years earlier farther north the Delano Police Department, created to disrupt the organizing of Cesar Chavez and the United Farm Workers.

146. Giorgio Agamben, *State of Exception,* trans. Kevin Attell (Chicago: University of Chicago Press, 2005), 1.

147. Butler does not use race in her analysis, although she does note that it is important to investigate "how sovereignty, understood as state sovereignty in this instance, works by differentiating populations on the basis of ethnicity and race, how the systematic management and derealization of populations function to support and extend the claims of sovereignty accountable to no law; how sovereignty extends its own power precisely through the tactical and permanent deferral of the law itself. In other words, the suspension of the life of a political animal, the suspension of standing before the law, is itself a tactical exercise, and must be understood in terms of the larger aims of power." Judith Butler, *Precarious Life: The Powers of Mourning and Violence* (New York: Verso, 2004), 68. Her description of petty sovereign officials is similar to Walter Benjamin's description of the police, for with the police "the separation of lawmaking and lawpreserving violence is suspended." Benjamin, "Critique of Violence," 286.

148. Butler, *Precarious Life,* 61–62.

149. Cheryl Harris identified these as the property (rights) of whiteness.

150. The same can be said of one of the earliest theories of natural domination in Western philosophy—namely, Aristotle's notion of natural slaves. See Wendy Brown's discussion of Aristotle's naturalization of slavery in *Manhood and Politics: A Feminist Reading in Political Theory* (Totowa, NJ: Rowman and Littlefield, 1988), ch. 1.

151. Horkheimer and Adorno, *Dialectic of Enlightenment,* xviii.

BIBLIOGRAPHY

Adamczak, Bini. *Kommunismus: Kleine geschichte, wie endlich alles anders wird*. Munster: UNRAST-Verlag, 2004.

Adichie, Chimamanda Ngozi. *Americanah*. New York: Alfred A. Knopf, 2013.

Adorno, Theodor W. *Against Epistemology: A Metacritique; Studies in Husserl and the Phenomenological Antinomies*. Translated by W. Domingo. Cambridge, MA: MIT Press, 1982.

———. *Negative Dialectics*. Translated by E. B. Ashton. New York: Routledge and Kegan Paul, 1973.

Agamben, Giorgio. *Homo Sacer: Sovereign Power and Bare Life*. Translated by Daniel Heller-Roazen. Stanford, CA: Stanford University Press, 1998.

———. *State of Exception*. Translated by Kevin Attell. Chicago: University of Chicago Press, 2005.

Ahmed, Sara. *Queer Phenomenology: Orientations, Objects, Others*. Durham, NC: Duke University Press, 2006.

Alcoff, Linda Martín. "Gadamer's Feminist Epistemology." In *Feminist Interpretations of Hans-Georg Gadamer*. Edited by Lorraine Code, 231–258. University Park: Pennsylvania State University Press, 2003.

———. *Visible Identities: Race, Gender and the Self*. New York: Oxford University Press, 2005.

Alexander, Michelle. *The New Jim Crow: Mass Incarceration in the Age of Colorblindness*. New York: New Press, 2010.

Althusser, Louis. "Ideology and Ideological State Apparatuses (Notes towards an Investigation)." In *Lenin and Philosophy and Other Essays*. Translated by Ben Brewster, 127–186. New York: Monthly Review Press, 1971.

Anderson, Perry. *The Origins of Postmodernity*. New York: Verso, 1998.

Anzaldúa, Gloria. *Borderlands/La Frontera: The New Mestiza.* 3rd ed. San Francisco: Aunt Lute Books, 2007.

———. "En Rapport, in Opposition." In *The Gloria Anzaldúa Reader.* Edited by AnaLouis Keating, 111–118. Durham, NC: Duke University Press, 2009.

Apel, Karl-Otto. *Understanding and Explanation: A Transcendental-Pragmatic Perspective.* Translated by Georgia Warnke. Cambridge, MA: MIT Press, 1984.

Arendt, Hannah. *The Human Condition.* Chicago: University of Chicago Press, 1958.

———. "What Is Freedom?" In *Between Past and Future: Six Exercises in Political Thought,* 143–172. New York: Viking Press, 1961.

Aristotle. *The Complete Works of Aristotle: The Revised Oxford Translations.* Edited by Jonathan Barnes. Vol. 2. Princeton: Princeton University Press, 1984.

———. *Metaphysics.* In Aristotle, *The Complete Works of Aristotle,* 1552–1728.

———. *Nicomachean Ethics.* In Aristotle, *The Complete Works of Aristotle,* 1729–1867.

Armitage, David. "John Locke, Carolina, and the *Two Treatises of Government.*" *Political Theory* 32 (2004): 602–627.

Arneil, Barbara. *John Locke and America: The Defence of English Colonialism.* New York: Clarendon Press, 1996.

Arrighi, Giovanni. *Adam Smith in Beijing: Lineages of the Twenty-First Century.* New York: Verso, 2007.

Ast, Friedrich. *Hermeneutics.* In *The Hermeneutic Tradition: From Ast to Ricoeur.* Edited by Gayle L. Ormiston and Alan D. Schrift, 39–56. New York: SUNY Press, 1990.

Atkins, A. W. H. "Theoria versus Praxis in the *Nicomachean Ethics* and the *Republic.*" *Classical Philology* 73, no. 4 (October 1978): 297–313.

Ayer, A. J. *Language, Truth and Logic.* New York: Dover, 1946.

Bacon, Francis. *New Organon.* Edited by Lisa Jardine and Michael Silverthorne. New York: Cambridge University Press, 2000.

Baker Miller, Jean. *Toward a New Psychology of Women.* Boston: Beacon Press, 1986.

Baldwin, James. *The Devil Finds Work.* New York: Knopf, 2011.

———. *The Fire Next Time.* New York: Vintage, 1963.

———. *Notes of a Native Son.* New York: Beacon Press, 1955.

Balibar, Étienne. *The Philosophy of Marx.* Translated by Chris Turner. New York: Verso, 1995.

Bartky, Sandra Lee. *Femininity and Domination: Studies in the Phenomenology of Oppression.* New York: Routledge, 1990.

Beauvoir, Simone de. *The Second Sex.* Translated by Constance Borde and Sheila Malovany-Chevallier. New York: Vintage, 2011.

Beck, Elizabeth. "The National Domestic Workers Union and the War on Poverty." *Journal of Sociology and Social Welfare* 18, no. 4. (Dec. 2001): 195–211.

Bell, David, and Gill Valentine, eds. *Mapping Desire.* New York: Routledge, 1995.

Benhabib, Seyla. *Situating the Self: Gender, Community and Postmodernism in Contemporary Ethics*. New York: Routledge, 1992.

Benjamin, Walter. "Critique of Violence." In *Reflections: Essays, Aphorisms, Autobiographical Writings*. Edited by Peter Demetz, 277–300. New York: Schocken, 1986.

———. "Fragment 74: Capitalism as Religion." In *Religion as Critique: The Frankfurt School's Critique of Religion*. Edited by Eduardo Mendieta. Translated by Chad Kautzer. New York: Routledge, 2005.

Bernasconi, Robert. "Kant as an Unfamiliar Source of Racism." In *Philosophers on Race: Critical Essays*. Edited by Julie Ward and Tommy Lee Lott, 145–166. Malden, MA: Blackwell, 2002.

———. "Who Invented the Concept of Race? Kant's Role in the Enlightenment Construction of Race." In *Race*. Edited by Robert Bernasconi, 11–36. Oxford: Blackwell, 2001.

Bernstein, Richard J. *Beyond Objectivism and Relativism*. Philadelphia: University of Pennsylvania Press, 1983.

———. *Praxis and Action: Contemporary Philosophies of Human Activity*. Philadelphia: University of Pennsylvania Press, 1971.

———. *The Restructuring of Social and Political Theory*. Philadelphia: University of Pennsylvania Press, 1976.

Biddy, Martin, and Chandra Talpade Mohanty. "Feminist Politics: What's Home Got to Do with It?" In *Feminist Studies/Critical Studies*. Edited by Teresa de Laurentiis, 191–212. Bloomington: Indiana University Press, 1986.

Bishop, Claire. *Artificial Hells: Participatory Art and the Politics of Spectatorship*. New York: Verso, 2012.

Blackstone, William. *Commentaries on the Laws of England*. Vol. 1. Chicago: University of Chicago Press, 1979.

———. *Commentaries on the Laws of England*. Vol. 2. Chicago: University of Chicago Press, 1979.

Bleicher, Josef. *Contemporary Hermeneutics: Hermeneutics as Method, Philosophy and Critique*. New York: Routledge, 1980.

Bluestone, Barry, and Bennett Harrison. *Deindustrialization of America: Plant Closings, Community Abandonment and the Dismantling of Basic Industry*. New York: Basic Books, 1983.

Bolden, Dorothy. "Dorothy Bolden Portrait." In *Nobody Speaks for Me! Self-Portraits of American Working-Class Women*. Edited by Nancy Seifer, 136–177. New York: Simon and Schuster, 1976.

Bordo, Susan. *Unbearable Weight: Feminism, Western Culture, and the Body*. Berkeley: University of California Press, 2003.

Bourdieu, Pierre. *In Other Words: Essays Towards a Reflexive Sociology*. Translated by Matthew Adamson. Stanford, CA: Stanford University Press, 1990.

————. *The Logic of Practice*. Translated by Richard Nice. Stanford: Stanford University Press, 1990.

————. *Outline of a Theory of Practice*. Translated by Richard Nice. New York: Cambridge University Press, 2013.

Bourdieu, Pierre, and Jean-Claude Passeron. *Reproduction in Education, Society and Culture*. Translated by Richard Nice. London: Sage, 1977.

Brecht, Bertolt. "On Chinese Acting." In *Brecht Sourcebook*. Edited by Carol Martin and Henry Bial, 13–20. New York: Routledge, 2000.

————. "A Short Organum for Theater." In *Brecht on Theatre: The Development of an Aesthetic*. Edited and translated by John Willett, 179–207. London: Methuen, 1964.

Brett, Annabel. *Liberty, Right and Nature: Individual Rights in Later Scholastic Thought*. Cambridge: Cambridge University Press, 1997.

Brodkin, Karen. *How Jews Became White Folks and What That Says about Race in America*. New Brunswick, NJ: Rutgers University Press, 1998.

Brown, Wendy. *Manhood and Politics: A Feminist Reading in Political Theory*. Totowa, NJ: Rowman and Littlefield, 1988.

————. *States of Injury: Power and Freedom in Late Modernity*. Princeton: Princeton University Press, 1995.

Brownmiller, Susan. *Against Our Will: Men, Women and Rape*. New York: Ballantine, 1993.

Brudney, Daniel. *Marx's Attempt to Leave Philosophy*. Cambridge, MA: Harvard University Press, 1998.

Buck-Morss, Susan. *Hegel, Haiti and Universal History*. Pittsburgh: University of Pittsburgh Press, 2009.

Burns, J. H. "Fortescue and the Political Theory of *Dominium*." *Historical Journal* 28, no. 4 (1985): 777–797.

————. "Jus Gladii and Jurisdictio: Jacques Almain and John Locke." *Historical Journal* 26, no. 2 (June 1983): 369–374.

Butler, Judith. *Bodies That Matter: On the Discursive Limits of Sex*. New York: Routledge, 1993.

————. *Excitable Speech: A Politics of the Performative*. New York and London: Routledge, 1997.

————. *Gender Trouble: Feminism and the Subversion of Identity*. New York: Routledge, 1990.

————. "Performative Acts and Gender Constitution: An Essay in Phenomenology and Feminist Theory." *Theatre Journal* 40, no. 4. (1988): 522–531.

————. *Precarious Life: The Powers of Mourning and Violence*. New York: Verso, 2004.

————. *The Psychic Life of Power: Theories in Subjection*. Stanford, CA: Stanford University Press, 1997.

————. *Undoing Gender*. New York: Routledge, 2004.

Casey, Edward S. *Getting Back into Place: A Philosophical History*. Berkeley: University of California Press, 1997.

Césaire, Aimé. *Discourse on Colonialism*. Translated by Joan Pinkham. New York: Monthly Review Press, 2000.

Chan, Jenny. "A Suicide Survivor: The Life of a Chinese Worker." *New Technology, Work and Employment* 28 (2013): 84–99.

Chan, Jenny, Esther de Haan, Sara Nordbrand, and Annika Torstensson. *Silenced to Deliver: Mobile Phone Manufacturing in China and the Philippines*. Stockholm: SOMO and SwedWatch, 2008.

Chan, Kam Wing. "China, Internal Migration." In *The Encyclopedia of Global Migration*. Edited by Immanuel Ness and Peter Bellwood, 1–46. New York: Blackwell Publishing, 2011.

Chandrasekaran, Rajiv. *Imperial Life in the Emerald City: Inside Iraq's Green Zone*. New York: Knopf, 2006.

Chibber, Vivek. *Postcolonial Theory and the Specter of Capital*. New York: Verso, 2013.

Claire, Eli. "Stolen Bodies, Reclaimed Bodies: Disability and Queerness." *Public Culture* 13, no. 3 (Fall 2001): 359–365.

Cleaver, Harry. *Reading* Capital *Politically*. San Francisco: AK Press, 2000.

Coleman, Janet. "*Dominium* in Thirteenth and Fourteenth-Century Political Thought and Its Seventeenth-Century Heirs: John of Paris and Locke." *Political Studies* 33 (1985): 73–100.

Collins, Patricia Hill. *Black Feminist Thought: Knowledge, Consciousness, and the Politics of Empowerment*. 2nd ed. New York: Routledge, 2002.

———. *Fighting Words: Black Women and the Search for Justice*. Minneapolis: University of Minnesota Press, 1998.

Combahee River Collective. "Combahee River Collective Statement." In *Home Girls: A Black Feminist Anthology*. Edited by Barbara Smith, 264–274. New Brunswick, NJ: Rutgers University Press, 2000.

Comte, Auguste. *The Positive Philosophy of Auguste Comte*. Cambridge Library Collection. Translated by Harriet Martineau. Vol. 1. New York: Cambridge University Press, 1990.

Cooke, Maeve. *Language and Reason: A Study in Habermas's Pragmatics*. Cambridge, MA: MIT Press, 1994.

Crenshaw, Kimberlé. "Demarginalizing the Intersection of Race and Sex: A Black Feminist Critique of Antidiscrimination Doctrine, Feminist Theory and Antiracist Politics." *University of Chicago Legal Forum* 139 (1989): 139–167.

Dalla Costa, Mariarosa, and Selma James. *The Power of Women and the Subversion of the Community*. 3rd ed. Bristol, UK: Falling Wall Press, 1975.

Dalton, Harlon. "Failing to See." In *White Privilege: Essential Readings on the Other Side of Racism*. Edited by Paula S. Rothenberg, 15–18. New York: Worth Publishers, 2005.

Daly, Chris. *An Introduction to Philosophical Method*. Buffalo, NY: Broadview Press, 2010.

Davis, Angela. *Are Prisons Obsolete?* New York: Seven Stories Press, 2003.

———. "From the Prison of Slavery to the Slavery of Prison: Frederick Douglass and the Convict Lease System." In *The Angela Y. Davis Reader*. Edited by Joy James, 74–95. Malden, MA: Wiley-Blackwell, 1998.

———. "Women and Capitalism: Dialectics of Oppression and Liberation." In *The Angela Y. Davis Reader*. Edited by Joy James, 161–192. Malden, MA: Wiley-Blackwell, 1998.

———. *Women, Race, and Class*. New York: Vintage, 1983.

Deleuze, Gilles. *Difference and Repetition*. Translated by Paul Patton. New York: Columbia University Press, 1994.

Deleuze, Gilles, and Félix Guattari. *Anti-Oedipus: Capitalism and Schizophrenia, Anti-Oedipus: Capitalism and Schizophrenia*. Translated by Robert Hurley, Mark Seem, and Helen R. Lane. Minneapolis: University of Minnesota Press, 1983 [1972].

Derrida, Jacques. "Declarations of Independence." *New Political Science* 7, no. 1 (1986): 7–15.

———. "Force of Law." *Cardozo Law Review* 11 (1990): 919–1045.

———. *Margins of Philosophy*. Translated by Alan Bass. Chicago: University of Chicago Press, 1982.

———. "Structure, Sign, and Play in the Discourse of the Human Sciences." In *Writing and Difference*. Translated by Alan Bass, 351–370. Chicago: University of Chicago Press, 1978.

Descartes, René. *Rules for the Direction of the Mind*. In *The Philosophical Writings of Descartes*. Translated by John Cottingham, Robert Stoothoff, and Dugald Murdoch, 7–78. Vol. 1. New York: Cambridge University Press, 1985.

———. *Second Meditation*. In *The Philosophical Writings of Descartes*. Translated by John Cottingham, Robert Stoothoff, and Dugald Murdoch, 16–23. Vol. 2. New York: Cambridge University Press, 1984.

Dewey, John. *Human Nature and Conduct: An Introduction to Social Psychology*. New York: Henry Holt and Co., 1922.

Dilthey, Wilhelm. *The Rise of Hermeneutics*. In *The Hermeneutic Tradition: From Ast to Ricoeur*. Edited by Gayle L. Ormiston and Alan D. Schrift, 101–114. New York: SUNY Press, 1990.

———. "The Understanding of Other Persons and Their Life-Expressions." In *The Hermeneutics Reader: Texts of the German Tradition from the Enlightenment to the Present*. Edited by Kurt Mueller-Vollmer, 152–164. New York: Continuum, 1988.

Douglass, Frederick. "The Kansas-Nebraska Bill Speech," October 30, 1854. In *Frederick Douglass: Selected Speeches and Writings*. Edited by Philip S. Foner, 298–311. Chicago: Chicago Review Press, 2000.

———. "The Significance of Emancipation in the West Indies." Speech, Canandaigua,

New York, August 3, 1857. In *The Frederick Douglass Papers*. Series One: Speeches, Debates, and Interviews, Volume 3: 1855–63. Edited by John W. Blassingame, 204. New Haven, CT: Yale University Press, 1986.

———. "What the Black Man Wants." Delivered at the Annual Meeting of the Massachusetts Anti-Slavery Society in Boston, April 1865. *The Life and Writings of Frederick Douglass*. Edited by Philip S. Foner, 157–165. Vol. 4. New York: International Publishers, 1955.

Dreger, Alice Domurat. *Hermaphrodites and the Medical Invention of Sex*. Cambridge, MA: Harvard University Press, 1998.

Du Bois, W. E. B. *Black Reconstruction in America, 1860–1880*. New York: Free Press, 1995 [1935].

———. *The Souls of Black Folk*. New York: Oxford University Press, 2007 [1903].

Dyer, Richard. "White." *Screen* 29, no. 4 (1998): 44–64.

Engels, Friedrich. "Letter to Joseph Bloch." In Marx and Engels, *Marx-Engels Reader*, 760–765; *Marx/Engels Collected Works*. Vol. 49, 33–36.

———. *The Origin of the Family, Private Property and the State*. New York: Penguin, 2010.

———. "Socialism: Utopian and Scientific." In Marx and Engels, *The Marx-Engels Reader*, 683–717; *Marx/Engels Collected Works*. Vol. 25, 254–271, 630–644.

Estes, Steve. *I Am a Man! Race, Manhood, and the Civil Rights Movement*. Chapel Hill: University of North Carolina Press, 2005.

Eze, Emmanuel Chukwudi. "The Color of Reason: The Idea of 'Race' in Kant's Anthropology." In *Postcolonial African Philosophy: A Critical Reader*. Edited by Emmanuel Chukwudi Eze, 103–140. Cambridge, MA: Blackwell, 1997.

Fanon, Frantz. *Black Skin, White Masks*. Translated by Charles Lam Markmann. London: Pluto Press, 2008 [1952].

———. *Wretched of the Earth*. Translated by Richard Philcox. New York: Grove, 2005.

Federici, Silvia. *Caliban and the Witch: Women, the Body and Primitive Accumulation*. Brooklyn, NY: Autonomedia, 2004.

———. *Revolution at Point Zero: Housework, Reproduction, and Feminist Struggle*. Oakland, CA: PM Press, 2012.

Feenstra, Robert. "*Dominium* and *ius in re aliena*." In *New Perspectives in the Roman Law of Property*. Edited by Peter Birks, 111–122. Oxford: Clarendon Press, 1989.

Ferguson, Roderick A. *Aberrations in Black: Toward a Queer of Color Critique*. Minneapolis: University of Minnesota Press, 2003.

Foucault, Michel. *Discipline and Punish: The Birth of the Prison*. Translated by Alan Sheridan. New York: Vintage, 1979.

———. *The Foucault Reader*. Edited by Paul Rabinow. New York: Pantheon Books, 1984.

———. *Herculine Barbin: Being the Recently Discovered Memoirs of a Nineteenth-Century French Hermaphrodite*. Translated by Richard McDougall. New York: Pantheon, 1980.

———. *History of Sexuality*. Translated by Robert Hurley. Vol. 1. New York: Vintage, 1978.

———. *Power/Knowledge: Selected Interviews and Other Writings, 1972–77.* Edited by Colin Gordon. New York: Vintage, 1980.

———. *Remarks on Marx: Conversation with Duccio Trombadori.* Translated by R. James Goldstein and James Cascaito. New York: Semiotext(e), 1991.

———. *"Society Must Be Defended": Lectures at the College de France, 1975–1976.* Translated by David Macey. New York: Picador, 2003.

———. "The Subject and Power." In *Michel Foucault: Beyond Structuralism and Hermeneutics.* Edited by Hubert L. Dreyfus and Paul Rabinow, 208–226. Chicago: University of Chicago Press, 1982.

———. "Truth and Power." In *The Foucault Reader.* Edited by Paul Rabinow, 51–75. New York: Pantheon Books, 1984.

Franklin, Benjamin. *The Political Thought of Benjamin Franklin.* Edited by Ralph Ketchum. Indianapolis, IN: Hackett Publishing, 2003.

Fraser, Nancy. *Unruly Practices: Power, Discourse, and Gender in Contemporary Social Theory.* Minneapolis: University of Minnesota Press, 1989.

Fraser, Nancy, and Axel Honneth. *Redistribution or Recognition? A Political-Philosophical Exchange.* Translated by Joel Golb, James Ingram, and Christiane Wilke. New York: Verso, 2004.

Freire, Paulo. *Pedagogy of the Oppressed.* Rev. 2nd ed. Translated by Myra Bergman Ramos. New York: Continuum, 1997.

Gadamer, Hans-Georg. *Hegel's Dialectic: Five Hermeneutical Studies.* Translated by P. Christopher Smith. New Haven, CT: Yale University Press, 1976.

———. *Truth and Method.* Rev. ed. Translated by Joel Weinsheimer and Donald G. Marshall. New York: Continuum, 2006.

Galeano, Eduardo. *Open Veins of Latin America: Five Centuries of the Pillage of a Continent.* Translated by Cedric Belfrage. New York: Monthly Review Press, 1997.

Gandio, Jason Del. *Rhetoric for Radicals: A Handbook for the 21st Century Activists.* Gabriola Island, BC: New Society Publishers, 2008.

Garland-Thomson, Rosemarie. "Misfits: A Feminist Materialist Disability Concept." *Hypatia* 26, no. 3 (Summer 2011): 591–609.

Gauthier, David. "The Social Contract as Ideology." *Philosophy and Public Affairs* 6, no. 2 (1977): 130–164.

Genovese, Eugene D. *Roll, Jordan, Roll: The World the Slaves Made.* New York: Vintage, 1976.

Giddens, Anthony. *The Constitution of Society: Outline of the Theory of Structuration.* Oxford: Polity, 1985.

Giddings, Paula. *When and Where I Enter: The Impact of Black Women on Race and Sex in America.* New York: William Morrow, 1984.

Gilroy, Paul. *The Black Atlantic: Modernity and Double-Consciousness.* New York: Verso, 1993.

Goffman, Erving. *The Presentation of Self in Everyday Life*. Edinburgh: University of Edinburgh, 1956.

Goldman, Emma. "There Is No Communism in Russia." In *Red Emma Speaks: An Emma Goldman Reader*. Edited by Alix Kates Shulman, 405–420. Amherst, NY: Humanity Books, 1996.

Gould, Stephen Jay. *The Mismeasure of Man*. New York: W. W. Norton and Company, 1996.

Graeber, David. *Debt: The First 5,000 Years*. Brooklyn, NY: Melville House, 2011.

Gramsci, Antonio. *Selections from the Prison Notebooks*. Edited by Quintin Hoare and Geoffrey Nowell Smith. New York: International Publishers, 1971.

Grondin, Jean. *Introduction to Philosophical Hermeneutics*. Translated by Joel Weinsheimer. New Haven, CT: Yale University Press, 1994.

Grotius, Hugo. *De Iure Praedae Commentarius*, I. Translated by Gladys L. Williams and Walter H. Zeydal. Carnegie Endowment for International Peace, Oxford University Press, 1950.

———. *The Freedom of the Seas [Mare Liberum]*. New York: Oxford University Press, 1916.

Habermas, Jürgen. *Communication and the Evolution of Society*. Translated by Thomas McCarthy. Boston: Beacon Press, 1979.

———. *Knowledge and Human Interests*. Translated by Jeremy J. Shapiro. Boston: Beacon Press, 1971.

———. *On the Pragmatics of Communication*. Translated by Barbara Fultner. Cambridge, MA: MIT Press, 1998.

———. *The Philosophical Discourse of Modernity: Twelve Lectures*. Translated by Frederick G. Lawrence. Cambridge, MA: MIT Press, 1987.

———. "A Review of Gadamer's *Truth and Method*." In *The Hermeneutic Tradition: From Ast to Ricoeur*. Edited by Gayle L. Ormiston and Alan D. Schrift, 213–244. New York: SUNY Press, 1990.

———. *Theory and Practice*. Translated by John Viertel. Boston: Beacon Press, 1973.

Hall, Stuart. "Ethnicity: Identity and Difference." *Radical America* 23 no. 4 (1989): 9–20.

Halperin, David M. *One Hundred Years of Homosexuality: And Other Essays on Greek Love*. New York: Routledge, 1990.

Hampton, Jean. *Hobbes and the Social Contract Tradition*. New York: Cambridge University Press, 1986.

Hanke, Lewis. *The Spanish Struggle for Social Justice in the Conquest of America*. Philadelphia: University of Pennsylvania Press, 1949.

Haraway, Donna J. *Primate Visions: Gender, Race, and Nature in the World of Modern Science*. New York: Routledge, 1989.

———. "Situated Knowledges: The Science Question in Feminism and the Privilege of Partial Perspective." In *Simians, Cyborgs, and Women: The Reinvention of Nature*, 183–202. New York: Routledge, 1991.

Harding, Sandra, ed. *The Feminist Standpoint Theory Reader: Intellectual and Political Controversies.* New York: Routledge, 2004.

———. "Introduction: Standpoint Theory as a Site of Political, Philosophic, and Scientific Debate." In Harding, *The Feminist Standpoint Theory Reader: Intellectual and Political Controversies,* 1–16.

———. "Rethinking Standpoint Epistemology: What Is 'Strong Objectivity'?" In Harding, *The Feminist Standpoint Theory Reader: Intellectual and Political Controversies,* 127–140.

Hardt, Michael, and Antonio Negri. *Multitude: War and Democracy in the Age of Empire.* New York: Penguin, 2004.

Harris, Cheryl I. "Whiteness as Property." *Harvard Law Review* 106, no. 8 (June 1993): 1710–1791.

Hardt, Michael, and Antonio Negri. *Empire.* Cambridge, MA: Harvard University Press, 2000.

Hartsock, Nancy C. M. "The Feminist Standpoint: Developing the Ground for a Specifically Feminist Historical Materialism." In *Discovering Reality: Feminist Perspectives on Epistemology, Metaphysics, Methodology, and Philosophy of Science.* Edited by Sandra Harding and Merrill B. Hintikka, 283–310. Norwell, MA: Kluwer, 1983.

Harvey, David. *The Condition of Postmodernity: An Enquiry into the Origins of Cultural Change.* Cambridge, MA: Blackwell, 1990.

———. *The New Imperialism.* Oxford: Oxford University Press, 2003.

———. "The Right to the City." *New Left Review* 53 (2008): 23–40.

Hauser, Philip M. "The Chaotic Society: Product of the Social Morphological Revolution." *American Sociological Review* 34, no. 1 (1969): 1–19.

Hedrick, Todd. "Race, Difference, and Anthropology in Kant's Cosmopolitanism." *Journal of the History of Philosophy* 46 (2008): 245–268.

Hegel, Georg W. F. *Aesthetics: Lectures on Fine Art.* Translated by T. M. Knox. Vol. 1. New York: Oxford University Press, 1975.

———. *Elements of a Philosophy of Right.* Translated by H. B. Nisbet. New York: Cambridge University Press, 1991.

———. *Encyclopaedia of the Philosophical Sciences in Basic Outline, Part I, Logic.* Edited and translated by Klaus Brinkmann and Daniel O. Dahlstrom. New York: Cambridge University Press, 2010.

———. "Introduction." In *Lectures on the Philosophy of World History.* Translated by H. B. Nisbet. Cambridge: Cambridge University Press, 1975.

———. *Lectures on the Philosophy of World History.* Edited and translated by Robert F. Brown and Peter C. Hodgson. Vol. 1. Oxford: Oxford University Press, 2011.

———. *Phenomenology of Spirit.* Translated by A. V. Miller. New York: Oxford University Press, 1977.

———. *Science of Logic.* Translated by George di Giovanni. New York: Cambridge University Press, 2010.

Heidegger, Martin. *Being and Time.* Translated by John Macquarrie and Edward Robinson. New York: Harper and Row, 1962.

Heinrich, Michael. *An Introduction to the Three Volumes of Karl Marx's Capital.* Translated by Alexander Locascio. New York: Monthly Review Press, 2004.

Hennessy, Rosemary. *Profit and Pleasure: Sexual Identities in Late Capitalism.* New York: Routledge, 2000.

Hennessy, Rosemary, and Chrys Ingraham, eds. *Materialist Feminism: A Reader in Class, Difference, and Women's Lives.* New York: Routledge, 1997.

Hitler, Adolf. *Hitler: Speeches and Proclamations, 1932–1945.* Edited by Max Domarus and translated by Mary Fran Gilbert. Vol. 1. Wauconda, IL: Bolchazy-Carducci Publishers, 1990.

Hobbes, Thomas. *Leviathan.* Edited and translated by Richard Tuck. New York: Cambridge University Press, 1991.

———. *On the Citizen.* Edited by Richard Tuck and Michael Silverthorne. New York: Cambridge University Press, 1998.

Hochschild, Arlie Russell. "Global Care Chains and Emotional Surplus Value." In *On the Edge: Living with Global Capitalism.* Edited by William Hutton and Anthony Giddens, 130–146. London: Jonathan Cape, 2000.

———. *The Managed Heart: Commercialization of Human Feeling.* Berkeley: University of California Press, 1983.

Holland, Nancy J., and Patricia Huntington, eds. *Feminist Interpretations of Heidegger.* University Park: Pennsylvania State University Press, 2001.

Holloway, John. *Change the World without Taking Power: The Meaning of Revolution Today.* London: Pluto Press, 2005.

Honneth, Axel. *Disrespect: The Normative Foundations of Critical Theory.* Malden, MA: Polity, 2007.

———. *Freedom's Right: The Social Foundations of Democratic Life.* Translated by Joseph Ganahl. New York: Columbia University Press, 2014.

———. *The Struggle for Recognition: The Moral Grammar of Social Conflicts.* Translated by Joel Anderson. Cambridge, MA: MIT Press, 1996.

hooks, bell. *Ain't I a Woman: Black Women and Feminism.* Boston, MA: South End Press, 1981.

———. *Black Looks: Race and Representation.* Boston, MA: South End Press, 1992.

———. *Feminist Theory: From Margin to Center.* Cambridge, MA: Southend Press, 2000.

———. "Killing Rage: Militant Resistance." In *Killing Rage: Ending Racism.* New York: Holt, 1996.

———. *Where We Stand: Class Matters.* New York: Routledge, 2000.

Horkheimer, Max. "Traditional and Critical Theory." In *Critical Theory: Selected Essays.* Translated by Matthew J. O'Connell, 188–243. New York: Continuum, 1975.

Horkheimer, Max, and Theodor W. Adorno. *Dialectic of Enlightenment: Philosophical*

Fragments. Edited by Gunzelin Schmid Noerr. Translated by Edmund Jephcott. Stanford, CA: Stanford University Press, 2002.

Hume, David. *An Enquiry Concerning Human Understanding.* 3rd ed. Edited by L. A. Selby-Bigge and revised by P. H. Nidditch. Oxford: Clarendon Press, 1975.

———. "Of National Characters." In *Hume: Political Essays.* Edited by Knud Haakonssen, 78–92. New York: Cambridge University Press, 1994.

———. *A Treatise on Human Nature.* Edited by L. A. Selby-Bigge. Oxford: Oxford University Press, 1978.

Huntington, Samuel P. *The Clash of Civilizations and the Remaking of World Order.* New York: Simon and Schuster, 1996.

Husserl, Edmund. *The Crisis of European Sciences and Transcendental Philosophy.* Translated by David Carr. Evanston, IL: Northwestern University Press, 1970.

———. "The Critique of Historicism." In *The Essential Husserl: Basic Writings in Transcendental Phenomenology.* Edited by Donn Welton, 22–25. Bloomington: Indiana University Press, 1999.

———. *Experience and Judgment.* Translated by James S. Churchill and Karl Ameriks. Evanston, IL: Northwestern University Press, 1973 [1938].

———. *Formal and Transcendental Logic.* Translated by Dorion Cairns. The Hague: Martinus Nijhoff, 1969.

———. *Logical Investigations, Two Volumes.* Translated by J. M. Findlay. New York: Routledge, 2001.

———. "Pure Phenomenology, Its Method and Its Field of Investigation." In *The Phenomenology Reader.* Edited by Dermot Moran and Timothy Mooney, 124–133. New York: Routledge, 2002.

Jagose, Annamarie. *Queer Theory: An Introduction.* New York: New York University Press, 1997.

James, William. *The Principles of Psychology.* Vol. 1. Cambridge: Harvard University Press, 1981.

———. *Valences of the Dialectic.* New York: Verso, 2009.

Jameson, Fredric. *Postmodernism or, the Cultural Logic of Late Capitalism.* New York: Verso, 1991.

Jefferson, Thomas. "Letter to Samuel Latham Mitchill, June 13, 1800." In *The Papers of Thomas Jefferson.* Edited by Barbara B. Oberg, 18–19. Vol. 32. Princeton: Princeton University Press, 2005.

———. *A Summary View of the Rights of British America.* In *The Works of Thomas Jefferson, 1771–1779,* Federal Edition. Edited by Paul Leicester Ford, 49–92. Vol. 2. New York and London: G. P. Putnam's Sons, 1904–1905.

Jordan, June. *Civil Wars: Observations from the Front Lines of America.* New York: Touchstone, 1995.

Jubilee Debt Campaign Report. *Life and Debt: Global Studies of Debt and Resistance.*

October 2013. http://jubileedebt.org.uk/reports-briefings/report/life-debt-global
-studies-debt-resistance.

Kant, Immanuel. "An Answer to the Question: 'What Is Enlightenment?'" In *Kant: Political Writings*. Edited by H. S. Reiss, 54–60. New York: Cambridge University Press, 1991.

———. *Anthropology from a Pragmatic Point of View*. In *Kant: Anthropology, History, and Education*. Edited and translated by Robert B. Louden, 227–429. New York: Cambridge University Press, 2006.

———. *Critique of Pure Reason*. Edited and translated by Paul Guyer and Allen Wood. New York: Cambridge University Press, 1998.

———. "Idea for a Universal History with a Cosmopolitan Purpose." In *Kant: Political Writings*. Edited by H. S. Reiss, 41–53. New York: Cambridge University Press, 1991.

———. *Metaphysics of Morals*. Edited and translated by Mary Gregor. New York: Cambridge University Press, 1996 [1797].

———. *Observations on the Feeling of the Beautiful and Sublime*. In *Kant: Anthropology, History, and Education*. Edited by Günter Zöller and Robert Louden, 18–62. New York: Cambridge University Press, 2007.

———. "Of the Different Races of Human Beings." In *Kant: Anthropology, History, and Education*. Edited by Günter Zöller and Robert Louden, 82–97. New York: Cambridge University Press, 2007.

———. "On the Use of Teleological Principles in Philosophy." In *Kant: Anthropology, History, and Education*. Edited by Günter Zöller and Robert Louden, 192–218. New York: Cambridge University Press, 2007.

———. "Review of Herder's Ideas on the Philosophy of the History of Mankind." In *Kant: Political Writings*. Edited by H. S. Reiss, 201–220. New York: Cambridge University Press, 1991.

———. "What Does It Mean to Orient Oneself in Thinking?" In *Religion and Rational Theology*. Edited and translated by Allen Wood and George di Giovanni, 1–18. Cambridge: Cambridge University Press, 1996.

Karkazis, Katrina. *Fixing Sex: Intersex, Medical Authority, and Lived Experience*. Durham, NC: Duke University Press, 2008.

Kautzer, Chad. "Kant, Perpetual Peace, and the Colonial Origins of Modern Subjectivity." *Peace Studies Journal* 6, no. 2 (March 2013): 58–67.

———. "Self-Defensive Subjectivity: The Diagnosis of a Social Pathology." *Philosophy and Social Criticism* 40, no. 8 (2014): 743–756.

———. "The Urban Roots of the Crisis: An Interview with David Harvey on Class, Crisis, and the City." *Radical Philosophy Review* 11, no. 2 (2009): 53–60.

Kautzer, Chad, and Eduardo Mendieta. "Law and Resistance in the Prisons of Empire: An Interview with Angela Davis." *Peace Review* 16, no. 3 (2004): 339–347.

Keene, Edward. *Beyond the Anarchical Society: Grotius, Colonialism and Order in World Politics*. Cambridge: Cambridge University Press, 2002.

Kimmel, Michael. "Masculinity as Homophobia: Fear, Shame, and Silence in the Construction of Gender Identity." In *Theorizing Masculinities*. Research on Men and Masculinities Series. Edited by H. Brod and M. Kaufman, 119–142. Thousand Oaks, CA: SAGE Publications, 1994.

Kimmel, Michael, and Matthew Mahler. "Adolescent Masculinity, Homophobia, and Violence: Random School Shootings, 1982–2001." *American Behavioral Scientist* 46, no. 10 (June 2003): 1439–1458.

Klein, Naomi. *The Shock Doctrine: The Rise of Disaster Capitalism*. New York: Picador, 2008.

Kleingeld, Pauline. *Kant and Cosmopolitanism: The Philosophical Ideal of World Citizenship*. Cambridge: Cambridge University Press, 2012.

Kristeva, Julia. *The Kristeva Reader*. Edited by Toril Moi. Oxford: Blackwell, 1986.

———. "A New Type of Intellectual: The Dissident." In *The Kristeva Reader*. Edited by Toril Moi, 292–300. Oxford: Blackwell, 1986.

Laclau, Ernesto, and Chantal Mouffe. *Hegemony and Socialist Strategy: Towards a Radical Democratic Politics*. New York: Verso, 1985.

Langton, Rae. *Sexual Solipsism: Philosophical Essays on Pornography and Objectification*. New York: Oxford University Press, 2009.

Las Casas, Bartolomé de. *In Defense of the Indians*. Edited and translated by Stafford Poole. DeKalb: Northern Illinois University Press, 1974.

Lazzarato, Maurizio. *The Making of the Indebted Man: An Essay on the Neoliberal Condition*. Translated by Joshua David Jordan. New York: Semiotext(e), 2012.

———. *Signs and Machines: Capitalism and the Production of Subjectivity*. Translated by Joshua David Jordan. New York: Semiotext(e), 2014.

Lefebvre, Henri. *Dialectical Materialism*. Translated by John Sturrock. London: Jonathan Cape, 1968.

Lenin, Vladimir. *The State and Revolution*. Edited and translated by Robert Service. New York: Penguin, 1992 [1918].

Lerner, Gerda. *The Creation of Patriarchy*. In *Women and History*. Vol. 1. Oxford: Oxford University Press, 1987.

Lincoln, Abraham. *Collected Works of Abraham Lincoln*. Edited by Roy P. Basler, Marion Dolores Pratt, and Lloyd A. Dunlap. Vol. 2. New Brunswick, NJ: Rutgers University Press, 1953.

Lipsitz, George. *The Possessive Investment in Whiteness*. Philadelphia: Temple University Press, 2006.

Locke, John. *An Essay Concerning Human Understanding*. Edited by Peter H. Nidditch. Oxford: Oxford University Press, 1975.

———. *Essays on the Law of Nature: The Latin Text with a Translation, Introduction and Notes, Together with Transcripts of Locke's Shorthand in His Journal for 1676*. Edited by W. von Leyden. Oxford: Oxford University Press, 1988.

———. *Two Treatises of Government.* Edited by Peter Laslett. Cambridge: Cambridge University Press, 1999.

Loick, Daniel. *Kritik der Souveränität.* Frankfurt: Campus Verlag, 2012.

Lorde, Audre. "Age, Race, Class, and Sex: Women Redefining Women." In Lorde, *Sister Outsider,* 114–123.

———. "The Master's Tools Will Never Dismantle the Master's House." In Lorde, *Sister Outsider,* 110–113.

———. *Sister Outsider: Essays and Speeches.* New York: Random House, 1984.

———. "There Is No Hierarchy of Oppressions." *Interracial Books for Children Bulletin* 14. Special Issue: Homophobia and Education: How to Deal with Name-Calling (1983): 9.

———. "The Uses of Anger: Women Responding to Racism." In Lorde, *Sister Outsider,* 124–132.

Lukács, Georg. *History and Class Consciousness: Studies in Marxist Dialectics.* Translated by Rodney Livingstone. Cambridge, MA: MIT Press, 1972.

———. *The Theory of the Novel: A Historico-Philosophical Essay on the Forms of Great Epic Literature.* Translated by Anna Bostock. Cambridge, MA: MIT Press, 1971 [1920].

Lutz, Donald S. "The Relative Influence of European Writers on Late Eighteenth-Century American Political Thought." *American Political Science Review* 78, no. 1 (1984): 189–197.

Luxemburg, Rosa. *The Accumulation of Capital.* Translated by Agnes Schwartzschild. New York: Routledge, 2003 [1913].

———. "Organizational Questions of Russian Social Democracy." In *The Rosa Luxemburg Reader.* Edited by Peter Hudis and Kevin B. Anderson, 248–265. New York: Monthly Review, 2004.

Lyotard, Jean-François. *The Postmodern Condition: A Report on Knowledge.* Translated by Geoff Bennington and Brian Massumi. Minneapolis: University of Minnesota Press, 1984 [1979].

Mabbe, Carleton. *Sojourner Truth: Slave, Prophet, Legend.* New York: New York University Press, 1995.

MacIntyre, Alasdair. *After Virtue: A Study in Moral Theory.* 3rd ed. Notre Dame, IN: University of Notre Dame Press, 2007.

MacKinnon, Catharine. *Feminism Unmodified: Discourses on Life and Law.* Cambridge, MA: Harvard University Press, 1988.

———. *Towards a Feminist Theory of the State.* Cambridge, MA: Harvard University Press, 1989.

MacMillan, Ken. *Sovereignty and Possession in the English New World: The Legal Foundations of Empire, 1576–1640.* Cambridge: Cambridge University Press, 2006.

Macpherson, C. B. *The Political Theory of Possessive Individualism: Hobbes to Locke.* Oxford: Oxford University Press, 1962.

Marcos, Subcomandante. *Ya Basta! Ten Years of the Zapatista Uprising.* Edited by Žiga Vodovnik. Oakland, CA: AK Press, 2004.

Marcuse, Herbert. "On Concrete Philosophy." In *Heideggerian Marxism.* Edited by Richard Wolin and John Abromeit, 34–52. Lincoln: University of Nebraska Press, 2005.

Martin, Emily. "The Egg and the Sperm: How Science Constructed a Romance Based on Stereotypical Male-Female Roles." *Signs: Journal of Women in Culture and Society* 16, no. 3 (1991): 485–501.

Martinez, Jacqueline M. "Culture, Communication, and Latina Feminist Philosophy: Toward a Critical Phenomenology of Culture." *Hypatia* 29, no. 1 (2014): 221–236.

Marx, Karl. *Capital: A Critique of Political Economy.* Translated by Ben Fowkes. Vol. 1. New York: Penguin, 1976.

———. *Capital: A Critique of Political Economy.* Translated by David Fernbach. Vol. 3. New York: Penguin, 1991.

———. "Contribution to the Critique of Hegel's *Philosophy of Right*: Introduction." In Marx and Engels, *The Marx-Engels Reader,* 53–65; *Marx/Engels Collected Works,* Vol. 3, 175–187.

———. "Critique of the Gotha Programme." In Marx and Engels, *The Marx-Engels Reader,* 535–541; *Marx/Engels Collected Works,* Vol. 24, 75–99.

———. "Critique of the Hegelian Dialectic and Philosophy as a Whole." In Marx and Engels, *The Marx-Engels Reader,* 106–125; *Marx/Engels Collected Works,* Vol. 3, 326–348.

———. *The Eighteenth Brumaire of Louis Bonaparte.* In Marx and Engels, *The Marx-Engels Reader,* 594–617; *Marx/Engels Collected Works,* Vol. 11, 99–197.

———. "Estranged Labour." In Marx and Engels, *The Marx-Engels Reader,* 70–81; *Marx/Engels Collected Works,* Vol. 3, 270–282.

———. *Grundrisse: Foundations of the Critique of Political Economy (Rough Draft).* Translated by Martin Nicolaus. New York: Penguin Books, 1973.

———. "Letter to Arnold Ruge." In Marx and Engels, *The Marx-Engels Reader,* 12–15.

———. "On the Jewish Question." In Marx and Engels, *The Marx-Engels Reader,* 26–52; *Marx/Engels Collected Works,* Vol. 3, 146–174.

———. Preface to *A Contribution to the Critique of Political Economy.* In Marx and Engels, *The Marx-Engels Reader,* 3–6; *Marx/Engels Collected Works,* Vol. 29, 261–266.

———. "Private Property and Communism." In Marx and Engels, *The Marx-Engels Reader,* 81–93; *Marx/Engels Collected Works,* Vol. 3, 293–305.

———. "Theses on Feuerbach." In Marx and Engels, *The Marx-Engels Reader,* 143–145; *Marx/Engels Collected Works,* Vol. 5, 3–5.

Marx, Karl, and Friedrich Engels. *German Ideology.* In Marx and Engels, *The Marx-Engels Reader,* 146–200; *Marx/Engels Collected Works,* Vol. 5, 19–539.

———. *Manifesto of the Communist Party.* In Marx and Engels, *The Marx-Engels Reader,* 469–500; *Marx/Engels Collected Works,* Vol. 6, 477–519.

————. *Marx/Engels Collected Works*. Vol. 3. New York: International Publishers, 1975.

————. *Marx/Engels Collected Works*. Vol. 5. New York: International Publishers, 1976.

————. *Marx/Engels Collected Works*. Vol. 6. New York: International Publishers, 1976.

————. *Marx/Engels Collected Works*. Vol. 11. New York: International Publishers, 1979.

————. *Marx/Engels Collected Works*. Vol. 22. New York: International Publishers, 1986.

————. *Marx/Engels Collected Works*. Vol. 24. New York: International Publishers, 1989.

————. *Marx/Engels Collected Works*. Vol. 25. New York: International Publishers, 1987.

————. *Marx/Engels Collected Works*. Vol. 29. New York: International Publishers, 1987.

————. *Marx/Engels Collected Works*. Vol. 49. New York: International Publishers, 2001.

————. *The Marx-Engels Reader*. 2nd ed. Edited by Robert C. Tucker. New York: W. W. Norton and Company, 1978.

Matthews, Nancy A. *Confronting Rape: The Feminist Anti-Rape Movement and the State*. New York: Routledge, 1994.

McAlister, Lyle N. *Spain and Portugal in the New World, 1492–1700*. Minneapolis: University of Minnesota Press, 1984.

McIntosh, Peggy. "White Privilege: Unpacking the Invisible Knapsack." In *White Privilege: Essential Readings on the Other Side of Racism*. Edited by Paula S. Rothenberg, 109–113. New York: Worth Publishers, 2005.

Mead, George Herbert. *Mind, Self, and Society: From the Standpoint of a Social Behaviorist, Works of George Herbert Mead*. Edited by Charles W. Morris. Vol. 1. Chicago: University of Chicago Press, 1962.

Meek, Ronald L. *Social Science and the Ignoble Savage*. Cambridge: Cambridge University Press, 1976.

Mees, Patricia. "The Ripple Effect of Title IX on Women's Health Issues: Treating an Increasingly Active Population." *Physician and Sports Medicine* 31, no. 4 (2003): 21–23.

Memmi, Albert. *The Colonizer and the Colonized*. Boston: Beacon Press, 1965.

Mendieta, Eduardo. "Geography Is to History as Woman Is to Man: Kant on Sex, Race, and Geography." In *Reading Kant's Geography*. Edited by Stuart Elden and Eduardo Mendieta, 345–368. New York: SUNY, 2011.

Merleau-Ponty, Maurice. *Phenomenology of Perception*. Translated by Donald A. Landes. New York: Routledge, 2012.

————. *The Primacy of Perception: And Other Essays on Phenomenological Psychology*. Edited by James M. Edie and translated by William Cobb. Evanston, IL: Northwestern University Press, 1964.

Mies, Maria. *Patriarchy and Accumulation on a World Scale: Women in the International Division of Labor*. London: Zed Books, 2014.

Mikkelsen, Jon M., ed. and trans. *Kant and the Concept of Race: Late Eighteenth-Century Writings*. Albany: SUNY Press, 2013.

Mill, John Stuart. *On Liberty and the Subjection of Women*. Edited by Alan Ryan. New York: Penguin, 2007.

———. *A System of Logic, Ratiocinative and Inductive.* 8th ed. New York: Harper and Brothers, 1882.

Miller, Jean Baker. *Toward a New Psychology of Women.* Boston: Beacon Press, 1986.

Mills, C. Wright. *White Collar: The American Middle Classes.* New York: Oxford University Press, 2002.

Mills, Charles W. "Kant's *Untermenschen.*" In *Race and Racism in Modern Philosophy.* Edited by Andrew Valls, 169–193. Ithaca, NY: Cornell University Press, 2005.

———. *The Racial Contract.* Ithaca, NY: Cornell University Press, 1997.

Mogul, Joey L., Andrea J. Ritchie, and Kay Whitlock. *Queer (In)Justice: The Criminalization of LGBT People in the United States.* Boston: Beacon Books, 2011.

Mohanty, Chandra Talpade. *Feminism without Borders: Decolonizing Theory, Practicing Solidarity.* Durham, NC: Duke University Press, 2003.

Montesquieu, Charles de. *The Spirit of the Laws.* Edited and translated by Anne M. Cohler, Basia C. Miller, and Harold S. Stone. New York: Cambridge University Press, 1989.

Morton, Donald, ed. *The Material Queer: A LesBiGay Cultural Studies Reader.* Boulder, CO: Westview Press, 1996.

Mueller-Vollmer, Kurt, ed. *The Hermeneutics Reader: Texts of the German Tradition from the Enlightenment to the Present.* New York: Continuum, 1988.

Muldoon, James. *The Americas in the Spanish World Order: The Justification for Conquest in the Seventeenth Century.* Philadelphia: University of Pennsylvania Press, 1994.

———, ed. *The Expansion of Europe: The First Phase.* Philadelphia: University of Pennsylvania Press, 1977.

Nicholson, Linda. "Gender." In *A Companion to Feminist Philosophy.* Edited by Alison Jaggar and Iris Marion Young, 289–297. Malden, MA: Blackwell, 1998.

Nicholson, Linda, and Nancy Fraser. "Social Criticism without Philosophy: An Encounter between Feminism and Postmodernism." In *Feminism/Postmodernism.* Edited by Linda J. Nicholson, 19–38. New York: Routledge, 1990.

Norton, Rictor. *A Critique of Social Constructionism and Postmodern Queer Theory,* June 1, 2002, expanded July 11, 2002, onward, updated June 19, 2008. www.rictornorton.co.uk/extracts.htm.

Nussbaum, Martha. "Objectification." *Philosophy and Public Affairs* 24, no. 4 (1995): 249–291.

Oliver, Kelly. *Witnessing: Beyond Recognition.* Minneapolis: University of Minnesota Press, 2001.

Omi, Michael, and Howard Winant. *Racial Formation in the United States: From the 1960s to the 1990s.* 2nd ed. New York: Routledge, 1994.

Ormiston, Gayle L., and Alan D. Schrift, eds. *The Hermeneutic Tradition: From Ast to Ricoeur.* New York: SUNY Press, 1990.

Pagden, Anthony. *The Fall of Natural Man: The American Indian and the Origins of Comparative Ethnology.* Cambridge: Cambridge University Press, 1986.

———. *Lords of All the World: Ideologies of Empire in Spain, Britain and France c. 1500–c. 1800*. New Haven: Yale University Press, 1995.

Pappas, Robin, and William Cowling. "Toward a Critical Hermeneutics." In *Feminist Interpretations of Hans-Georg Gadamer*. Edited by Lorraine Code, 203–227. University Park: Pennsylvania State University Press, 2003.

Paterson, Kevin, and Bill Hughs. "Disability Studies and Phenomenology: The Carnal Politics of Everyday Life." *Disability and Society* 14, no. 5 (1999): 597–610.

Perelman, Michael. *The Invention of Capitalism: Classical Political Economy and the Secret History of Primitive Accumulation*. Durham, NC: Duke University Press, 2000.

Plato. *Complete Works*. Edited by John M. Cooper and D. S. Hutchinson. Indianapolis: Hackett, 1997.

———. *Republic*. In Cooper and Hutchinson, *Complete Works*, 971–1223.

———. *Theatetus*. In Cooper and Hutchinson, *Complete Works*, 157–234.

Polanyi, Karl. *The Great Transformation: The Political and Economic Origins of Our Time*. New York: Beacon, 2001 [1944].

Queer Nation Manifesto. "Queers Read This" distributed at the New York Gay Pride Day parade, 1990. www.historyisaweapon.com/defcon1/queernation.html.

Rabinow, Paul, and William M. Sullivan. "The Interpretive Turn." In *Interpretive Social Science: A Second Look*. Edited by Paul Rabinow and William M. Sullivan, 1–30. Berkeley: University of California Press, 1987.

Rancière, Jacques. *The Emancipated Spectator*. Translated by Gregory Elliott. New York: Verso, 2009.

Reis, Elizabeth. "Impossible Hermaphrodites: Intersex in America, 1620–1960." *Journal of American History* 92, no. 2 (Sept. 2005): 411–441.

Rich, Adrienne. *Blood, Bread and Poetry: Selected Prose, 1979–1985*. New York: Norton, 1986.

———. "Compulsory Heterosexuality and Lesbian Existence." *Signs* 5, no. 4 (Summer 1980): 631–660.

Robinson, Cedric J. *Black Marxism: The Making of the Black Radical Tradition*. London: Zed Press, 1983.

Roediger, David R. *The Wages of Whiteness: Race and the Making of the American Working Class*. New York: Verso, 2007.

Ross, Andrew. *Creditocracy and the Case for Debt Refusal*. New York: OR Books, 2013.

Rubin, Gayle. "Thinking Sex: Notes for a Radical Theory of the Politics of Sexuality." In *The Lesbian and Gay Studies Reader*. Edited by Henry Abelove, Michèle Aina Barale, and David M. Halperin, 3–44. New York: Routledge, 1994.

———. "The Traffic in Women: Notes on the 'Political Economy' of Sex." In *Toward an Anthropology of Women*. Edited by Rayna Reiter, 157–210. New York: Monthly Review Press, 1975.

Russel, Bertand. *History of Western Philosophy*. London: Routledge, 1996.

Rutherford, Donald. "Innovation and Orthodoxy in Early Modern Philosophy." In *The Cambridge Companion to Early Modern Philosophy*. Edited by Donald Rutherford, 11–38. New York: Cambridge University Press, 2006.

Said, Edward. *Orientalism*. New York: Penguin, 2003.

Sartre, Jean-Paul. *Anti-Semite and Jew: An Exploration of the Etiology of Hate*. Translated by George J. Becker. New York: Schocken, 1995.

———. *Being and Nothingness: An Essay on Phenomenological Ontology*. Translated by Hazel E. Barnes. New York: First Washington Square Press, 1992 [1943].

———. *Search for a Method*. Translated by Hazel E. Barnes. New York: Vintage, 1968.

———. *The Transcendence of the Ego: An Existentialist Theory of Consciousness*. Translated by Forrest Williams and Robert Kirkpatrick. New York: Hill and Wang, 1991.

Schleiermacher, Friedrich. *Hermeneutics and Criticism: And Other Writings*. Edited and translated by Andrew Bowie. New York: Cambridge University Press, 1998.

Schott, Robin. "Whose Home Is It Anyway? A Feminist Response to Gadamer's Hermeneutics." In *Gadamer and Hermeneutics*. Edited by Hugh Silverman, 202–209. New York: Routledge, 1991.

Schütz, Alfred. *The Problem with Social Reality*. Vol. 1 of *Collected Papers*. Edited by Maurice Natanson. The Hague: Martinus Nijhoff, 1962.

Sedgwick, Eve Kosofsky. *The Epistemology of the Closet*. Berkeley: University of California Press, 1990.

Sheth, Falguni A. *Toward a Political Philosophy of Race*. New York: SUNY Press, 2009.

Shiva, Vandana. *Biopiracy: The Plunder of Nature and Knowledge*. Cambridge, MA: South End Press, 1997.

Sitrin, Marina, ed. *Horizontalism: Voices of Popular Power in Argentina*. Oakland: AK Press, 2006.

Skinner, Quentin. *The Foundations of Modern Political Thought*. Vol. 2. Cambridge: Cambridge University Press, 1978.

Smith, Adam. *An Inquiry into the Nature and Causes of the Wealth of Nations*. Vol. 1. Edited by R. H. Campbell and A. S. Skinner. Volume 2 of the *Glasgow Edition of the Works and Correspondence of Adam Smith*. Indianapolis: Liberty Fund, 1981.

Soames, Scott. *Philosophical Analysis in the Twentieth Century: The Dawn of Analysis*. Princeton, NJ: Princeton University Press, 2003.

Sohn-Rethel, Alfred. *Intellectual and Manual Labour: A Critique of Epistemology*. London: Macmillan, 1978.

Sokolowski, Robert. *Introduction to Phenomenology*. New York: Cambridge University Press, 2004.

Stalin, Joseph. "Dialectical and Historical Materialism." In *The Essential Stalin: Major Theoretical Works, 1905–52*. Edited by Bruce Franklin, 300–333. Garden City, NY: Anchor Books, 1972.

Strike Debt. *The Debt Resisters' Operations Manual*. Brooklyn: Common Notions, 2014.

Takaki, Ronald T. *Iron Cages: Race and Culture in Nineteenth-Century America*. New York: Oxford University Press, 2000.

Taylor, Charles. "Interpretation and the Sciences of Man." *Review of Metaphysics* 25, no. 1 (September 1971): 3–51.

———. "The Politics of Recognition." In *Multiculturalism: Examining the Politics of Recognition*. Edited by Amy Gutmann, 25–73. Princeton: Princeton University Press, 1992.

———. *Sources of the Self: The Making of Modern Identity*. Cambridge, MA: Harvard University Press, 1989.

Taylor, F. W. *The Principles of Scientific Management*. New York: Harper and Brothers, 1911.

Thompson, Edward Palmer. *The Poverty of Theory and Other Essays*. In *The Essential E. P. Thompson*. Edited by Dorothy Thompson, 445–480. New York: New Press, 2001.

Tierney, Brian. *The Idea of Natural Rights: Studies on Natural Rights, Natural Law and Church Law 1150–1625*. Atlanta: Scholars Press for Emory University, 1997.

Tocqueville, Alexis de. *Democracy in America*. Vol. 1. New York: Vintage, 1990.

Truth, Sojourner. *Narrative of Sojourner Truth*. New York: Penguin, 1998.

Tuck, Richard. *Natural Rights Theories: Their Origin and Development*. New York: Cambridge University Press, 1979.

———. *The Rights of War and Peace: Political Thought and the International Order from Grotius to Kant*. New York: Oxford University Press, 1999.

Tully, James. *An Approach to Political Philosophy: Locke in Contexts*. Cambridge: Cambridge University Press, 1993.

———. *A Discourse of Property: John Locke and His Adversaries*. Cambridge: Cambridge University Press, 1980.

Tuscano, Alberto. "The Open Secret of Real Abstraction." *Rethinking Marxism* 20, no. 2 (2008): 273–287.

Tyson, Sarah. "Experiments in Responsibility: Pocket Parks, Radical Anti-Violence Work, and the Social Ontology of Safety." *Radical Philosophy Review*, forthcoming.

Uggen, Christopher, Sarah Shannon, and Jeff Manza. "State-Level Estimates of Felon Disenfranchisement in the United States, 2010." A Sentencing Project Report. http://felonvoting.procon.org/sourcefiles/2010_State_Level_Estimates_of_Felon _Disenfranchisement.pdf.

Vattel, Emerich de. *The Law of Nations; or, Principles of the Law of Nature Applied to the Conduct and Affairs of Nations and Sovereigns*. Translated by Joseph Chitty. London: Stevens and Sons, 1834.

Vico, Giambattista. *The First New Science*. Edited and translated by Leon Pompa. New York: Cambridge University Press, 2002.

Vitoria, Francisco de. *Vitoria: Political Writings*. Edited by Anthony Pagden and Jeremy Lawrance. Cambridge: Cambridge University Press, 1991.

Waldron, Jeremy. *God, Locke, and Equality: Christian Foundations in Locke's Political Thought.* Cambridge: Cambridge University Press, 2002.

Wallerstein, Immanuel, Calestous Juma, Evelyn Fox Keller, Jürgen Kocka, Dominique Lecourt, V. Y. Mudimbe, Kinhide Mushakoji, Ilya Prigogine, Peter J. Taylor, and Michel-Rolph Trouillot, eds. *Open the Social Sciences: Report of the Gulbenkian Commission on the Restructuring of the Social Sciences.* Stanford, CA: Stanford University Press, 1996.

Warner, Michael. "Queer and Then." *Chronicle of Higher Education.* January 1, 2012. http://chronicle.com/article/QueerThen-/130161/.

Weber, Max. *Economy and Society: An Outline of Interpretive Sociology.* Edited by Guenther Roth and Claus Wittich. Vol. 1. Berkeley: University of California Press, 1978.

Westfall, Richard S. *The Construction of Modern Science: Mechanisms and Mechanics.* New York: Cambridge University Press, 1977.

Willet, Cynthia. *Maternal Ethics and Other Slave Moralities.* New York: Routledge, 1998.

Williams, Robert A., Jr. *The American Indian in Western Legal Thought: The Discourses of Conquest.* New York: Oxford University Press, 1990.

Wittgenstein, Ludwig. *Philosophical Investigations.* Rev. 4th ed. Translated by G. E. M. Anscombe, P. M. S. Hacker, and Joachim Schulte. Oxford: Blackwell Publishing, 2009.

Wittig, Monique. "One Is Not Born a Woman." In *The Lesbian and Gay Studies Reader.* Edited by Henry Abelove, Michèle Aina Barale, and David M. Halperin, 103–109. New York: Routledge, 1994.

Wood, Allen. "The Marxian Critique of Justice." *Philosophy and Public Affairs* 1, no. 3 (Spring 1972): 244–282.

Wood, Ellen Meiksins. "The Agrarian Origins of Capitalism." In *Hungry for Profit: The Agribusiness Threat to Farmers, Food, and the Environment.* Edited by Fred Magdoff, John Bellamy Foster, and Frederick H. Buttel, 23–42. New York: Monthly Review Press, 2000.

———. *Democracy against Capitalism: Renewing Historical Materialism.* New York: Cambridge University Press, 1995.

———. *Empire of Capital.* London: Verso, 2003.

Wood, Neal. *John Locke and Agrarian Capitalism.* Berkeley: University of California Press, 1984.

Wylie, Alison. "Why Standpoint Matters." In *Science and Other Cultures: Issues in Philosophies of Science and Technology.* Edited by Robert Figueroa and Sandra Harding, 26–48. New York: Routledge, 2003.

Yekani, Elahe Haschemi, Eveline Kilian, and Beatrice Michaelis, eds. *Queer Futures: Reconsidering Ethics, Activism, and the Political.* Burlington, VT: Ashgate, 2013.

Young, Iris Marion. "House and Home: Feminist Variations on a Theme." In *Feminist Interpretations of Heidegger.* Edited by Nancy J. Holland and Patricia Huntington, 252–288. University Park: Pennsylvania State University Press, 2003.

————. *Inclusion and Democracy*. New York: Oxford University Press, 2002.

————. *Justice and the Politics of Difference*. Princeton, NJ: Princeton University Press, 1990.

————. "Throwing Like a Girl: A Phenomenology of Feminine Body Comportment, Motility, and Spatiality." In *On Female Body Experience: "Throwing Like a Girl" and Other Essays*, 27–45. New York: Oxford University Press, 2005.

Zack, Naomi. "Race and Philosophic Meaning." In *Race and Racism*. Edited by Bernard Boxill, 43–57. New York: Oxford University Press, 2001.

Žižek, Slavoj. *Less Than Nothing: Hegel and the Shadow of Dialectical Materialism*. New York: Verso, 2012.

INDEX

Ableism, 16, 70, 77

Abstract individualism, 9, 13

Abstract labor, 60–62

Accumulation: by dispossession, 66–67, 134, 156n81; flexible, 43; primitive, 66–67, 102, 109, 116–118, 169n130

ACT UP (AIDS Coalition to Unleash Power), 78

Adamczak, Bini, 158n96

Adichie, Chimamanda Ngozi, 109

Adorno, Theodor, 10, 12, 21, 35, 39, 134, 179n122, 180n133

Affective labor, 47–48, 93–94

Agamben, Giorgio, 112, 119, 127, 171n17

Agrarian capitalism, 173n46, 174n58

Ahmed, Sara, 85–86

Alcoff, Linda Martín, 18, 28, 85, 148n91, 162n26

Alexander, Michelle, 132

Alienation, 33, 37, 39, 48–51, 53–56, 87, 89–92, 153n29; and commodity fetishism, 56; in Marxism, 50–55, 153n29, 154n37, 165n76; and objectification, 87–88, 90–92; of property, 124; related to affective labor, 48

Alter-globalization movement, 43, 73–74

Althusser, Louis, 170n16

Americans with Disabilities Act, 168n114

Analytic philosophy, 15

Anarchism, 19, 72, 74

Anger, 1–2, 17–18

Anghie, Antony, 175n64

Anthony, Susan B., 167n107

Antidialogue, 87

Antiracism: hermeneutics of race, 110–122; overview, 105–110; whiteness as property, sovereignty, and fetish, 122–134

Anzaldúa, Gloria, 75, 78, 84, 160n8, 166n97

Aquinas, Thomas, 115–116, 123

Arendt, Hannah, 114, 127–128, 138n36

Aristotle, 1, 6–9, 22, 113, 120, 135n3, 137n25, 141n5, 147n77, 168n115; forms of knowing, 7–8; habit, 141n5; laws of classical logic, 147n77; methodology, 22; natural slaves, 181n150; polis (*civitas*), 9; *theōria*, 6–7; understanding of human praxis, 139n61

Ast, Friedrich, 25–26

Aufhebung (sublation), 34

Autonomism, 73; feminist, 73; Marxist, 158n110

Autonomy: and fetish character of white subjectivity, 125–127; in hermeneutics of race, 113–116, 119–120

Ayer, A. J., 139n57

Bacon, Francis, 9–10, 12–13, 113
Bakunin, Mikhail, 72, 158n107
Baldwin, James, 105, 122, 177n86
Balibar, Étienne, 4
Bare life, 112, 119
Bartky, Sandra, 91–92
Beauvoir, Simone de, 33, 39, 75, 80, 82, 85–86, 88, 90, 95; demands of masculinity, 95; dialectical structure of gender and sexuality, 86; gender and sexuality socialization, 85; gender assignment, 82; influence of Hegel's dialectical method, 39; norms of gender and sexuality, 86; objectification, 88–90; phenomenology of body, 33; sex and gender differentiation, 80
Becoming-other, 35
Benjamin, Walter, 123, 126, 181n147
Bernstein, Richard J., 172n34
Biological determinism, 80, 108, 111
Biopiracy, 67
Bio-power, 92, 103
Black Codes, 131–132
Blacks: black feminism, 76–77, 160n10; civil rights struggle, 105–107; hermeneutics of race, 121–122; racial classification of Enlightenment, 111–112. See also Race
Blackstone, William, 98–99, 115
Body: in critical hermeneutics, 28; dysappearance, 33, 84; female, violence against, 101; in historical materialism, 42; Marx's concept of alienation, 54; normalization of gender and sexuality, 79–86; objectification, 89–90; phenomenologies of, 32–33
Bolden, Dorothy, 107–108

Bondage, dialectic of lordship and, 38, 88–89, 120, 128, 179n117
Borderland, 78, 84, 101
Bordo, Susan, 89, 164n67
Bourdieu, Pierre, 18, 78, 141n5, 161n15
Bradwell v. State of Illinois (1873), 97–99
Brecht, Bertolt, 21, 141n9
Bremer, Paul, 67
Brown, Wendy, 99–101, 168n119
Brown v. Board of Education (1954), 131
Buckley v. Valeo (1976), 157n92
Burns, J. H., 174n53
Burwell v. Hobby Lobby, 573 US (2014), 168n114
Butler, Judith, 12, 17, 33, 39, 77, 80–84, 89, 103, 133, 141n5, 147n79, 161n14, 162n30, 162n31, 181n147; gender and sexuality, 77, 80, 103; influence of Hegel's dialectical method, 39; intelligible genders, 83–84; metaphysics of substance, 162n30; othering, 89; performativity, 162n31; popular sovereignty, 133–134; power relations, 17; prediscursive establishment of sex difference, 81–82; queer phenomenology, 33; race, 181n147; sense of nonidentity, 147n79; subordination and subject formation, 12

Capital. See Capitalism
Capital: A Critique of Political Economy (Marx), 41–42, 49, 59, 66, 153n32
Capital accumulation, 48, 63, 66, 68–69, 91. See also Capitalism
Capitalism: agrarian, 173n46, 175n58; alienation, 50–55, 90–91; anticapitalism, 70; communism, 70–74; domination in, 69–70; exchange-value, 58–59; feminist and queer theory, 99–103; fetishism, 55–58; hermeneutics of value, 55–58; historical materialism, 40–44; inequality, production of

in, 65–67; mythology of, 176n71; overview, 46–50; phenomenology of labor, 50–55; post-capitalism, 70–74; subjectivity in, 68–70; surplus value and class conflict, 62–70; undermining of self-sufficiency under, 66–67; use-value, 58; value of labor, 59–62

Cartesian (mind-body) dualism, 10, 31, 99–100

Casey, Edward, 82

Catholic Church, 142n20

Césaire, Aimé, 39, 105

Childbirth, as disability, 168n114

China: communism in, 72; industrialization in, 46–47, 67; urbanization in, 151n4

Chinese, juridical racialization of, 129

Chinese Exclusion Act (1882), 129, 179n131

Cisgender, 80, 82, 86. *See also* Queer politics

Citizens United v. Federal Election Commission (2010), 157n92

Civil Rights Act (1964), 131, 168n114

Civil rights movement, 105–107, 131–132. *See also* Race

Civil society, versus nature, 99–103

Civitas (polis), 9, 101, 127, 138n36

Class conflict, 49–50, 60, 62–63, 68

Class consciousness, 29, 37, 40, 51

Classical logic, laws of, 35, 147n77

Classical philosophical tradition, 5–9

Cleaver, Harry, 158n110

Closed dialectical method, 39

Collective action, orientation toward, 3–4

Collins, Patricia Hill, 20, 84, 137n20, 160n10, 164n62

Colonialism: assertion of sovereignty, 127–128; debates over *dominium*, 173n48; and hermeneutics of race, 109–122

Commodification of affect, 47–48

Commodities: C-M-C formula, 64; commodity values, 153n23; labor power as, 65; M-C-M formula, 64–65; use-value and exchange-value of, 59

Commodity fetishism, 55–58, 125–126

Commodity-Money-Commodity (C-M-C) formula, 64

Communism, 51, 70–74, 170n6

Communist Manifesto (Marx and Engels), 40, 63, 68, 71, 110

Compulsory heterosexuality, 78, 95

Comte, Auguste, 14

Concrete labor, 60–61

Conflict theory, 19, 39

Conquest, 139n52

Consciousness: class, 29, 37, 40, 51; double, 87–89; false, 96; in Hegel's dialectics, 35–36; historically effected, 87; intentionality of, 31; in Marxism, 52–53; phenomenology as study of that which appears to, 30–31; of self, 35–36, 147n87

Contemplative notion of philosophy, 3, 6–7

Contradiction, 34, 53–54

Controlling images, 84

Cooke, Maeve, 144n39

Copernican Revolution of Kant, 143n23

Corporate personhood, 69–70, 157n92

Crenshaw, Kimberlé, 159n5

Criminal justice system, 132

Critical methodology: dialectics, 33–40; hermeneutics, 24–28, 77–78; materialism, 40–45; overview, 20–24; phenomenology, 30–33; standpoint method, 28–30

Critical resistance, 4–6, 104. *See also* Critical methodology

Critical social theory, 3–4, 6

Cultural hegemony, 94, 96, 130–131, 179n117

Cultural imperialism, 87, 130–131

Dalla Costa, Maria, 73

Dalton, Harlon, 108

Daly, Chris, 139n58

Dasein, 26
Davis, Angela, 19, 102–103, 167n113, 168n121, 180n145
Debt, 44–45
Deductive method, 10
Deindustrialization, 43–44, 47
Deleuze, Gilles, 148n95
Dependency of women, 98–99
Deployment of sexuality, 103–104
Derrida, Jacques, 126, 148n95
Descartes, René, 9–10, 113, 138n43
Desires, management of, 84–85
Determination. *See* Self-determination
Determinism, biological, 80, 108, 111
Dewey, John, 21, 37, 141n5
Dialectic of Enlightenment, 109
Dialectic of immanence and transcendence: communism, 71; defined, 21; feminist and queer theory, 92; relation of theory and praxis, 35, 39–40
Dialectic of lordship and bondage, 38, 88–89, 120, 128
Dialectic of negativity, 50
Dialectical theater, 21
Dialectics (*dialektikē tekhnē*): of gender and sexuality, 86–89, 93–94; hermeneutics of race, 110; historical materialism, 40–43; Marx's analysis of class conflict, 62; Marx's concept of alienation, 53–54; mutual recognition, 34–39; overview, 33–35; relation of theory and praxis, 39–40
Dialogue, 159n114
Dictatorship: association of Marxist communism with, 71–72; of proletariat, 72; racial, 127–128
Difference, radical philosophy as embracing, 5
Dilthey, Wilhelm, 25–26, 30, 143n28
Disability: critical phenomenology, 33; pregnancy and childbirth treated as, 168n114

Disciplinary power, 91–92
Dispossession, 66–67
Dissident intellectuals, 136n16
Division of labor: and commodity fetishism, 57; gendered, 101–102, 107; in historical materialism, 42–43; labor theory of value, 60–62
Domination: and assertion of sovereignty, 126–128; in capitalism, 69–70; in function of wife, 99; gender and sexual identities produced through, 103–104; in Hegel's dialectics, 36–38; Hitler's idea of right to dominate, 178n106; and objectification, 86–92; role in masculinity, 94–95. *See also* White supremacy
Dominium, 12, 115–119, 123–124, 127, 173n48, 177n100; and colonialism, 117–118; defined, 115; self-, 114–116, 118, 123; Spanish debates over, 173n48; and whiteness, 123–124, 127, 177n100
Double consciousness, 87–89
Douglass, Frederick, 19, 127–128, 160n7
Dred Scott v. Sandford (1857), 97–98, 121–122, 128
Du Bois, W. E. B., 69, 87–88, 106, 131, 170n6, 180n142; color-line as problem of Twentieth Century, 106; death of, 170n6; double consciousness, 87–88; incarceration of blacks, 180n142; white privilege, 69, 131
Dualism, Cartesian, 10, 31, 99–100
Dyer, Richard, 106
Dys-appearance, 33, 84

Economic means, production of inequality by, 68–69
Economy, in feminist and queer theory, 101–102
Emancipatory intent: feminist and queer theory, 92; radical philosophy, 4–5, 16–19

Embodiment, 19, 25, 28, 32–33, 54–55, 85, 89–90, 101, 167n113, 168n119
Enclosure, 66–67
Encomienda system, 116
Engels, Friedrich, 13, 40–43, 61–64, 68, 70–73, 101–102, 155n61, 158n97; class conflict, 63, 68; communication technologies, 61; communism, 70–73; discussion of ideology, 130; family as private service, 101–102; historical materialism, 40–43; naturalization, 102; scientific method, 13; unpaid labor, 64; utopian versus scientific, 158n97
Enlightenment: general discussion, 9–11; hermeneutics of race, 109–120
Epic theater, 21, 141n9
Epistēmē (knowledge of universals), 7, 25, 142n16
Epistemology: inverted, 130; of ignorance, 130, 134; overview, 23; social, 28–29
Epochē, 31
Equal Employment Opportunity Commission, US, 168n114
Estrangement effect (*Verfremdungseffekt*), 21, 141n9
Ethnicity, 76, 108, 160n9, 181n147
European colonialism. *See* Colonialism
Exchange-value, 42, 58–59, 64–65
Excluded middle, law of, 147n77
Existential phenomenology, 30, 32–33
Existentiale, 143n30
Externalization, 50–54, 144n38
Extra-economic means, production of inequality by, 66–68
Extra-juridical nonwhite racialization, 129–130
Extra-legal violence, 101, 129
EZLN (Zapatista National Liberation Army), 44, 73

False consciousness, 96
Family wage, 43, 107

Fanon, Frantz, 33, 39, 90
Federici, Silvia, 73, 169n130
Femininity, 82–83. *See also* Gender
Feminism: autonomist, 73; black, 76–77, 160n10; bodies, performance, and normalization, 79–86; law, patriarchy, and labor, 97–104; masculinity, 92–96; objectification, 86–92; overview, 75–79; violence associated with masculinity and heterosexuality, 94–97
Feminist standpoint theory, 29–30
Ferguson, Roderick, 161n21
Fetish, whiteness as, 122–134, 178n104
Fetishism, commodity, 55–58, 125–126
Fichte, Johann Gottlieb, 30
Fifteenth Amendment, 167n107
Finance capital, 56
Financialization, 44–45, 63
Flexible accumulation, 43
Force, in Hegel's dialectics, 37
Forced labor, 67–68, 132
Forces of production, 41–44. *See also* Means of production
Fordism, 43, 150n115
Foucault, Michel: accumulation of knowledge, 150n112; adversarial stance, 88; bio-power, 92, 103; conflict theory, 19; deployment of sexuality, 103–104; disciplinary power, 91–92; knowledge and power relations, 6; regimes of truth, 140n66; resistance to gender oppression, 94; specific intellectuals, 136n16; war, 166n91
Fourteenth Amendment, 97–98, 157n92
Foxconn, 46–48, 67, 152n6
Franciscans, 115
Franklin, Benjamin, 59–60, 127
Fraser, Nancy, 6, 40
Freedom: feminist and queer theory, 100–101; in hermeneutics of race, 112–116, 119; in historical materialism, 42; individual, dialectic of, 34–39; in Marxism, 51, 73;

Freedom *(continued)*
and popular sovereignty, 127–128; as sovereignty, 109
Freire, Paulo, 40, 87, 91, 139n52, 149n103, 159n114; alienation, 91; antidialogue, 87; conquest, 139n52; dialogue, 159n114; historical materialism, 40; pedagogy of oppressed, 149n103
Fusion of horizons, 27

Gadamer, Hans-Georg, 22, 26–28, 87
Gage, Frances D., 159n3
Galilei, Galileo, 9, 32
Gay politics. *See* Queer politics
Geduldig v. Aiello, 417 US 484 (1974), 168n114
Geist (spirit), 25, 38
Gender: and civil rights struggle, 107; differentiation between sex and, 80–81; division of labor, 101–102; historical nature of, 77–78; intelligible, 83–84, 89; intersectionality of sexuality and, 79; masculinity, 92–96; norms of, 84–85; oppression, 92–97; prediscursive establishment of sex difference, 81–82, 103; social structure of, 77–78; socialization, 84–85. *See also* Feminism; Queer politics
Gender assignment, 80, 82
General formula of capital, 64–65
Genovese, Eugene D., 179n117
The German Ideology (Marx and Engels), 102, 130
Giddings, Paula, 76
Gilroy, Paul, 109
Gitmo, 133
Globalization, 43–44
Goldman, Emma, 158n108
Gramsci, Antonio, 43, 94, 136n16
Grotius, Hugo, 117

Habermas, Jürgen, 7–8, 27–28, 144n38
Habit, 17–19, 20–21, 26–27, 30, 32, 37, 38, 79–80, 86, 89, 92–93, 103, 113, 141n5
Habitus, 18
Haitian slave revolt, 38
Hall, George, 129
Haraway, Donna, 28–29, 145n45
Harding, Sandra, 29
Hardt, Michael, 47, 155n63
Harris, Cheryl I., 124–125, 177n100, 178n104, 181n149
Hartsock, Nancy, 29–30
Harvey, David, 43, 67, 150n115, 151n4
Health care, 49, 158n94, 168n114
Hegel, Georg Wilhelm Friedrich, 17, 30, 33–39, 50–51, 53, 88–89, 100, 120–121, 128, 141n5, 147n71, 147n75, 147n87, 148n91, 148n95, 153n22, 168n118, 176n80, 177n88; dialectic of lordship and bondage, 38, 88–89, 120, 128; dialectical method, 33–40; habit, 141n5; hermeneutics of race, 121; human self-consciousness, 147n87; influence on Marx, 50–51; labor of the negative, 17; Marx's comments on *Phenomenology,* 152n21; phenomenology, 30; postmodern critiques of, 148n95; sphinx, 100–101; subject and substance, 153n22; views on philosophy, 147n75
Hegemony, 94, 96, 130–131, 179n117
Heidegger, Martin, 26–27, 32, 143n30
Hennessy, Rosemary, 95, 104
Hermeneutic circle, 25–26, 34
Hermeneutics: of feminist and queer projects, 77–78; general discussion, 24–28; of race, 110–122. *See also* Value hermeneutics
Herrenrecht (right to dominate), 178n106
Heteronomy, 114
Heteronormativity: gender and sexuality

socialization, 84–85; and queer politics, 78–79; and radical feminism, 76–77

Heterosexuality: compulsory, 78, 95; as social system, 96; violence associated with, 94–97

Hierarchical nature of race, 18, 28, 78, 108–109, 112, 125, 132, 170n14

Hierarchy of oppression, 76–77

Hispanics, juridical racialization of, 130

Historical materialism: class conflict, 62–63; commodity fetishism, 57; communism, 70–71; general discussion, 40–44. See also Marx, Karl

Historical methods. See Critical methodology

Historically effected consciousness, 27, 87

Historicism, 30

Hitler, Adolf, 178n106

Hobbes, Thomas, 8–9, 11–12

Hochschild, Arlie, 47

Holloway, John, 1, 56

Homo sacer, 112

Homophobia, 95. See also Queer politics

Homosexuality, 103. See also Queer politics

Honneth, Axel, 40, 137n18, 144n38, 148n93

hooks, bell, 2, 69, 104, 159n5, 168n120

Horizons, fusion of, 27

Horizontalism, 4, 38, 73–74, 142n18, 159n114

Horkheimer, Max, 10, 12, 134, 138n46, 140n65, 179n122

Howe, Julia Ward, 167n107

Hughs, Bill, 33

Hume, David, 111–112, 176n76

Husserl, Edmund, 15, 30–32, 52–53

Ideal speech situation, 27–28

Identity, law of, 35

Ideology, 130–131, 157n91, 171n16

Illyricus, Matthias Flacius, 142n20

Immanence, and self-relation of objectification, 90

Immanence and transcendence, dialectic of: communism, 71; defined, 21; feminist and queer theory, 92; relation of theory and praxis, 35, 39–40

Immanent potential, 21, 40–41, 71, 92

Immigrants, undocumented, 133

Imperialism: cultural, 87, 130–131; military, 67–68

Incarceration (prisons), 3, 19, 67–68, 94, 101, 130, 132–133, 180n144

Individual freedom, dialectic of, 34–39

Individualism: abstract, 9, 13; possessive, 65–66, 68–69, 115

Inductive scientific reasoning, 10

Industrialization, 46–47, 67

Inequality, production of in capitalism, 65–67

Intellectuals, 136n16

Intelligible genders, 83–84, 89

Intentionality: of consciousness, 31; inhibited, 83

Interdependency: in Hegel's dialectics, 36–37; prefigurative, 5

Interdisciplinary component of radical philosophy, 5

Internalization, reflective, 52

International Working Men's Association, 158n107

Interpretation, 24–26, 143n28, 143n35; interpretive horizon, 28; interpretive method, 15–16

Intersectionality (intersectionalist theory): antiviolence work, 97; need for, 93; overview, 159n5; queer politics, 78–79; radical feminism, 76–77

Intersexed bodies, 80

Intersubjectivity, 32, 52, 69, 90, 114, 125

Iraq, invasion of, 67, 133

Jagose, Annamarie, 166n103
James, William, 20, 141n3, 141n5
Jameson, Fredric, 44
Jefferson, Thomas, 118–119, 123
Jim Crow laws, 130–132
Juridical discourse in political science, 12
Juridical racialization, 129–130

Kant, Immanuel, 8, 11, 20, 25, 30,
    111–114, 119–120, 122, 137n33,
    143n23; autonomy, 114; Copernican
    Revolution, 143n23; freedom as
    sovereignty, 119; habit, 20; marriage,
    11; phenomenology, 30; *poiēsis,* 8;
    reason, 113; transcendental subject,
    25; universal knowledge, 25; unsocial
    sociability, 119–120; white supremacy,
    111–112, 122
Kautzer, Chad, 177n94, 180n145
Kepler, Johannes, 9
Kimmel, Michael, 94–96
King, Coretta Scott, 107
King, Dr. Martin Luther, Jr., 106–107,
    170n6
Klein, Naomi, 67
Knowledge: historical evolution of
    concept, 7–9; knowledge interests,
    144n38; perspectival, 28–30;
    production of, in radical philosophy,
    6; in standpoint method, 28–30;
    situated, 28–30; subjugated, 5;
    subordinate, 145n48
Kristeva, Julia, 136n16

Labor: abstract, 60–62; affective, 47–48,
    93–94; concrete, 60–61; division of,
    42–43, 57, 60–62, 101–102, 107;
    forced, 67–68, 132; in historical
    materialism, 42–43; law, patriarchy
    and, 97–104; Marxist phenomenology
    of, 50–55; of the negative, 17;
    objectification of, 52–53; organized,
    68; power, 64–66, 91; value of,

in Marxism, 59–62; wage-labor,
    42–43, 64, 101–102, 107. *See also*
    Reproductive labor
Labor theory of property, 117
Labor theory of value, 59–62
Langton, Rae, 165n71
Language, in hermeneutics, 24, 27–28
Las Casas, Bartolomé de, 173n48
Latinos, juridical racialization of, 130
Law: and assertion of sovereignty, 126–
    127; of classical logic, 35, 147n77;
    patriarchy, and labor, 97–104; violence
    beyond, 96
Law of excluded middle, 147n77
Law of identity, 35
Law of non-contradiction, 147n77
Law of value, 60–62
Lawlessness, 127, 131, 133–134, 176n78
Lazzarato, Maurizio, 45
Lebenswelt, 32
Lefebvre, Henri, 42
Legal personhood, 11–12, 39, 68–70,
    157n92
Lenin, Vladimir, 72–73, 158n105
Lerner, Gerda, 164n58
LGBTQ (lesbian, gay, bisexual,
    transgender, and queer), 78. *See also*
    Queer politics
Liberalism, 99–103
Life-world, 32
Lipsitz, George, 123, 131
Locke, John, 59, 113–119, 123–124,
    132, 174n49, 174n51, 174n52,
    174n56, 175n58, 175n60, 175n61,
    178n102; agrarian capitalism, 175n58;
    colonialism, 116–118; entailment of
    freedom as sovereignty, 119; influence
    on international law, 175n61; labor
    theory of value, 59–60; natural law,
    174n52, 174n56; property, 123–124,
    178n102; reason, 113; state of nature,
    116–119, 174n49, 174n51
Loick, Daniel, 179n121

Lorde, Audre, 1, 5, 17, 76, 134, 160n9
Lordship and bondage, dialectic of, 38, 88–89, 120, 128
Lucy, Bill, 170n7
Lukács, Georg, 23, 40–41, 56, 81, 90–91, 153n25; alienation, 90–91; commodities, 55–56; dialectics, 40; historical materialism, 41; methodology, 23; prediscursive foundations, 81–82
Luther, Martin, 142n20
Luxemburg, Rosa, 46, 66, 73, 158n109
Lyotard, Jean-François, 148n95, 150n119

MacIntyre, Alasdair, 139n61, 180n133
MacKinnon, Catharine, 86, 90, 165n75
Macpherson, C. B., 65, 114–115
Magnuson Act of 1943, 179n131
Mahler, Matthew, 96
March on Washington for Jobs and Justice, 106
Marcuse, Herbert, 20
Marx, Karl, 149n110, 155n63; alienation, 50–55, 90–91, 154n37, 165n76; anti-philosophy, 4; autonomist Marxism, 158n110; capitalist mythology, 176n71; commodities, 153n32, 154n41; commodity values, 153n23; communism, 70–74; critical philosophy as self-clarification, 21; dialectical logic, 34, 37, 39–40; discussion of ideology, 130; exchange-value, 58–59; fetishism, 55–58, 125–126; on Hegel's *Phenomenology*, 152n21; hermeneutics of value, 55–58; historical materialism, 40–43; knowledge interests, 144n38; naturalization, 102; overview, 46–50; phenomenology of labor, 50–55; post-capitalism, 70–74; process creating capital-relation, 156n72; rights,

156n88, 157n91; surplus value and class conflict, 62–70; use-value, 58; utopian versus scientific, 158n97; value of labor, 59–62
Masculinity: as form of rule, 100; general discussion, 92–96; violence associated with, 94–97. *See also* Feminism; Patriarchy
Mass production, 43, 150n115
Master-slave dialectic, 36–37, 136n16, 168n120
Materialism: class conflict, 62–63; communism, 70–71; general discussion, 40–45
McIntosh, Peggy, 109
M-C-M (Money-Commodity-Money) formula, 64–65, 155n70
Means of production: capitalism, 54–55, 63–65; cultural imperialism, 130–131; dispossessing, 66; materialism, 41–44; Paris Commune, 71; Soviet Union, 72
Mechanistic philosophy, 10–11, 139n61
Mediation, 34–36, 88, 149n95, 153n22
Mees, Patricia, 163n50
Memmi, Albert, 118
Mendieta, Eduardo, 171n25, 180n145
Merchant's capital, 155n70
Merleau-Ponty, Maurice, 33, 54, 79, 83, 86, 141n5, 146n68, 162n22; alienation, 54; bodily schema, 146n68; body, 33, 79, 83, 86, 162n22
Metaphysics, 23, 31, 142n17, 162n30
Methods/methodology, 4, 10, 20–24. *See also* Critical methodology
Militarized police forces, 180n145
Mill, John Stuart, 92–94, 143n28, 165n85, 165n86
Miller, Jean Baker, 145n48
Mills, C. Wright, 47, 152n13
Mills, Charles W., 112, 130
Mind-body (Cartesian) dualism, 10, 31, 99–100
Mitsein, 88–89

Mode of production, 41
Mohanty, Chandra Talpade, 41, 88, 160n9
Money-Commodity-Money (M-C-M) formula, 64–65, 155n70
Montesquieu, Charles de, 110–112, 121
Multiculturalism, 108
Multiracial class struggle, 106–107
Mutual (or social) recognition, 34–39, 51, 53, 70, 73, 80, 89, 90, 106, 114, 125, 144n38, 148n93, 177n80

National Coalition of Anti-Violence Programs, 97
National Domestic Workers Union, 107
Natural law, 116–117, 119, 134, 174n56
Natural right to property, 116–118
Natural sciences, 9–16
Natural slaves, 181n150
Nature: and sovereignty, 12; state of, 12, 101, 116–119, 132,174n49, 174n51
Negation, 34, 37–38
Negative dialectics, 39
Negri, Antonio, 47, 155n63
Neoliberalism, 43–44
New Deal, 63, 68
Nicholson, Linda, 160n11, 161n16
Nicomachean Ethics (Aristotle), 22, 137n25, 141n5
Nomothetic science, 13–14
Non-contradiction, law of, 147n77
Noncriminal violence, 101, 109, 129
Nonidentity, 21, 34–39, 87, 94, 147n79
Nussbaum, Martha, 165n71

Objectification: in feminist and queer theory, 86–92; forms of, 165n71; of labor, 52–53; of self, 83; of subjects, 11–13
Objectivity: othering, objectification and, 90; in phenomenology of Husserl, 32; in philosophy of Descartes, 10; in positivism, 14

Occupy Wall Street, 45, 63, 74
Ockham, William of, 115
Oikos (household), 101, 138n36
Omi, Michael, 19
Open dialectical method, 39
Open Marxism, 73
Opposition, and concept of alienation, 53–54
Oppression: forms of, 136n14; gender, 92–97; intersectionality of privilege and, 76–77; pedagogy of oppressed, 40, 149n103. See also Domination
Organic intellectuals, 136n16
Organized labor, 68
Othering, 16, 35–38, 48, 75, 78, 79, 84, 86–90, 95, 114, 119–120, 125, 128, 134, 153n22, 160n8

Paris Commune, 71
Passeron, Jean-Claude, 161n15
Paterfamilias, 127, 178n112
Paterson, Kevin, 33
Patriarchy: and assertion of sovereignty, 127; and civil rights struggle, 107; link to law and labor, 97–104; Mill's critique of, 92–94; and other structures of domination, 69. See also Feminism
Pedagogy of oppressed, 40, 149n103
People v. Hall (1854), 129
Perelman, Michael, 66
Performativity, 85–86, 162n31
Personality market, 47–48
Personhood: corporate, 69–70, 157n92; and European colonialism, 118; legal, 11–12; in Locke's labor theory of property, 117; subpersonhood, 112, 125
Perspectival knowledge, 28–30
Phenomenological reduction, 31, 52
Phenomenology: appearance in, 31; existential, 30, 32–33; of femininity, 82; feminist and queer theory, 79–86;

general discussion, 30–33; Hegel's dialectical method, 33–40; of labor, Marxist, 50–55; transcendental, 30–32

Phenomenology of Spirit (Hegel), 34–35, 50, 147n75, 148n91, 152n21, 153n22

Philosophy: analytic, 15; classical tradition, 5–9; defined, 3; influence of scientific revolution on, 14–15; methods of, 139n58. *See also* Radical philosophy

Phronēsis (practical knowledge), 7–9, 11, 17, 22–23, 27, 49

Picture-thinking, law of identity as, 35

Plato, 1, 3, 10, 23, 33, 135n3, 142n16

Plessy v. Ferguson (1896), 131

Pluralistic component of radical philosophy, 5

Poiēsis (productive or technical knowledge), 7–9, 11, 49–50

Polanyi, Karl, 66

Police forces, militarized, 180n145

Polis (*civitas*), 9, 101, 127, 138n36

Political economy, 53

Political science, 11–13

Politics, historical evolution of concept, 7–9

Poor People's Campaign, 106–107

Positive dialectical method, 39

Positivism: Hegel's view of, 35; overview, 14; and phenomenology of Husserl, 32; resistance to, 15–16

Possessive individualism, 65–66, 68–69, 115

Post-capitalism, 70–74

Postcolonial feminism, 77

Postmodernism, 44, 148n95, 150n119

Power: to exert symbolic violence, 161n15; Hume's viewpoint on, 176n76; in radical philosophy, 6, 17. *See also* Domination; Oppression; White supremacy

Practical interests, 6–7, 144n38

Practical knowledge. *See Phronēsis*

Practical means, in radical philosophy, 4

Praxis: and alienation, 50–51; dialectic of immanence and transcendence, 39–40; Marxism, 49–53, 153n22; and objectification, 91; in phenomenology of Husserl, 32; in radical philosophy, 4–5, 16–19; transition from Aristotelian to mechanist view, 139n61

Prediscursive foundations, 81–82, 103

Prefigurative politics, 5, 73

Pregnancy as disability, 167n114

Pregnancy Discrimination Act (1978), 167n114

Prejudices, in Gadamer's philosophy, 27

Primitive accumulation, 66–67, 116, 118, 169n130

Prisons. *See* Incarceration

Private work, and gendered division of labor, 101–102

Privatization of public resources, 67

Privilege: intersectionality of oppression and, 76–77; mainstream discourses about gender and sexuality, 78. *See also* White privilege

Privileges or Immunities Clause, Fourteenth Amendment, 97–98

Production: forces of, 41–44; in historical materialism, 41–42; of knowledge, in radical philosophy, 6; labor theory of value, 60–61; mass, 43, 150n115; mode of, 41; relations of, 41; surplus value and class conflict, 63–64. *See also* Means of production

Productive knowledge. *See Poiēsis*

Proletariat, dictatorship of, 72

Property: alienability of, 124; hermeneutics of race, 115–119; whiteness as, 122–134

Protestant Reformation, 24

Psychological wage, 69

Public work, and gendered division of labor, 101–102

Punctual self, 113, 116–117, 172n35

Punishment: slavery as, 132; for violations of laws of nature, 117–118

Queer, defined, 78
Queer Nation Manifesto, 78
Queer of color critique, 161n21
Queer phenomenology, 33
Queer politics: bodies, performance, and normalization, 79–86; law, patriarchy, and labor, 97–104; masculinity, 92–96; objectification, 86–92; overview, 75–79; violence associated with masculinity and heterosexuality, 94–97. See also Sexuality
Queergender, 80
Quine, Willard V. O., 15

Race: hermeneutics of, 110–122; hierarchical nature of, 109; overview, 105–110; queer of color critique, 161n21; science of, 107–108; whiteness as property, sovereignty, and fetish, 122–134
Racial segregation, 131
Racism, structural, 69
Radical (radix), 2–3
Radical philosophy: antiviolence work, 97; and classical philosophical tradition, 5–9; conflict theory, 19; defined, 2–4; emancipatory praxis, 4–5, 16–19; overview, 1–2; pluralistic and interdisciplinary component of, 5; and scientific revolution, 9–16
Rage, 1–2, 17–18
Rancière, Jacques, 141n9
Rape, 101; Rape Crisis Centers, 97; spousal rape, 101
Real abstraction, 155n59
Reason, 112–115, 172n34
Recognition, 34–39, 90, 106, 148n93, 177n80
Reconciliation, 34, 51
Reconstruction, 131–132
Reduction, phenomenological, 31, 52

Reflective internalization, 52
Reflexive method, 15–16. See also Critical methodology
Reformation, Protestant, 24
Reification, 90–91, 178n104
Relations of production, 41
Reproductive labor: autonomist feminist critiques of, 73; as class oppression, 94; family wage, 107; gendered division of labor, 43, 101–102; Marx's exclusion of, 64; use-values, 42
Resistance: and the body, 86, 88; critical, 1–2, 4–5, 17–18, 40–41, 68, 73, 78; dialectic of immanence and transcendence, 71, 92; to gender oppression, 94; interpretive, 24
Ricardo, David, 60
Rich, Adrienne, 78, 96
Rights (natural; human): history of, 156n88; Marx's critique of, 157n91; philosophical discourse of, 11–12; right to dominate (Herrenrecht), 178n106
Roosevelt, Franklin D., 68
Rubin, Gayle, 161n12, 162n23
Russell, Bertrand, 14–15
Rustin, Bayard, 170n6

Said, Edward, 180n134
Santa Clara County v. Southern Pacific Railroad Company (1886), 157n92
Sartre, Jean-Paul, 4, 33, 39, 137n27, 145n53, 163n37; consciousness, 163n37; influence of Hegel's dialectical method, 39; phenomenology, 32–33; philosophy, 4–5, 137n27
Schütz, Alfred, 15–16
Scientific management, 150n116
Scientific method, 5–6, 8–16
Scientific revolution, 9–16
Scott, Dred, 121–122, 177n80
The Second Sex (Beauvoir), 33, 75, 85
Sedgwick, Eve Kosofsky, 161n20
Segregation, racial, 131

Self: in late Enlightenment thinking, 113; objectification of, 83; punctual, 113, 116–117, 172n35
Self-centralism, 158n109
Self-consciousness, 35–36, 147n87
Self-critique, 17, 21, 38
Self-determination, 4, 38, 75, 113, 124
Self-dominium (self-mastery), 114–116, 118, 123
Self-negation, 37–38, 90, 93–94, 113–114
Self-owning subject, 65–66
Self-relation of objectification, 90
Self-sufficiency, 66–67
Sepúlveda, Juan Ginés de, 174n48
Service sector work, 47–48
Sexuality: bio-power, 92, 103; deployment of, 103–104; gender and, 79–81; masculinity as form of rule, 100; norms of, 84–85; prediscursive establishment of sex difference, 81–82, 103; queer of color critique, 161n21; social structure of, 77–78; socialization, 84–85. See also Feminism; Queer politics
Sheth, Falguni, 170n14
Shiva, Vandana, 67
Shock doctrine, 156n84
Sitrin, Marina, 142n18
Situated knowledge, 28–30
Skinner, Quentin, 174n53
Slavery: Aristotle's naturalization of, 181n150; assertion of sovereignty, 127–128; and capitalism, 102; dual power of slaveholders, 179n117; hermeneutics of race, 110–122; as punishment, 132
Smith, Adam, 60, 62, 154n52
Smith, Dorothy E., 29
Soames, Scott, 15
Social epistemology, 28–29
Social identities, 76–77
Social pathology, 92–93, 100, 108, 120, 177n94. See also White supremacy

Social recognition. See Recognition
Social sciences, 11, 13–15
Social structure: critical hermeneutics, 27–28; feminist and queer theory, 92; of gender and sexuality, 77–78, 94; gender oppression, 93; general discussion, 18–19; horizontalism, 73–74; othering, 89; standpoint method, 28–29. See also Race
Socially necessary labor time (law of value), 60–62
Society (societas), 9, 138n36
Socrates, 3; Socratic method, 33
Sokolowski, Robert, 146n59
Sovereign power, 12
Sovereign subject, 99, 109, 128, 133–134
Sovereignty: hermeneutics of race, 114–119; popular, 125, 127–128, 133–134; violence as exercise of, 96; whiteness as, 109–110, 122–134
Spaces of rule, 99, 104
Species-being, 51–52
Sphinx, 100–101
Spirit (Geist), 25, 38
Sports, women's participation in, 85
Stalin, Joseph, 72
Standpoint method, 28–30
Stanton, Elizabeth Cady, 167n107
State: in communism, 71–73; popular sovereignty, 133–134
State of exception, 116, 133
Stone, Lucy, 167n107
Stonewall riots, 96, 166n103
Strike Debt, 45
Struggle for recognition, 36–37
Subject formation, 12–13, 47–48
Subjectivity: bodies as situating and enabling, 79–80; in capitalism, 68–70; capitalist reproduction of, 42–43; in Hegel's dialectics, 38; in interpretive method, 15–16; in phenomenology of Husserl, 32; in philosophy of Descartes, 10; in positivism, 14

Sublation (*Aufhebung*), 34
Subordination, relation to subject formation, 12–13; subordinate knowledge, 145n48
Subpersonhood, 112, 125, 127
Substance, metaphysics of, 162n30
Suffragist movement, 75–76, 167n107. *See also* Feminism
Surplus value, 42, 49, 59, 62–70

Takao Ozawa v. United States (1922), 129
Taylor, Charles, 113–114, 117, 172n35
Taylorism, 91, 150n116
Technē, 8
Technical knowledge. *See Poiēsis*
Technical knowledge interest, 144n38
Thales of Miletus, 3
Theaetetus (Plato), 135n3, 142n16
Theater: dialectical, 21; epic, 21, 141n9
Theorists, role in political struggles, 136n16
Theōria (theory), 6–8, 39–40, 137n25
Thirteenth Amendment, 132
Thompson, E. P., 48
Till, Emmett, 99
Title IX, 85, 163n50
Tocqueville, Alexis de, 118
Totalitarianism, 71–72
Transcendence: ambiguous, 82–83; of body, 82–83; dialectic of immanence and, 21, 35, 39–40, 71, 92
Transgender, 77, 78, 80. *See also* Queer politics
Treaty of Guadalupe Hidalgo, 130
Trotsky, Leon, 72
Truth, Sojourner, 75–76, 159n3

Undocumented immigrants, 130, 133
United States v. Bhagat Singh Thind (1923), 129
Universal knowledge (*epistēmē*), 7–10, 25, 142n16; universalistic thinking, 10–11
Unsocial sociability, 119–120, 128

US Equal Employment Opportunity Commission, 168n114
Use-value, 42, 58–61, 64–65

Valorization (*Verwertung*), 56, 65
Value hermeneutics: class conflict, 62–70; exchange-value, 58–59, 64–65; overview, 49, 55–58; surplus value, 59, 62–70; use-value, 42, 58–61, 64–65; value of labor, 59–62
Vattel, Emerich de, 175n61
Verfremdungseffekt (estrangement effect), 21, 141n9
Vico, Giambattista, 142n22
Violence: anti-violence work, 97; and assertion of sovereignty, 126–127; associated with masculinity and heterosexuality, 94–97; extra-legal or noncriminal, 101, 129; symbolic, 78, 161n15; systematic forms of, 96; against violations of laws of nature, 117–118
Vitoria, Francisco de, 116, 173n48
Voting, exclusion of women from, 167n107. *See also* Feminism
Voting Rights Act (1965), 131

Wage-labor, 42–43, 64–67, 100–102, 107
Wallerstein, Immanuel, 13–14
Weber, Max, 15–16
White privilege, 69, 106, 109, 131
White supremacy: and double consciousness, 87–88; hermeneutics of race, 110–122; Hitler's idea of right to dominate, 178n106; naturalized gender complex, 99; and other structures of domination, 69; overview, 105–110; prediscursive foundations of, 82; and radical feminism, 76–77; whiteness as property, sovereignty, and fetish, 122–134
"Whiteness as Property" (Harris), 124
Wife, domination in function of, 98–99, 101, 103. *See also* Feminism

Wilkins, Roy, 170n6
Winant, Howard, 19
Wittgenstein, Ludwig, 23
Women. *See* Feminism
Women's Suffrage Movement, 75–76,
   167n107

Young, Iris Marion: cultural imperialism,
   87; forms of oppression, 136n14;
   gender and sexuality socialization,

85; gendered division of labor, 101;
institutionalized forms of oppression,
19; phenomenology, 33, 82–83,
163n34; self-relation of objectification,
90
Yu, Tian, 46–47, 67

Zapatista National Liberation Army
   (EZLN), 44, 73
Zedong, Mao, 72